THE LITERARY GOURMET

MENUS FROM MASTERPIECES

•

WRITTEN AND EDITED BY

LINDA WOLFE

•

WITH DRAWINGS BY FREDERICK E. BANBERY

A Fireside Book
Published by Simon & Schuster Inc.
New York London Toronto Sydney Tokyo

Fireside
Simon & Schuster Building
Rockefeller Center
1230 Avenue of the Americas
New York, New York 10020
Copyright © 1962, 1985 by Linda Wolfe
First Fireside Edition, 1989
Published by arrangement with the author.
FIRESIDE and colophon are registered trademarks
of Simon & Schuster Inc.
Manufactured in the United States of America
1 3 5 7 9 10 8 6 4 2 Pbk.
Library of Congress Cataloging in Publication Data
Wolfe, Linda.
The literary gourmet.
Reprint. Originally published: New York:
Harmony Books, 1985.
"A Fireside Book."
Includes index.
1. Cookery, International. 2. Literary cookbooks.
I. Title.
[TX725.A1W584 1989]   641.59   88-23933
ISBN 0-671-67353-X Pbk.

ACKNOWLEDGMENTS

EXCERPTS

From "The Prologue" to *The Canterbury Tales* by Geoffrey Chaucer, new version by Neville Coghill. Reprinted by permission of John Farquharson, Ltd., London.

From *The Ingenious Gentleman Don Quixote de la Mancha* by Cervantes, translated by Samuel Putnam. Copyright, 1949, Samuel Putnam, renewed copyright © 1977 by Hilary Putnam. Reprinted by permission of Viking Penguin Inc.

From *Drunkard (L'assommoir)* by Emile Zola, translated by Arthur Symons. Reprinted by permission of Granada Publishing Limited, London.

"A Woman's Kingdom" from *The Party and Other Stories* by Anton Chekhov, translated by Constance Garnett. Copyright, 1917, Macmillan Publishing Company, renewed, 1945, by Constance Garnett.

"Swann's Way" from *Remembrance of Things Past* by Marcel Proust, translated by C.K. Scott-Moncrieff. Copyright, 1928, and renewed, 1956, by The Modern Library, Inc. Reprinted by permission of Random House, Inc.

"Tit for Tat" from *The Old Country* by Sholom Aleichem, translated by Julius and Frances Butwin. Copyright, 1946, copyright renewed 1974 by Crown Publishers, Inc.

From *To the Lighthouse* by Virginia Woolf. Copyright, 1927, by Harcourt, Brace & World, Inc. Copyright, 1955, by Leonard Woolf. Reprinted by permission of Harcourt Brace Jovanovich, Inc.

From *Of Time and the River* by Thomas Wolfe. Copyright, 1935, Charles Scribner's Sons: renewal copyright © 1963 Paul Gitlin Administrator, C.T.A. Reprinted by permission of Charles Scribner's Sons.

"Breakfast" from *The Long Valley* by John Steinbeck. Copyright, 1938, copyright © renewed, 1966, by John Steinbeck. Reprinted by permission of Viking Penguin Inc.

"A Rich Man Dines" from *The Complete Works of Horace*, translated by Dr. C.J. Kraemer. Modern Library edition.

From "A Baghdad Cookery-Book, Translated from the Arabic," an article by A.J. Arberry in *Islamic Culture*, Vol. 13, 1939 (Hyderabad, India).

"The Fifth Tale on the First Day" from *The Decameron* by Giovanni Boccaccio, translated by Frances Winwar. Modern Library edition.

From *The Epicure in Imperial Russia* by Marie Alexandre Markevitch. Published in a limited edition by The Colt Press, San Francisco, 1941.

From *Dine with the Dutch* by Marty Hartree. (Pamphlet) London, 1945.

From *Old Holland Dishes* by Mrs. J.B. Hornbeck. (Pamphlet) Muskegon, Michigan, 1936.

RECIPES

From *The Roman Cookery Book: A Critical Translation of Apicius, The Art of Cooking* by Barbara Flower and Elizabeth Rosenbaum. Reprinted by permission of George G. Harrap & Company, Limited, London.

From *The Goodman of Paris* by Eileen Power. Reprinted by permission of Routledge & Kegan Paul, Ltd., London.

ACKNOWLEDGMENTS

From *The Dictionary of Cuisine* by Alexandre Dumas; edited, abridged and translated by Louis Coleman. Copyright © 1958 by Louis Coleman. Reprinted by permission of Simon & Schuster, Inc.

From *The Art of Jewish Cooking* by Jennie Grossinger. Copyright © 1958 by Random House, Inc. Reprinted by permission of Random House, Inc.

The author's gratitude is also expressed to the following sources:
Mrs. Mina and Mrs. Emma Kaufman, The Chateaubriand Restaurant, Mrs. John William Harless, and Mrs. Lucius Morgan, Jr.

CONTENTS

Part II. Sugar and Spice: The Medieval World and the Age of Elizabeth 25

ARABIAN NIGHTS, The History of the Barber's
Sixth Brother   33

  MENU: *Goose with sweet sauce, dressed with vinegar,*
          honey, raisins and dried figs   40
        Lamb fattened with pistachio nuts   41
        Cakes   42

GIOVANNI BOCCACCIO, from The Decameron
(1348–53)   44

  MENU: *One chicken course after another*
        Capons stewed   48
        Giblets   49
        Pigge or chicken in sauge   50
        Capon brewet   51
        Farced chikens, colored or glazed   51

GEOFFREY CHAUCER, from The Canterbury Tales
(c. 1387–1400)   52

  MENU: *Bake meat pie of fish*   54
        Bake meat pie of flesh   55
        Partridge   56
        Bream   56
        Pike   57
        Sauces with sting   58
          Vert sauce   58
          Sauce Aliper   58

WILLIAM SHAKESPEARE, from The Taming
of the Shrew (c. 1594)   59

  MENU: *Neat's foot*   63
        Tripe   64
        Beef and hot mustard   64

MIGUEL DE CERVANTES, from Don Quixote (1615)   66

  MENU: *Roast partridges*   72
        with Sardine sauce   72

Part III. La Cuisine Classique: The Old World, 1700 to Today

INTRODUCTION
TO
REVISED EDITION

Nowadays, they sell croissants at Burger King. And Kiwi fruit at the A&P. When *The Literary Gourmet* was first published back in 1962, however, America's great infatuation with food was still in its infancy. The book began to make its way. Several newspapers called it one of the outstanding books of the year, and one ranked it with a handful of cookbooks—among them *Larousse Gastronomique*, Irma Rombauer's *The Joy of Cooking*, and Elizabeth David's *French Provincial Cooking*—that have since become classics in the field. But *The Literary Gourmet* wasn't really a cookbook. Or, at least, it wasn't just a cookbook. It was a book about food in literature and history as much as it was about food in the oven or on top of the stove. It was for reading as much as it was for cooking. At the time, there wasn't much of an audience for things like this, and all too soon—or so I felt—*The Literary Gourmet* went out of print.

In the ensuing years, it attained a certain fame among collectors of food books, and as shops specializing in such books began to flourish I often received letters asking me where copies of *The Literary Gourmet* might be obtained. Unfortunately, I didn't know.

All of this is by way of saying how delighted I am that the book is being republished in today's more sophisticated culinary atmosphere.

The Literary Gourmet was my first book. I had gotten the idea for it because I had long been noticing that the writers I most admired, and from whom I was forever trying to learn literary lessons, invariably used scenes of dining in their works. Sometimes they included them simply to provide concreteness or to create the semblance of reality. Sometimes, however, the scenes existed for more subtle purposes—to enable the author to uncover gracefully a character's psychological quirks or his social attitudes.

I studied the writers I was reading for clues about how to make a world set down on paper seem authentic, and how to signal, with a minimum of detail, the essential aspects of a character's personality. And I used their tricks in my own writing. And then, one day, I thought, "Why not a book?" I could recall, without even having to open the books, hundreds of scenes that had been built, by the world's foremost writers, around food.

This, then, was how the idea for *The Literary Gourmet* came about. Getting the book done was something else. To begin, an editor-friend warned me that without recipes, the book wouldn't do. People reading about dishes served up by great authors would want, perforce, to re-create them. But how to tell them how? It was then that the idea for obtaining recipes from cooks and cookbooks contemporaneous with the authors occurred to me, and I began my research.

Later, the recipes had to be adapted and tested. I did the best I could, but a truly great chef was needed to bring these antique meals back to contemporary burners. What greater chef than Albert Stockli? The Swiss-born Stockli was then chef at a brand-new magnificent restaurant, The Four Seasons. My editor said she would arrange to have Stockli and The Four Seasons test the recipes.

I couldn't believe my good fortune, but soon afterward, an energetic young woman named Mimi Sheraton called me. She was, she told me, a consultant for The Four Seasons and had been asked to supervise the testing of the recipes in *The Literary Gourmet*. In the ensuing weeks, she studied the recipes in detail, examining their proportions and techniques, deciding which ones needed further clarification, and even cooking some of them in her own kitchen. And then at last, she told me that The Four Seasons was ready to do its testing. Did I want to come over and see how it was done?

I went, and saw Stockli waving his mixing spoon like a baton over my orchestra of soups and stews and sauces. It was a tremendously exciting experience for a writer who until then had been working all alone, chiefly in the rare books room of the New York Public Library, to see her cullings become, at the fingers of this wizard, cuisine.

That's the story of *The Literary Gourmet*. Sadly, Albert Stockli died some years ago. Happily, Mimi Sheraton went on to become a world-renowned restaurant critic and cookbook author. And as for myself, I went on to write other books. But *The Literary Gourmet* remained a favorite of mine. I hope others will favor it too.

Linda Wolfe
New York City

FOREWORD

This book is both a literary anthology and a cookbook, a combination that is not as odd as it may sound. For centuries authors have been wining and dining their fictional characters, serving up meals that have satisfied a rich variety of literary purposes.

Food, with its kaleidoscope of odors and textures, colors and flavors, has given writers prime equipment for creating the semblance of reality that is the first requirement of their job. Thus they have concocted many a pioneer pudding and peasant soup and aristocratic herb sauce in order to make their heroes' lives sound actual and real. But some of their depictions of meals and table talk and manners have been so fine that much of what we know best of ancient life, or even of the more recent life of the French nobility or English gentry or American homesteaders, we know through the carefully detailed dinner scenes of fiction writers and poets.

Food has provided them with turning points in their plots: lovely ladies have been headed down the primrose path to sin with a sirloin steak, as Theodore Dreiser does it in *Sister Carrie*, or with a platter of quail in plumage, as Gustave Flaubert does it in *Madame Bovary;* shrewish heroines have been subdued with the offer of teacakes or mustard sauce on beef; sated lovers have renewed their passion over deviled chicken; and fictional families in trouble have been held together with a pan of freshly-baked biscuits or a well-roasted goose.

But most importantly, at mealtimes men are most vulnerable, and this in itself has been a magnet for literary imagination. When the famous gourmet Brillat-Savarin said, "Show me what a man eats and I will tell you what he is," he merely turned into a maxim the powerful method of insight that writers have always practiced. From Cervantes' Sancho Panza, who pragmatically is willing to forsake the promise of nobility for a plate of simple stew, to Tolstoy's Levin, who ascetically longs for Russian cabbage soup though he is served with the finest French luxuries, to Thomas Wolfe's Eugene Gant, who raids a refrigerator as if he were raping a woman, behavior toward food has been used by writers to demonstrate the innermost workings of their characters' personalities. Even the ancient Biblical story of Jacob and Esau first shows Esau's fatal flaw of rashness through the very nature of the food that tempts that hasty man to betray himself: not a milk-fed kid or some fine honey cakes, but pottage, mere lentil pottage.

All these and many other celebrated literary meals are presented in *The Literary Gourmet*. From the great wealth of fictional dinner parties I have selected my favorites, those that go beyond the mere description of food and feasting to portray a society long-gone, to tell a story, or to unveil the intricacies of a personality during the intimacy of eating. For the reader, the book provides the complete dinner scenes so that the selections can be read and enjoyed for their own sake. For the cook, the book provides recipes for the dishes so that these famous meals may be sampled today. The recipes come primarily from historical cooks and cookbooks of the authors' own times, to preserve the authenticity of their birth, but they have been adapted for modern-day cooking.

The dinners themselves have a built-in air of festivity and

tradition. They can be served successfully today because so often the great writers, with their uncanny ability to hit upon the essence of things, selected dishes that were ideally suited to the purpose of particular entertainments: seductively spicy ones for lovers' encounters, gentle and relaxing ones for conversational meals between friends, nourishing ones for family nights. Time has simply not produced a better menu for flattering a friend than the one Ben Jonson devised for a comrade in 1616, nor for stimulating flagging married love than the one Guy de Maupassant proposed in 1880, nor for conveying the welcoming spirit of Christmas than the traditional dinners in Charles Dickens' *A Christmas Carol* or Anton Chekhov's "A Woman's Kingdom."

The recipes come from worlds far removed from our own, worlds in which women were warned that a hair in the soup might be sufficient cause for divorce or that an unswept kitchen might bring the wrath of God personally down upon the offender, but they have lost none of their charm or taste. Indeed, many of the dishes, like fifteenth-century "bake-meat pie of flesche" or seventeenth-century "grand sallet," taste not just as good as but better than their twentieth-century counterparts like chicken pie and fruit salad. You will find dozens of such ancestors of your favorite foods.

Finally, in selecting the recipes I attempted to cull them from as many different sources as possible, hoping in that way to provide not only an anthology of the literature of dining but an anthology of the history of cooking as well. Cooking, unlike any other discipline, has been unkind to its masters, letting them fall into obscurity as library-lepers. And it has been equally unkind to its present-day practitioners, letting them go through their paces ill informed of their heritage. But there were a host of remarkable men and women who contributed to the art of cooking and who deserve to be remembered today. I have presented as many of them as I could, the great professionals like Urbain-Dubois, chef to the Court of Germany, and Sir Patrick Lamb, who cooked for half a dozen crowned heads of England, the haughty amateurs like Alexandre Dumas and the fat Baron Brisse, as well as mere pioneer housewives and sentimental English ladies and old Dutch grannies.

Here then are the practitioners of two of the most august and ancient arts. They speak in the singular tones of their own century, their country and their class and I have interrupted them only politely and in parentheses. I put you, with confidence, into their capable hands.

L. W.

A NOTE TO THE COOK

Apple Charlotte has barely changed a crust in two centuries. Small
birds cooked the Italian way in the eighteenth century closely
resemble cut-up chickens cooked the Italian way today. Simmered
meat *en daube*, still a popular French dish, can be found in a
fourteenth-century cookbook. The great recipes of the past, handed
down from generation to generation, century to century, still find
their way onto today's tables, their cooking time slightly length-
ened or shortened, an obscure herb dropped, a fashionable new
ingredient added. Some things have changed; we no longer eat
dormice or flamingos, as the Romans did, nor grease our pans
with the fatty tail of a sheep, as the medieval Arabs did. But it
is surprising how many procedures and combinations of the past
resemble rather than differ from our own. We are fed, both sym-
bolically and in reality, upon the achievements of our ancestors.

However, although the essential combinations have remained
similar, the method of communicating a recipe from one cook to
another has changed radically. Cookbooks today pride themselves

upon exactitude. But until recently most cookbook authors assumed that everyone knew how long to roast a cut of meat, in how hot an oven to bake a cake. "Cook it till it be ynow," said the medieval chefs. "It must be put on at sunrise in order to be eaten at three o'clock," said the early nineteenth-century chefs, unconcerned with the varying hour of sunrise. And often the cookbooks did not state the exact amounts of ingredients. "Cook larks with a little whole mace, a piece of sweet butter, and a handful of parsley," writes the seventeenth-century Sir Hugh Plat. Or, even when the cooks of the past are explicit, they talk in terms odd for us. The thirteenth-century Arab Muhammad speaks of throwing in a *dirham* of this, an *uqiya* of that, a *ratl* of yet another thing, and his measurements do not quite approximate any of our own; nineteenth-century cooks were in the habit of saying "add a saltspoon of shallots" or a "wineglassful of cream," measurements that we no longer honor; English cooks mean a measurement more generous than ours when they say pint. And ingredients themselves were different in different centuries and countries. Sometimes milk was creamier or fruit softer or flour less refined or meat tougher, so that even when a cook's proportions are precise and familiar, his instructions do not always apply properly to our own commodities.

Contemporary collections of old recipes usually follow one of two courses. Either they modernize the recipes, deleting the classic methods and ingredients and inventing new proportions and combinations (a second cousin, always, to the original, never a closer relative), or they print the recipes as they appeared originally, with no attempt to indicate proportions in those that did not themselves possess any. Both methods have their value, but both have their pitfalls too. The first emasculates the recipes; the second inhibits the modern cook. I have tried to strike a balance between the two. To preserve the original greatness of the old recipes, the individuality of their creators and the individuality of the people who will cook them today, I have left the instructions virtually unchanged. The modern cook will find it easy and enjoyable to supply his or her own parallels to instructions like "add butter at least the size of an egg," or "roll out the dough until it is about as thick as a crown piece." But wherever complexities exist which seem so bewildering that the cook might be held back from the enjoyment of the meal, suggestions for adapting the recipe or for making it similar to a parallel modern dish have been offered. These comments, always in parentheses, supply ingredients important to our taste buds and overlooked by the old cooks (how often even the greatest of chefs forgot about salt!), explain how cooking styles have changed (medium-sized chickens in the eighteenth century, roasted before huge open fires, were cooked for only thirty minutes; vegetables in the disease-fearful nineteenth century were always boiled too long for our taste), and offer suggested proportions, wherever feasible, for ingredients left vague in the original.

Cooking times, serving portions and oven temperatures have been added to many of the recipes. Hints as to when the old cooks' exact proportions would produce a dish too sweet or too sour, too thin or too thick, for modern-day palates, appear throughout. These parenthetical changes and comments, which represent my own taste preferences, are meant as a guide for the cook accustomed to modern cookbook techniques. There were, however, some cases in which I was unable to make the recipes as exact or as thorough as an inexperienced cook might desire without thoroughly rewriting the instructions and altering the procedure, a thing I was loath to do. Thus, while some of the recipes are quite simple and can be successfully cooked by the most untried chef, others will require experience, the reader's own ability to fall back upon modern parallels and supply favorite procedures or quantities.

With only a few exceptions, like cranes, some tiny birds and an occasional wild boar, all the ingredients in the book or close substitutes for them may be easily purchased. And every recipe may be cooked and eaten. Making them has given me and will, I hope, give you not just enjoyable cooking hours but something equally precious in these days when history seems about to stop: a sense of how man's everyday works live on, despite death and change and calamity.

PART I

•

POTTAGE AND PEACOCKS' TONGUES

•

THE ANCIENT WORLD

At Egyptian feasts a tiny wooden mummy lying in a coffin was handed from guest to guest. "Look upon this," the host would say. "Look upon this and eat and drink your fill. For when thou art dead, thus wilt thou be."

Down through the centuries this has been the spirit of man's feasting. "Let us eat and drink, for tomorrow we die." "Drink! for you know not whence you came, nor why; Drink! for you know not why you go nor where." "Go thy way, eat thy bread with joy, and drink thy wine with a merry heart . . . for there is no work, nor device, nor knowledge, nor wisdom, in the grave, whither thou goest." "Look upon this, and eat and drink your fill!"

Death is the end. But to feast is to slap the very face of death. How can it harm us when we have proved ourselves, even for the brief moments of a meal, not in fear of its first, its ancient and underlying, punishment: starvation.

In Biblical times men experienced famine after famine, enduring. There was never much food, even when the treacherous rivers did not overflow, even when the rains came on schedule. The starving sold their birthright for a mess of pottage, endured humiliation for the mere promise of a meal, died with their begging bowls in their hands. But

1

when there was food, even just the barest of food, men feasted.

A myriad of occasions provided excuses. Sometimes feasts were grandiose, like the one that terminated Ahasuerus' three month carnival. For seven days and nights all loyal subjects, the great and the small alike, were allowed to partake of the king's splendor. He stuffed them with delicacies, let them drink as much wine as they could hold, wooed them by giving out golden cups no two of which were alike. The nobles and the king himself reclined on golden and silver couches and got so uproariously drunk that the queen would have nothing to do with them and consequently lost her throne.

But this was more like a dream than reality. More frequent were the feasts that were a part of daily life. Weddings, betrothals, the return of a relative, even the day upon which a child gave up the mother's breast and chewed its first solid food, were celebrated by feasting and conviviality. Often covenants and oaths were not considered sealed until the participants had taken a meal together. Religious ceremonies and sacrifices ended in banqueting. And the coming of a stranger always meant the sharing of food, sometimes more elaborate than anything the family ate while alone.

Throughout the ancient east hospitality was an almost sacred duty. The wayfarer was protected by God, might indeed be God. Had not the Lord appeared to Abraham in the guise of three dusty travelers? Suppose that founder of a people had not jumped up and run to greet them? Abraham had after all been sitting wearily before his tent, exhausted by his day's labor and the intense heat of the sun. But exhaustion faded before the call of hospitality. He hurried to the travelers and, despite their poor and dirty aspect, bowed low to the ground before them. "I will fetch a morsel of bread, and comfort ye your hearts," he suggested.

His words were self-effacing. Just as we say "take potluck" to the unexpected visitor, then work feverishly to produce a nourishing meal, Abraham's morsel of bread turned out to be a tender calf he selected from his flock, a special sauce he personally concocted to go with it, and cakes made of fine meal by Sarah, who obediently lit the fire and baked them upon the hearth even though it was the hottest time of the desert day.

In Egypt, too, visitors were accorded generous treatment. When a particularly important guest was expected, the entire household might be busy weeks in advance preparing his welcome. The house was cleaned and scrubbed, wine was chosen, beer was brewed and bread was baked. The Egyptians have left many paintings depicting the making of their food and drink. The bread bakers knead their dough into thin round shapes, sprinkle it with spices, garnish it with almonds. The wine makers rhythmically tread the grapes while musicians sit amongst them easing their task by playing accompaniment for the necessary foot motions.

Once the beer and the wine and the bread were made it was time to choose the ox, often so fattened that it could barely walk. Geese were spitted and roasted. Water was poured into enormous jars to cool. Pastry makers turned out elaborate desserts, sometimes even using snow in their concoctions, an amazing feat in that torrid climate.

Later the entertainers would arrive, musicians and acrobats and dancers. Perhaps they were like the troop on one painting: four beautiful female musicians, dressed in graceful robes and ornate necklaces almost as full and as long as blouses. Discreetly they avoid watching the two naked girls who dance exquisitely to the unheard sound of their instruments.

At last the guest was heard approaching. The host rushed forth to greet him at the gates. They exchanged eloquent compliments: "The evil that men speak of thee doth not exist. . . ."

The Greeks welcomed their guests in the same spirit. A traveler was to be fed first, questioned about why he had come only after he was full. In Homer's time women and menials had not yet crept into the kitchens of heroes, and men could have their meat exactly as they liked it. Achilles and Patroclus themselves prepared supper for Agamemnon's envoys, roasting their beef and mutton and pork on long skewers, much the way the Near Easterners do today. Made personally by the host, such a meal became a special tribute to the dignity of the guest.

Much later dining grew more elaborate. The Greeks forgot the little polished wooden tables that had served as their ancestors' only plates, the hard chairs that had supported them. These were replaced by ornate tableware, carved tables and gem-encrusted couches. Slaves washed the diners' feet and placed garlands on their heads. Many different kinds of food were eaten and much spiced wine was drunk. But after dinner, after musicians had quieted the guests with the gentle sounds of the flute and young girls had excited them by somersaulting through hoops lined with upright swords, Socrates and other men like him said, "Let us now entertain ourselves."

It was an original, a pleasing concept. If the stomach were kept a little less than full, and the brain a little less than benumbed with wine, there were perhaps new pleasures to be had. Following Socrates' lead, the learned discoursed graciously about politics, art and love.

The Romans, who copied so much from the Greeks, were never able to emulate this. The coda to their banquets was to become not philosophy but the vomitorium.

There had been excess before the Romans. The very words "to feast" derive in Greek from the verb "to drink," and many feasts in all parts of the ancient world had ended in excessive drunkenness. Both Egyptian and Greek artists painted celebrations at which the participants grew so ill that friends and servants were kept busy fetching bowls to hold beneath dribbling chins. The Bible too had many dire morning, that they may follow strong drink; that continue until night, warnings, like that of Isaiah, against those "that rise up early in the till wine inflame them!"

But the Romans developed indulgence of the palate and the stomach beyond anything the ancient world had before experienced. It happened gradually. In the beginning the Romans were energetic and militarily wise. They made themselves masters of the known world. But little by little no luxury was too great, no carnality too vulgar, and no penitence possible. What does one do with the world when one owns it? One eats it.

They imported their cooks first from Greece. Then they drew them from other outlying regions. Soon they were able to taste all the pleasures of all the places, and their concept of the exotic paled. They ate many of the meats we now eat, like pork, veal, lamb and ducks. But they ate cranes and peacocks also, and Heliogabalus once offered two hundred gold pieces to anyone who would bring back to him, ostensibly for dinner, the legendary phoenix.

The length of the Mediterranean and even the shores of the Black Sea were turned inside out in search of the beautiful red-legged flamingo. Its thick and oily tongue was highly prized. Pickled, it was a delicacy without which no Roman banquet could succeed. Ostrich brains were another delight. Sometimes six hundred ostriches were killed for a single imperial meal and only their brains were served. The Romans seem to have been titillated by killing so huge a bird to obtain so small and exquisite a pleasure.

A man's life had about as much value as an ostrich's life. There is a story about a certain Pollio whose slave broke a glass bowl while serving dinner. Good crystal was hard to come by in those days; slaves were not. When the bowl shattered, Pollio was so infuriated that he ordered the slave thrown to his voracious eels as punishment. Only the intercession of the unusually righteous emperor Augustus prevented the murder. But Augustus was an early ruler and his influence did not curb the trend upon which Rome had already embarked.

Augustus' own contemporary, the noble Antony, could not control his love of indulgence. Forgetful that in the morning he had an oration to deliver, he drank and ate so furiously all night at a wedding that when at last he stood in front of the populace he was unable to speak and, sick to his stomach, hid behind his gown and threw up. Because he could not bear the sight of poverty, he took his entire golden table service with him wherever he traveled. For his dinner eight wild boars were kept roasting in the kitchen. When a visitor remarked to Antony's cook that a great number of guests must be expected the cook laughed at this naïveté. Only twelve were coming, he explained, but every item had to be served perfectly done, for if anything was ill-timed even to a moment Antony would declare it spoiled and have the entire dish thrown out. Replacements had thus to be kept always on hand. But because the other side of his impulsiveness was generosity, Antony had no trouble finding cooks. Word quickly passed among the professionals that Antony had once rewarded a chef who prepared him a particularly satisfying supper with a full possession of a town of some thirty-five thousand inhabitants.

He and Cleopatra entered into a culinary competition early in their courtship, decorating their feasts with thousands of lighted tree branches and designing dishes meant to outcost any hitherto prepared. The contest was won by Cleopatra who dissolved one of her expensive pearl earrings in a goblet of lemon juice.

Later, even when Antony wanted to live simply it became impossible for him. He was very fond of fishing but Cleopatra objected to the sport. One day when he went fishing on the Nile she instructed her slaves to hook his lines with presalted fish. Antony pulled them up. Everybody roared with laughter. Cleopatra turned away her noble profile and said scornfully, "General, leave the fishing rod to Egyptians; your game is cities, provinces and kingdoms."

Thus the Romans, whose game was indeed cities, provinces and kingdoms, abandoned the simple pleasures like fishing and evolved ever more intemperate ones. They loved fish and to keep this easily spoiled food fresh they had it brought to them live in buckets. The rich would then place the fish in home ponds so that they would be readily on hand when needed. Often these fish became great pets before their demise and were given names and fed by hand. This makes even more astonishing the story Seneca, one of Rome's profoundest observers, relates about red mullets. When important guests came to dinner they were allowed to choose the mullet they wanted and to see it killed before their eyes, much the way we to this day choose a lobster in fine seafood restaurants. But for the Romans death had become such a stimulating obsession that killing the fish ceased to be merely a way of insuring freshness. Rather, the guests avidly concentrated upon the death of the mullet. It was placed on a white marble table, the better to reveal its changing death-agony colors. "Look how it reddens," one guest would cry ecstatically, "there is no vermilion like it!" And another would exclaim over the exquisite grayness that followed as the inanimate body faded to a single pale hue. Then, appetized, the guests would dine.

Heliogabalus, who had first entered the city in a chariot drawn by naked girls, was the most pleasure-minded of all the Romans and used to feed even his dogs on pheasants and peacocks' tongues. The general Lucullus kept a whole series of dining halls in his home so that meals of different degrees of luxury could be served in settings appropriate to the person entertained. Perfumes were wafted past the noses of guests throughout mealtimes. Every dish was spiced to extremity. Never was one spice used or even three but always the entire contents of the cook's cabinet were paraded into the sauces.

We know more about Roman cooking than we do about that of any other ancient people. Though cookbooks undoubtedly existed in the ancient world, few have come down to us. There are some Greek recipes and there are descriptions of food throughout the Bible and in Arabian and Greek literature. There are the paintings of Egypt. But Rome has bequeathed us a complete, detailed cookbook with recipes for the preparation of all items of a meal: meat, fish and fowl, soups and sauces, even desserts and wines. The book is attributed to Apicius, a famous gourmet who wrote during the first century A.D. and literally lived for the pleasures of the table. When he discovered that he had spent most of his fortune on food and entertainment he decided that life was no longer worthwhile. He had enough money to survive, but, rather than scrimp on his food, he killed himself.

His cookbook, the little good that he had done, lived after him. It was edited and re-edited in later centuries, so that the book now credited to Apicius is actually the work of a fourth- or fifth-century cook who added recipes for simple households and rephrased Apicius' elegant language.

A typical Apician sauce for slices of meat calls for pepper, lovage, caraway, mint, spikenard, bay leaf, egg yolk, honey, vinegar and oil. These are added to *garum,* the basic Roman sauce, as ubiquitous as our catchup. And *garum* was made by salting the entrails, gills, juice and blood of tuna fish and letting them soak up the hot sun for two months. Even turnips, that poor man's food, were seasoned with plenty of cumin, somewhat less rue, and asafetida, honey, vinegar, *garum,* wine and a little oil. While this combination of flavors is excellent in any single sauce, every dish received virtually the same treatment.

Ultimately vomitoria were invented so that guests could mercifully rid themselves of one course to make room for another. Throats were tickled with long feathers to aid the process and sometimes emetics were even taken when an invitation to a dinner was received, just to make sure the greedy stomach would be ready.

Ultimately the age-old rule of hospitality collapsed. Roman writers frequently describe hosts who "serve their guests with other wines than those they drink themselves, or substitute inferior wine for better in the course of the repast." At one man's table "very elegant dishes were served up to himself and a few more of the company; while those placed before the rest were cheap and paltry." Another man fed himself marvelous wines "whose date and name have been effaced by the soot which time has gathered on the aged jar," but gave his guests "bits of hard bread that have turned moldy."

Ultimately too the emperors used their gastronomical concerns to indicate their contempt of the country and the whole task of governing it. Domitian humiliated his cabinet by forcing them to attend him at his villa to help solve a serious problem. When they arrived he kept them waiting for hours. The problem, it finally appeared, was that the emperor had just purchased a giant fish, too large for any dish he owned, and he needed the learned brains of his ministers to decide whether the fish should be minced or whether a larger pot should be sought. The emperor Claudius one day rode hurriedly to the Senate and demanded they deliberate the importance of a life without pork. Another time he sat in his tribunal ostensibly administering justice but actually allowing the litigants to argue and orate while he grew dreamy, interrupting the discussions only to announce, "Meat pies are wonderful. We shall have them for dinner."

Seneca had written warningly of the Romans' food excesses.

"Where is the lake, the sea, the forest, the spot of land that is not ransacked to gratify our palates? Our infirmities are the price of the pleasures to which we have abandoned ourselves beyond all measure and restraint. Are you astonished at our innumerable diseases? Count the number of our cooks!" He was referring to infirmities of the body but surely also to the rampant diseases of the soul.

When Rome fell to the barbarian invasions its cuisine fell too. No other kingdom on earth could support such extravagances. Some sauces had been good and tasty. Certainly the way the Romans handled spice was enticingly artful in any single dish. But the dream of variety produced its monstrous opposite. Roman cookery took on a soporific sameness when foods as different as conger eel and dormice followed thrushes and turtledoves and the wombs of sterile sows, each seasoned with the same minimal pepper, lovage, origan, cumin, rue, asafetida, honey, vinegar and *garum*. The food of the next thousand years would be simpler, heavily spiced but not with the abandonment of the conspicuously consumptive Romans. Occasionally a boar or a bird would even be roasted and served whole and allowed to disclose its own humble flavor.

THE BIBLE

THE STORY OF JACOB AND ESAU

*Esau, a much maligned man, has been called greedy and dull-witted
for so despising his birthright as to sell it for soup. But God had warned
his mother that she would give birth to two children and that contrary
to custom the elder would serve the younger. Esau's fate was never his
to handle and his story becomes one of the most troubling ones in the
Bible. Here is a man at the mercy of his mortality; starving, he sells his*

birthright. Here is a man at the mercy of his simplicity; loving, he is never suspicious of his conniving brother until it is too late. Here is a man denied by God, despised by his mother, and disappointed even by the helpless father he had revered: "Bless even me also, O my father," weeps Esau, a son hungry for food and for love.

And these are the generations of Isaac, Abraham's son: Abraham begat Isaac and Isaac was forty years old when he took Rebekah to wife, the daughter of Bethuel the Syrian of Padan-aram, the sister to Laban the Syrian. And Isaac entreated the Lord for his wife, because she was barren: and the Lord was entreated of him, and Rebekah his wife conceived.

And the children struggled together within her; and she said, "If it be so, why am I thus?" And she went to inquire of the Lord. And the Lord said unto her, "Two nations are in thy womb, and two manner of people shall be separated from thy bowels; and the one people shall be stronger than the other people; and the elder shall serve the younger." And when her days to be delivered were fulfilled, behold, there were twins in her womb. And the first came out red, all over like an hairy garment; and they called his name Esau. And after that came his brother out, and his hand took hold on Esau's heel; and his name was called Jacob: and Isaac was threescore years old when she bare them. And the boys grew: and Esau was a cunning hunter, a man of the field; and Jacob was a plain man, dwelling in tents. And Isaac loved Esau, because he did eat of his venison; but Rebekah loved Jacob.

And Jacob sod pottage: and Esau came from the field, and he was faint: and Esau said to Jacob, "Feed me, I pray thee, with that same red pottage; for I am faint": therefore was his name called Edom. And Jacob said, "Sell me this day thy birthright." And Esau said, "Behold, I am at the point to die: and what profit shall this birthright do to me?" And Jacob said, "Swear to me this day"; and he sware unto him: and he sold his birthright unto Jacob.

Then Jacob gave Esau bread and pottage of lentiles; and he did eat and drink, and rose up, and went his way: thus Esau despised his birthright.   •   •   •

And it came to pass, that when Isaac was old, and his eyes were dim, so that he could not see, he called Esau his oldest son, and said unto him, "My son." And he said unto him, "Behold, here am I." And he said, "Behold now, I am old, I know not the day of my death: Now therefore take, I pray thee, thy weapons, thy quiver and thy bow, and go out to the field, and take me some venison; and make me savoury meat, such as I love, and bring it to me, that I may eat; that my soul may bless thee before I die."

And Rebekah heard when Isaac spake to Esau his son. And Esau went to the field to hunt for venison, and to bring it. And Rebekah spake unto Jacob her son, saying, "Behold, I heard thy father speak unto Esau thy brother, saying, 'Bring me venison, and make me savoury meat, that I may eat, and bless thee before the Lord before my death.' Now therefore, my son, obey my voice according to that which I command thee. Go now to the flock, and fetch me from thence two good kids of the goats; and I will make them savoury meat for thy father, such as he loveth: and thou shalt bring it to thy father, that he may eat, and that he may bless thee before his death."

And Jacob said to Rebekah his mother, "Behold, Esau my brother is a hairy man, and I am a smooth man. My father peradventure will feel me, and I shall seem to him as a deceiver. And I shall bring a curse upon me, and not a blessing." And his mother said unto him, "Upon me be thy curse, my son: only obey my voice, and go fetch me them."

And he went, and fetched, and brought them to his mother: and his mother made savoury meat, such as his father loved. And Rebekah took goodly raiment of her eldest son Esau, which were with her in the house, and put them upon Jacob her youngest son: and she put the skins of the kids of the goats upon his hands, and upon the smooth of his neck: and she gave the savoury meat and the bread, which she had prepared, into the hands of her son Jacob. And he came unto his father, and said, "My father." And he said, "Here am I; who art thou, my son?" And Jacob said unto his father, "I am Esau thy firstborn; I have done according as thou badest me: arise, I pray thee, sit and eat of my venison, that thy soul may bless me." And Isaac said unto his son, "How is it that thou hast found it so quickly, my son?" And he said, "Because the Lord thy God brought it to me."

And Isaac said unto Jacob, "Come near, I pray thee, that I may feel thee, my son, whether thou be my very son Esau or not." And Jacob went near unto Isaac his father; and he felt him, and said, "The voice is Jacob's voice, but the hands are the hands of Esau." And he discerned him not, because his hands were hairy, as his brother Esau's hand: so he blessed him.

And he said, "Art thou my very son Esau?" And he said, "I am." And he said, "Bring it near to me, and I will eat of my son's venison, that my soul may bless thee." And he brought it near to him, and he did eat: and he brought him wine, and he drank. And his father Isaac said unto him, "Come near now, and kiss me, my son." And he came near, and kissed him: and he smelled the smell of his raiment, and blessed him, and said, "See, the smell of my son is as the smell of a field which the Lord hath blessed: therefore God give thee of the dew of heaven, and the fatness of the earth, and plenty of corn and wine. Let people serve thee: and nations bow down to thee: be lord over thy brethren, and let thy mother's sons bow down to thee: cursed be everyone that cursed thee, and blessed be he that blesseth thee."

And it came to pass, as soon as Isaac had made an end of blessing Jacob, and Jacob was yet scarce gone out from the presence of Isaac his father, that Esau his brother came in from his hunting. And he also had made savoury meat, and brought it unto his father, and said unto his father, "Let my father arise, and eat of his son's venison, that thy soul may bless me." And Isaac his father said unto him, "Who art thou?" And he said, "I am thy son, thy firstborn Esau." And Isaac trembled very exceedingly, and said, "Who? where is he that hath taken venison, and brought it me, and I have eaten of all before thou camest, and have blessed him? Yea, and he shall be blessed."

And when Esau heard the words of his father, he cried with a great and exceeding bitter cry, and said unto his father, "Bless me, even me also, O my father." And he said, "Thy brother came with subtilty, and hath taken away thy blessing." And he said, "Is not he rightly named Jacob? For he hath supplanted me these two times: he took away my birthright; and, behold, now he hath taken away my blessing." And he said, "Hast thou not reserved a blessing for me?" And Isaac answered and said unto Esau, "Behold, I have made him thy lord, and all his brethren have I given to him for servants; and with corn and wine have I sustainèd him: and what shall I do now unto thee, my son?"

And Esau said unto his father, "Hast thou but one blessing, my father? Bless me, even me also, O my father!" And Esau lifted up his voice and wept.

MENU:

Red pottage of lentils

No cookbooks have come down to us from Biblical times and I have relied, in making this recipe for lentil pottage, on Biblical encyclopedias and concordances.

RED POTTAGE OF LENTILS

2 cups lentils
2-3 quarts water
meat (leftover poultry bones or
   soup meat or what you will)

chopped onions and garlic,
   sautéed in olive oil
salt to taste

All these ingredients were used in soups by the ancient Hebrews. For a dish that will resemble the pottage for which Esau sold his birthright, soak the lentils overnight in cold water to cover; drain them and place in a deep kettle with water; add meat and simmer soup and meat gently for 3-4 hours. A half hour before the pottage is done, add the sautéed chopped onions and garlic. Taste; add salt if needed.

(Serves 8-10)

HORACE

THE SATIRES: RICH MAN DINES

c. 29 B.C.

Horace's report of a wealthy Roman's unhappy dinner party makes an all-important point about how to be a good host. Nasidienus, the host in "Rich Man Dines," is made miserable when a canopy falls down upon his table, shedding black dust all over the dishes. He grows even more distressed when he discovers that the calamity is more devastating to his own ego than to his guests' pleasure. But they had been

irritated by his too-perfect meal. They had been longing for a faux pas
or an accident, anything to alleviate the pall of too much pretension.

*Horace seems to warn that the duties of a host demand the dis-
play of humor and dignity as well as fine food. A further secret to be
mastered is offered by one of the wiser visitors at the ancient dinner.
"A host," he says, "is like a general; adversity reveals his genius, prosperity hides it."*

HORACE. How did you enjoy your dinner with the rich Nasidienus?

FUNDANIUS. Vastly. I never had a better time.

HORACE. Tell me, if you don't mind, what was the first dish to appease
   your ravenous appetites?

FUNDANIUS. First there was a Lucanian boar, captured, so the host told
   us, when the south wind was softly blowing. Around it were
   pungent rape, lettuce, radishes, skirret, fish-pickle, Coan lees and
   everything to whet the appetite. When these were removed, a
   neatly dressed slave carefully wiped the maplewood table with
   a purple napkin. Another swept up the crumbs and anything that
   could offend the guests. Then, like an Attic maiden bearing Ceres'
   sacred emblems, came forward a dusky Indian with Caecuban
   wine, and a Greek with Chian unmixed with brine. Then said the
   host, "If you prefer Alban, Maecenas, or Falernian, we have both."

HORACE. Oh, the curse of being so rich! But who were your supper
   companions with whom you had so good a time, Fundanius? I
   am eager to know.

FUNDANIUS. I was at the head of the table. Next to me was Viscus of
   Thurii, and beyond him, if I recall, Varius. Then Vibidius and
   Servilius Balatro, uninvited guests whom Maecenas had brought
   him. Nomentanus was next to him; beyond him Porcius, who made
   us laugh by gulping down cheese cakes whole. Nomentanus was
   there to point his forefinger at anything that might escape our
   notice. As for the rest of us, people of no importance, we supped
   on birds, shellfish, and fish that had a flavor very different from
   anything we knew. I, for instance, soon discovered this when I
   was handed the livers of a plaice and a turbot—a dish I had never
   tasted before.

After this he informed me that honey-apples are red if they are
gathered when the moon is waning. What difference that makes you
had better learn from him.

Then Vibidius whispered to Balatro, "We will die unavenged unless we drink him bankrupt," and called for larger cups.

At that our host grow pale, as he had a horror for hard drinkers, either because their talk is too free, or because hot wines dull a delicate taste.

Vibidius and Balatro tilted whole decanters into Allifan goblets. Everybody followed suit except the guest on the lowest couch, who took care to drink little.

Then a lamprey, with shrimp sauce, was brought in, stretched full length on a platter. At this the host remarked, "It was caught before spawning. If caught after spawning its meat is poorer. Here is the recipe for the sauce: oil of the first pressing from Venafrum; roe from the juices of the Spanish mackerel; wine five years old, but domestic, poured in while the sauce is simmering—after the sauce is cooked, Chian is the best wine to pour in—white pepper, and vinegar made from fermenting Lesbian wine. I was the first to point out that green rockets and bitter elecampane should be boiled in the sauce. Curtillus says to add sea-urchins unwashed, for the shell-fish's natural brine is better than any pickle."

Just then the canopy fell heavily from the ceiling upon the platter, bringing with it more black dust than the north wind raises on the plains of Campania. We feared something worse was about to happen, but finding there was no danger we recovered our composure. Rufus laid his head on the table and wept as if his son had been cut off in his prime. What would have been the end I don't know, if Nomentanus had not comforted his friend by a philosopher's reflection, "Ah, Fortune, what god is more cruel to us than thou! How thou delightest ever to make sport of human life!"

Varius could hardly smother a laugh with his napkin. Balatro, who sneers at everything, remarked, "Such is life, and therefore the reward of fame will never compensate you for your labor to attain it. To think that you must be racked with every kind of annoyance to entertain me sumptuously—lest the bread be burned, or badly seasoned sauce be served, and that your slaves be properly and neatly dressed when they wait on table! Then, too, such accidents as this—the canopy's coming down as it did just now or some numbskull's falling and breaking a dish. But a host is like a general: adversity reveals his genius, prosperity hides it." To this Nasidienus replied, "Heaven grant you all that you pray for! You are so kind and considerate a guest!" and called for his sandals.

Then on each couch was heard the buzz of people whispering into each other's ears.

HORACE. I know of no play I would rather have seen. But tell me, what did you find to laugh at next?

FUNDANIUS. While Vibidius was asking the waiters whether the flagon also was broken, since the cups were not brought to him when he called for them, and while we were laughing at pretended jests, with Balatro egging us on, back came Nasidienus with changed countenance as if to mend misfortune by his art. Then followed the servants bearing on a huge platter the limbs of a carved crane sprinkled with plenty of salt and meal, and the liver of a white goose fattened on rich figs, and hares' legs torn off, much nicer so than if they were eaten with the loins. Then we saw blackbirds served with the breast burnt, and pigeons without the rumps—all nice enough if the host had not explained their laws and properties. But off we ran, taking it out on him by tasting nothing at all, as though it had all been poisoned with Canidia's breath, deadlier than African serpents.

MENU:

Wild boar

Birds

(Partridge, hazelhen
or turtledove)

Shellfish

Lamprey with shrimp sauce

Crane

Hare

Blackbirds and pigeons

The recipes come from the western world's oldest cookbook, The Art of Cooking, *believed to be the work of the first-century Roman Apicius, a gourmet who killed himself when he realized he had spent virtually his entire fortune on food and drink. But long after his death his elaborate recipes continued to delight generations of Romans. The version of Apicius that we know today was probably written out as much as four centuries after his death, added to and modified and adapted for a middle-class audience. This book has recently received an excellent new translation by Elisabeth Rosenbaum and Barbara Flower who went far beyond the safe call of a translator's duty to try out many of Apicius' disturbing recipes.*

Their conclusion, after a number of very enjoyable meals, was that Roman cooking did not deserve the disdain so frequently heaped upon it. As to the Roman cookery book itself, it "was not meant for beginners," they wrote. "The lack of indication of quantities in most recipes makes a basic knowledge of cookery necessary. But we found that with common sense and a little imagination one cannot go wrong on the quantities."

Some of the spices and herbs mentioned in the recipes are no longer available; others are very hard to come by. But in testing the recipes the translators observed that one or another of the herbs might be safely omitted without crucially altering the taste. As to quantities, let your own preferences guide you, remembering that to emulate the Romans you will need to loosen your normal control when tilting the herb bottles. Here is a glossary of some of the Roman terms and ingredients:

Liquamen *or* garum *was a factory-made sauce, apparently used instead of salt. Few modern cooks will care to authentically reproduce* garum, *which was made by soaking the entrails, gills, juice and blood of tuna fish in salt for two months. Plain table salt, soy sauce, or a dab of Chinese shrimp paste or oyster sauce may be used as a substitute.*

Defrutum, caroenum, passum *and* mulsum *were special wine or winelike preparations. For* defrutum, *the fresh pressed juice of the grape reduced by boiling, substitute grape juice boiled down to two-thirds its original volume. For* caroenum, *a reduced wine, substitute white or red wine also boiled down to two-thirds its volume. For* passum, *a specially prepared sweet wine, substitute a very sweet Spanish wine. And for* mulsum, *a wine the Romans mixed with honey, add two tablespoons of honey to a bottle of dry white wine.*

Asafetida, *an ingredient still in use in some areas of the world but long rejected by most cooks for its unpleasant odor, is available in drugstores. "It is very strong and must be used with utmost caution," writes Elisabeth Rosenbaum. "The tiniest drop gives just enough flavour. If more than a minute quantity is taken the entire dish may be spoiled. But, used with care, it gives a delicious flavour, especially in combination with fish."*

WILD BOAR

FROM *The Art of Cooking,* 1st–5th century A.D., Apicius

In the absence of wild boars, try this sweet sauce on ham, suckling pig or fresh pork loin.

a boar	honey
salt	*liquamen*
grilled cumin	*caroenum*
ground pepper	*passum*

pan juice from the boar

Boar is prepared in the following manner: Sponge it and sprinkle with salt and grilled cumin, and leave it like that. The next day put it in the oven. When it is cooked pour over (a sauce made of) ground pepper, the pan juice from the boar, honey, *liquamen, caroenum* and *passum.*°

°If you wish to use boar, buy only a leg (a whole boar weighs 60-80 pounds). Marinate the leg in the sauce ingredients above and leave in refrigerator for five days. Then roast in a 450° oven for 40 minutes, reduce heat to 350° and continue roasting for about 25 minutes per pound, basting with the marinade.

BIRDS

FROM *The Art of Cooking,* 1st-5th century A.D., Apicius

a partridge, hazelhen or
turtledove (or Cornish game
   hen or squab)
pepper
lovage

mint
rue seeds
liquamen
wine
oil

For partridge, hazelhen, turtledove: (Brown the bird in butter. Make a sauce of) pepper, lovage, mint, seed of rue, *liquamen,* wine and oil. (Pour cver bird and braise in covered pot till done.)

SHELLFISH

FROM *The Art of Cooking,* 1st–5th century A.D., Apicius

(shellfish)
pepper
lovage
parsley
dried mint

cumin
honey
vinegar
liquamen
bay leaf

Dressing for all kinds of shellfish: Pepper, lovage, parsley, dried mint, plenty of cumin, honey, vinegar, *liquamen.* If you wish add also a bay leaf. . . . (Simmer briefly and serve. The sauce can be dramatically heightened by adding to it ground figs previously soaked in water, a touch of bottled horseradish and/or a little fish fumet.)

LAMPREY WITH SHRIMP SAUCE

FROM *The Satires, c.* 29 B.C., Horace

This recipe is Horace's own. His garrulous rich man describes how to make the dish, but unfortunately the canopy-disaster occurs before the recipe is completed, so we never find out how long to simmer the sauce. Nor do we know whether the absence of shrimp in the shrimp sauce occurs because Nasidienus hadn't yet gotten around to it or, as seems more likely, "lamprey with shrimp sauce" meant lamprey served with the sauce that was generally served on shrimp.

boiled lamprey (or eel)
olive oil
mackerel roe
Italian wine, preferably
   Chianti
white pepper

wine vinegar
green rockets (also called cress
   or rugola)
bitter elecampane (sorrel)
unwashed sea-urchins

For the sauce: (combine) oil of the first pressing from Venafrum (olive oil), roe from the juices of the Spanish mackerel, wine five years old, but domestic, poured in while the sauce is simmering—after the sauce is cooked, Chian is the best wine to pour in—white pepper, and vinegar made from fermenting Lesbian wine. Green rockets and bitter elecampane should be boiled in the sauce. Add sea-urchins unwashed, for the shellfish's natural brine is better than any pickle. (Do not cook after adding sea-urchins as cooking them will turn the sauce bitter. Pour sauce over skinned, cut-up and boiled eel.)

CRANE

FROM *The Art of Cooking,* 1st–5th century A.D., Apicius

a crane, duck or chicken	stoned damsons (plums)
pepper	*mulsum*
dried onion	vinegar
lovage	*liquamen*
cumin	*defrutum*
celery seed	oil

For crane, duck or chicken: Take pepper, dried onion, lovage, cumin, celery seed, stoned damsons, *mulsum,* vinegar, *liquamen, defrutum* and oil. Cook. (Simmer the sauce and pour over roasted poultry or stew the birds in this sauce.)

When you cook a crane see to it that the head does not touch the water, but is outside it. When the crane is cooked wrap it in a warm cloth and pull its head: it will come off with the sinews, so that only the meat and the bones remain. [This is necessary] because one cannot eat it with the sinews.

HARE

FROM *The Art of Cooking*, 1st–5th century A.D., Apicius

a hare (or rabbit)	asafetida root
oil	dried onion
liquamen	mint
stock	rue
a bunch of leeks	celery seed
coriander	honey
dill	*defrutum*
pepper	vinegar
lovage	cornflour (cornstarch)
cumin	

Clean the hare, bone, truss, put in the pan. Add oil, *liquamen,* stock, a bunch of leeks, coriander, dill. (Simmer.) While it is cooking put in the mortar pepper, lovage, cumin, coriander seed, asafetida root, dried onion, mint, rue, celery seed; pound. Moisten with *liquamen,* add honey, some of the cooking liquor, blend with *defrutum* and vinegar, bring to the boil (in a separate pot). When boiling, thicken with cornflour. Undo the hare, pour the sauce over, sprinkle with pepper, and serve.

BLACKBIRDS AND PIGEONS

FROM *The Art of Cooking*, 1st–5th century A.D., Apicius

birds (use squab or duck)	wine
pepper	*liquamen*
lovage	oil
thyme	*defrutum*
dried mint	mustard
filbert nut	optional: pastry made of
Jericho date	oil and flour
honey	
vinegar	

For "high" birds of any kind. (Stew them in) pepper, lovage, thyme, dried mint, filbert nut, Jericho date, honey, vinegar, wine, *liquamen*, oil, *defrutum*, mustard.

You give a bird a greater flavor and make it more nourishing, and keep all the fat in, if you wrap it in pastry made of oil and flour and cook it in the oven.

PART II

•

SUGAR AND SPICE

•

THE MEDIEVAL WORLD AND THE AGE OF ELIZABETH

England may have muttered about the extravagance of King Richard II, but at least one spot in the kingdom was merry: the back kitchens of the royal castle. Richard's master chefs were proud of their monarch's spendthrift habits. He was, they said, "the best and ryallest viander of all Christian Kynges." To pay Richard tribute and show for all posterity what a fine table he had set, his chefs wrote down the many recipes they had conceived and cooked for him. Their 1390 cookbook, *The Forme of Cury* (cookery), has a modern flair. Concerned about nutrition, the chefs advertise that they will teach a man not just how to make a crafty soup or stew, but a wholesome one as well, for they have consulted the many wise physicians and philosophers dwelling in the court. Concerned about efficiency, they include a kind of index or table of contents, so that a hungry man may find "without tarrying what meat he lusts for to have."

The instructions are sometimes odd; birds and fish are placed in "litell coffyns" or piecrusts and baked to a second death; sauces are made with vinegar as their only liquid and soaked bread as their only thickener. But most of the recipes ring familiar. Poultry and fish are simmered with slivered almonds and chopped dates and raisins. Saffron turns the dish a pacific yellow. Cinnamon, ginger and nutmeg add interest and distinction.

Indeed the recipes in *The Forme of Cury,* and in all other medieval cookbooks, closely resemble oriental and Arabic recipes still prepared today. They reveal that there was something more to the careful phrase, "best and royalest viander of all Christian kings," than first meets the eye. Richard may easily have outvianded King Charles VI of France and King John I of Portugal and all the other kings of the Christian world. But somewhere in the East, somewhere among the lucky infidels, they had it better than he did.

Unlike the infidel monarchs, the Christian kings had to scrounge for their pepper and cinnamon, be cajoled with "gifts" of saffron and nutmeg. Like France's Louis the Young, who in 1163 received not gems but a handy packet of spices from an *abbé* with an important favor to ask, they had to swallow their pride in order to swallow their dinners. For even if they were not so beautiful or as long-lasting as jewels, spices were at times just as necessary, depending upon how many caravans had been lost in a particular decade. They were essential for covering up the disastrous effects of lack of refrigeration. But medieval man came to love the taste of spice for itself alone, adding cinnamon and ginger not just to perishables like meat and fish but even to his favorite wines. Cooking without spice was as inconceivable in the thirteen hundreds as cooking without salt is today. Richard would have found America's bland food, however well preserved, unpalatable.

Because the ingredients were so ubiquitous in all medieval recipes and because they had to be imported from so far away, their cost was exorbitant. Arab traders ran the monopoly, buying the spices in Asia and hazardously transporting them back to the Levantine over roundabout sea routes and tedious land routes.

Too many middlemen, Europe complained. The thousands of miles of distance were bad enough, but paying profits to nonbelievers was beyond toleration. Europe wanted its own path to the east.

In 1415 Prince Henry the Navigator of Portugal conceived the idea of reaching India by sailing around the bottom of Africa. For the rest of his long life he sent ship after ship to sail down along Africa's west coast to find a way to the East. It was slow, miserable work for the superstitious sailors who believed all the tales as old as Odysseus of bloody and boiling seas and greedy monsters that could swallow a ship whole. And the real sufferings, the scurvy and sickness and starvation that plagued them perpetually, were enormous beyond conception.

Year after dreadful year progress occurred. One captain rounded a cape on the Moroccan coast and brought home gold and slaves. But this was not what the medieval world was after. Henry pressed his captains on. In 1488 another explorer rounded the tip of Africa and headed north. They called the cape "Good Hope." But the route to the East was still just a hope.

Columbus attempted it and failed. He believed the world was round and that India could be reached by sailing westward. When he arrived at the Bahamas, he thought he was in Japan. The Spanish, who had sponsored the voyage, gloated because their Portuguese neighbors had been struggling eastward unsuccessfully for eighty years. But the Portuguese calmly pointed out that Columbus too had brought back no spices.

Then in 1498 Vasco da Gama sailed around the Cape of Good Hope and arrived on the western shores of India. Despite dangerous opposition from the Arab traders who recognized that now their long-standing monopoly would collapse, he loaded aboard his ship a heavy cargo of spices. Two years after they had left home, Da Gama's leaking ships sailed back into port where his cargo brought a market price sixty times greater than what he had paid for it. The way to the East was opened, and Europe could begin a new future free of caravans and Arabs.

Colonization soon followed the discoveries, and the virtues of the worlds encountered in the search for spice were revealed and relished. Africa provided gold and slaves; America provided corn and potatoes and cocoa. Magellan circled the globe. The Middle Ages were over— the world was round.

Oddly, once their possession had been achieved, spices began to grow less important. They were still widely used. The Elizabethans put sage, cinnamon, nutmeg and mace into their butter. When Sir Francis Drake reached the Spice Islands in the latter part of the sixteenth century, the first cargo he attempted to haul home to England was six tons of cloves. But a comparison of the recipes of the two periods shows that while the medieval cook catholically demanded five or six or even seven different herbs and spices in a dish, the Elizabethan chef often stuck to two or three. Like the sadness after love, it was a phenomenon cruelly human, this turning from the desired object once attained.

Still, the defection was gradual. Essentially eating habits in Shakespeare's day remained the same as they had been two hundred years earlier in Chaucer's. In the medieval world there were frequent fast days when appealing food had to be prepared despite extensive proscriptions. The marvelous medieval talent for disguise and "counterfet," a necessity that later blossomed into an art separate and apart from its origin, seems to have first sprung from this constraint. Thus the medieval cooks would make "two capons of one" by removing the skin of a capon and serving Bird One without skin and Bird Two as a skin stuffed with something other than authentic capon flesh. Thus they would make an egg resemble a cabbage. Or make white wine into red wine right at the table by throwing powdered flowers into the wine-glass. They seemed to take a childlike delight in such counterfeiting. The recipe for turning white wine into red cautions the mischiefmaker to do it while no one is looking, as if to say, "Won't they be surprised!"

This delight went much further, into the realm of fantastic, selfless creation. Elaborate "subtleties" came into favor—sculptures made of paste or jelly or custard that were not to be eaten but to be admired and talked about. Much later, in the nineteenth century, this visual approach to cuisine was to be immortalized by the great French chef Carême. But the medieval men who practiced it were nameless, just like their brother-creators of churches and paintings. Art was anonymous. It offered its practitioners no personal immortality. And the subtlety-makers must have had a particular dedication. Not only was immortal-ity never to be theirs, but even the materials in which they worked were destined for prompt decay. Still, they molded great suns and lions from pink jelly and chicken. Or shaped the four seasons in pastry. At the coronation of King Henry the Fifth they whipped up a dinner of antelopes, swans and eagles, each with the scriptures written out on "her bylle." At the installation of Clifford, Bishop of London, they ex-ceeded themselves. They built a castle in the midst of a custard, and in the castle they molded a demon confronting a learned doctor in a pulpit. So minute was the cooks' attention to detail that this poor jellied Faust even wore a pious Latin inscription on his green hood!

The Elizabethans continued this tradition. But they molded in marchpane (marzipan). They made castles from it and creatures like mermaids, dolphins, eagles or camels, and even fortifications complete with drummers, trumpeters and soldiers. Queen Elizabeth had an in-ordinate love of sweets and often received gifts made of marchpane. Her subjects and servitors, though reputedly fond of her, nevertheless gave the often toothaching queen a marchpane rendition of St. Paul's, a marchpane chessboard, and a myriad other minor sweets as a New Year's gift one winter.

Both the medieval host and the Elizabethan host loved to serve food in its most fanciful form. Peacocks in their plumage, swans with silvered bodies and gilded beaks resting on a field of green pastry were common. One writer tells of an elaborate medieval feast in France at which an enormous pastry was hauled in. When the baron began to carve it, twenty little birds dashed out and began flying recklessly about the crowded hall, just like the "four and twenty blackbirds baked in a pie." Unfortunately, these little birds were part of an entertainment. The baron's falconers unleashed their hawks, who pounced upon the unlucky birds, much to the delight of the audience.

The Elizabethans liked this kind of culinary playfulness too, and were known to bake peacocks and pheasants inside a pie crust, the bodies buried in butter and flour but the gilded bills protruding at one end and the handsome tailfeathers thrust out at the other.

In both ages there were recipe books, quite a few of which have come down to us. The most delightful medieval cookbook, because it is the most personal, is one written late in the fourteenth century by an elderly Parisian bourgeois for his child-bride. She was a girl of fifteen. He was well into his sixties. Moreover, she was an orphan, with no wise female relatives to teach her how to run a household, and he was a wealthy man, accustomed to his comforts. The bride made his life even more complicated by cleverly choosing their honeymoon as the time to make him promise to be indulgent to her youth and never correct her in front of the servants. At a loss about how to turn the child into the kind of woman he wanted, he devised the idea of teaching her through writing a book. Nothing could be more private than that.

Both behavior and cookery came under his scrutiny. "Have a care that you be honestly clad," he warns his wife, "without too much or too little frippery . . . as happens with certain drunken, foolish or witless women, who have no care for their honour, nor for the honesty of their estate or of their husbands, and who walk with roving eyes and head horribly reared up like a lion. . . ." He generously asks that she learn proper behavior not for himself alone, but for the sake of that husband who will one day inherit her when he is dead. And he tells her where to get the best bargains in fish and herbs and how to prepare his favorite puddings, sausages, soups and roasts. Always considerate, when a recipe seems too complex for her youthful skill, he excuses her. "It is not a work for a citizen's cook, nor even for a simple knight's; and therefore I leave it."

By the late 1500's the printing press had come along and a rash of cookbooks appeared. Unmistakably a woman's item, these books were beautiful. Like missals, they were tiny, made to be carried in the palm of a dainty hand or tucked deep inside a belt. Their paper was so fine it barely crumbles today. Their design was so elaborate that some books bore ornate borders of flowers on every one of their two by three pages.

Because of the competition, the authors were forced to attract their audience by offering more than merely recipes. They tried the trick of denouncing their competitors: all previous cookbooks "instructed how to marre rather than make good Meate," warned John Murrel's 1631 *Two Bookes of Cookery & Carving*. They invited criticism: "Reade, Practice and Censure," announced bold Sir Hugh Plat in his 1609 *Delightes for Ladies*. They included such sure feminine enticements as ways to distill perfumes. And they gave "infallible and approved" remedies for maladies. A woman could learn how to cure a husband suffering from the bite of a mad dog, or a child suffering from pleurisy. She could learn to make a "tart that is a courage to man or woman." She could even learn how to stay thin. Thomas Dawson's 1587 *Good Huswife's Jewell* told weight-conscious Elizabethans about a controlled-diet drink, "For to make one slender take Fennell, and seeth it in water, a very good quantity, and wring out the juyce thereof when it is sod, and drinke it firste and laste. . . ."

In both the late Middle Ages and the time of Elizabeth, great ceremony accompanied dining for those that could afford it. We undoubtedly eat better quality food these days, but with far less splendor. In the Middle Ages feasts were spread upon tables set with gold and silver cups in the shape of lions and dragons. At every place a lovely individual cake of fine flour appeared and pewter or silver porringers were shared by every two guests (an improvement over an earlier custom of a common drinking vessel, shared by the assemblage). Throughout the meal minstrels would make music. In Elizabethan England the same kind of ceremony continued. While Elizabeth was being served dinner, twelve trumpets and two kettledrums resounded. The elegant Sir Francis Drake had his meals served to the sound of trumpets even at sea.

The pageantry in the lordly homes became particularly brilliant at Christmastime. The great halls were no longer much used in Elizabeth's day and served primarily as a servants' mess hall. But at Christmas the family would eat there once again, sitting high on the dais and close to a good fire. They were fed many courses, each preceded by music. Perhaps there would be the traditional boar's head, revered not just because of the taste of its meat but for its symbolic importance, some Elizabethans believing the boar had taught man how to plough the fields through its habit of digging at the earth with its tusks. Perhaps there would be a peacock, brought in by the family's pretty daughter, and the men would take the "Peacock Vow"—pledging, with one hand on the back of the proud bird, that they would always be brave, always defend the rights of women.

The poor, of course, fared badly. While the rich fed upon the brown meats of beef, mutton, game and pork, the poor lived on what were euphemistically known as "white meats"—milk, butter and cheese. Their bread was made of coarse barley, rye or oats and in times of want farmers were even known to have made their bread from acorns. In the Middle Ages the poor crowded round the gates of castles that were giving feasts, hoping to receive table scraps which were, indeed, sometimes tossed to the many dogs, sometimes to them. They were fortunate because medieval man had not yet thought of plates to eat upon. Rather, he had his meat served onto loaves of bread called "trenchers," used exclusively as a surface upon which food might lie. At the end of a feast these gravy-soaked trenchers were collected and distributed at the gates. And in Elizabeth's time the poor were fortunate because a custom of politeness prevented the wealthy from drinking wine throughout their meals. Wine cups were placed upon a sideboard and whenever a guest wished a drink, he could call for a cup, sip some mouthfuls from it and hand it back to the servant who then dumped the remainder into a bowl of dregs destined for the poor.

It was a painful period in which to be underprivileged. As it does today, prosperity raged all around the unfortunate. Venetian glass had come into vogue, and the rich decked out their tables with it, careless of its high destructibility. Even those unable to afford it longed for the kind of dramatic wastefulness and indulgence the possession of glass implied. They purchased cheap imitations made of burnt stone which, says one contemporary writer, "went the same way—to shards—anyway." Other new extravagances were on their way too. Forks, which had been known previously but not used, were described in 1611 by Tom Coryate as being seen in Italy in the homes of all the fastidious and really nice people. "The Italians," he wrote, "doe alwaies at their meales use a little forke, when they cut their meate. . . . The reason of this their curiosity is, because the Italian cannot by any means indure to have his dish touched with fingers, seeing all men's fingers are not alike clene." Coryate was considered eccentric in his fondness for this gentility, but there was no way of stopping it. Young girls were cautioned not to wipe their mouths on the tablecloth, and the squires who waited on table were instructed not to spit across the board or beyond it. Table manners were becoming ever more fashionable, do what men might.

England was prosperous now. She had colonies and a navy. The time had come for refinements and change.

Hard liquor began to get some modest use. Writers disagreed about its effects, just as they do today. "Prolongs health, dissipates superfluous matters, revives the spirits, and promotes youth," said one; "hurtful," decreed another, "to all that are of a hot nature and complexion."

Potatoes were brought in from the New World. The Elizabethans welcomed them, but saved their enthusiasm for that particular gift of the West Indies: sugar. In the Middle Ages it had come from the Levant in small, irregular lumps, but, as it was very expensive, most people had used honey as their sweetener. Now it was available in quantity. Huge loaves of it were imported and ever newer sweets were invented. The whole nation went mad for sugar. Elizabeth carried candy and comfits with her wherever she went. Not just fruits and nuts but even marigolds and roses and gillyflowers were preserved in sugar.

England became known as a land preoccupied with the good eating of sugar and spice and everything nice. She prided herself upon her consumption. "We do not, thanks be to God and the liberty of our princes," wrote William Harrison in 1587, "dine or sup with a quarter of a hen, or make repast with a cock's comb as they do in some countries; but if occasion serve, the whole carcasses of many capons, hens, pigeons and suchlike do oft go to wrack besides beef, mutton, veal and lamb." Such riches gave England a reputation for both generosity and extravagance, a reputation which was to draw upon her the blessing (or the plague, some said) of French cooks come to practice their art in a land where provisions abounded. The next culinary step forward would be engineered by the French.

ARABIAN NIGHTS

THE HISTORY OF THE BARBER'S SIXTH BROTHER

The Arabian Nights comes to us early in our youth. It enters the recesses of our minds and there remains, despite age and the movies, as the supreme world of fantasy: our very dreams occur in its shape. For there is something richer and more profound about this world, even when first explored in expurgated editions, than in any of the fantasy of our Western heritage. Here are words the very sounds of which summon up dreams: myrtle, tamarisk, ambergris. Here is an entire culture, the rich and the poor, the learned and foolish, the wicked and the godly. Here are the delights of love, of food and wine, of friendship and riches, but here also are the most absolute cruelties and anguish. The Arabian Nights *can be more gentle than* Alice in Wonderland, *more horrifying than* Grimm's Fairy Tales. *It was composed over a period of many centuries from tales that had been told not just in Arabia but in Persia and India as well; when it was written down it was already ancient, and the lasting quality of its stories proven.*

In the form we know it, the tales in the Arabian Nights *are told by Scheherazade, the noble daughter of a vizier in the court of a caliph who takes a new bride each night and kills her the following morning. Scheherazade braves death in a bold attempt to stop this madness. She agrees to be the caliph's bride-for-a-day, but devises a plan of starting a story each evening and refusing to finish it until the next. Her plan is successful. So engrossed does the caliph become that he continually postpones her death and, ultimately, abandons his murderous ways with women.*

The story reprinted here, "The Barber's Story of His Sixth Brother," teeters for a while on the verge of horror. There is something ominous about the Barmecide's joke. One should not humiliate and tantalize the starving so. Yet, after all, like a dream which we safely pilot from nightmare start to happy end, it turns out to be just a joke, just that, and everyone eats happily ever after.

The history of my sixth brother is the only one that now remains to be told: and he was called Schacabac, the hare-lipped. He was at first sufficiently industrious to employ the hundred drachms of silver which came to his share, on the division between him, me, and his other brothers, in a very advantageous manner; but at length, by reverse of fortune, he was reduced to the necessity of begging his bread. In this occupation he acquitted himself with great address, his chief aim being to procure admission, by bribing the officers and domestics, into the houses of the great, and, by having access to their persons, to excite their compassion.

He one day passed a very magnificent building, through the door of which he observed a spacious court, where he saw a vast number of servants. He went up to one of them, and inquired of him to whom the house belonged. "My good man," answered the domestic, "where can you come from to ask such a question? Any one you would meet would tell you it belonged to a Barmecide." My brother, to whom the liberal and generous dispositions of the Barmecides was well known, addressed himself to the porters, for there were more than one, and requested them to afford him some charity. "Come in," answered they, "no one prevents you, and speak to our master; he will send you back well satisfied."

My brother did not expect so much kindness; and, after returning many thanks to the porters he, with their permission, entered the palace, which was so large that it took him some time to find the apartment belonging to the Barmecide. He at length came to a large square building, of a very beautiful style of architecture, into which he entered by a vestibule that led to a fine garden, the walks of which were formed of stones of different colours, very pleasant to the eye. The apartments, which surrounded this building on the ground floor, were almost all open, and shaded only by some large curtains in order to keep off the sun, and which, when the heat began to subside, they drew aside to admit the fresh air.

My brother would have been highly delighted to remain in so pleasant a spot, had his mind been sufficiently at ease to enjoy it. He advanced still further, and entered a hall which was very richly furnished, and ornamented with foliage, painted in azure and gold. He perceived a venerable old man, whose beard was long and white, sitting on a sofa, and in the most distinguished place. Hence he judged him to be the master of the house. In fact, it was the Barmecide himself, who, in an obliging manner, told him that he was welcome, and asked him what he wished. "My lord," answered my brother in a lamentable tone, in order to excite his pity, "I am a poor man, who stands very much in need of the assistance of such powerful and generous persons as you." He could not have done better than address himself to the person he did, for he was possessed of a thousand amiable qualities.

The Barmecide was much astonished at my brother's answer; and, putting both his hands to his breast, as if to tear his habit as a mark of commiseration: "Is it possible," he cried, "that I should live at Bagdad, and that such a man as you should be so much distressed as you say you are? I cannot suffer this." At this exclamation my brother, thinking he was going to give him a singular proof of his liberality, wished him every blessing. "It shall never be said," replied the Barmecide, "that I abandon you; nor do I intend that you shall again leave me."

"Sir," replied my brother, "I swear to you that I have not even eaten anything this day."

"What!" cried the Barmecide, "is it true, that at this late hour you have not yet broken your fast? Alas, poor man, he will die with hunger! Hello there, boy!" he added, raising his voice, "bring us instantly a basin of water, that we may wash our hands."

Although no boy made his appearance, and my brother observed neither basin nor water, the Barmecide nevertheless began to rub his hands, as if some one held the water for him, and while he was doing this he said to my brother: "Come close, and wash along with me." Schacabac by this supposed that the Barmecide was fond of fun, and as he himself liked a little raillery, and was not ignorant of the submission the rich expect from the poor, he approached him and did the same.

"Come," said the Barmecide, "now bring us something to eat, and mind you do not keep us waiting." He had no sooner said this than he began, although nothing had been brought, to eat as if he had taken something in his plate, and pretended to be eating, calling out at the same time to my brother: "Eat, I entreat you, my guest; make yourself quite at home. Eat, I beg of you: you seem, for a hungry man, to have but a poor appetite."

"Pardon me, my lord," replied Schacabac, imitating his motions at the same time very accurately, "you see I lose no time, and understand my business very well."

"What think you of this bread?" said the Barmecide; "don't you find it excellent?"

"In truth, my lord," answered my brother, who in fact saw neither bread nor meat, "I never ate anything more white or delicate."

"Eat your fill, then," rejoined the Barmecide: "the slave who made this bread cost me, I assure you, five hundred pieces of gold." Then continuing to praise the female slave who was his baker, and boasting of his bread, which my brother devoured only in imagination, he said: "Boy, bring us another dish."

"Come, my friend," he continued to my brother, though no other boy appeared, "taste this fresh dish, and tell me if you have ever eaten any boiled mutton and barley better than this."

"Oh, it is admirable!" answered my brother: "I therefore, you see, help myself very plentifully."

"It affords me great pleasure," added the Barmecide, "to see you, and I entreat you not to suffer any of these dishes to be taken away, since you find them so much to your taste." He presently called for a goose with sweet sauce, and dressed with vinegar, honey, dried raisins, grey peas and dried figs; this was brought in the same manner as the mutton had been. "This goose is nice and fat," said the Barmecide; "here, take only a wing and a thigh, for you must nurse your appetite; there are many more things yet to come." In short, he called for many other dishes of different kinds, of which my brother, all the time dying with hunger, constantly pretended to eat. But what he boasted of most was a lamb that had been fattened with pistachio nuts and which, when ordered, was served up in the same manner as the other dishes had been.

"Now this," said he, "is a dish you never meet with anywhere but at my table, and I wish you to eat your fill of it." As he said this, he pretended to take a piece in his hand, putting it to my brother's mouth: "Take and eat of it," he said, "and you will not think ill of my judgment in boasting of this dish."

My brother held his head forward, opened his mouth, pretended to take the piece and to eat and to swallow it with the greatest pleasure. "I was quite sure," said the Barmecide, "you would think it excellent."

"Nothing can be more so," replied Schacabac, "in short, no table can be more deliciously served than yours."

"Now bring the ragout," said the other; "and I do not think you will be less pleased with that than with the lamb. Well, what do you think of it?"

"It is wonderful," answered my brother: "we have in this at the same time the flavour of amber, cloves, nutmegs, ginger, pepper and sweet herbs; yet they are so well balanced that the presence of one does not injure the flavour of the rest. How delicious it is!"

"Do justice to it, then," cried the Barmecide, "and eat heartily of it, I beg. Hello, boy!" cried he, raising his voice, "bring us a fresh ragout."

"Oh no, by no means," said Schacabac, "for in truth, my lord, I cannot eat any more."

"Let the dessert, then," said the Barmecide, "be served, and the fruit brought." He then paused a few moments, in order to give the servants time to change the dishes, when resuming his speech, he said: "Taste these almonds; they are just gathered, and very good."

They then both pretended to take the skin off the almonds, and eat them. The Barmecide after this invited my brother to partake of many other things. "Here are, you see," he said, "all sorts of fruit, cakes, dried comfits, and preserves; take what you please." Then stretching out his hand, as if he were going to give him something: "Take this lozenge," he said, "it is excellent to assist digestion." Schacabac pretended to take it and eat it, saying, "Here is no want of musk in this, my lord?"

"I have them made at home," said the Barmecide, "and neither for these nor anything else in my house is any stint made of aught that can ensure its goodness." And still continuing to persuade my brother to eat, he said, "for a man who was almost starving when he came here, you have really eaten hardly anything."

"My lord," replied Schacabac, whose jaws were weary of masticating nothing, "I assure you I am so full that I cannot eat another morsel of your cheer."

"Well then," cried the Barmecide, "after having eaten so heartily, it is necessary to drink a little. You have no objection to good wine?"

"My lord," replied my brother, "excuse me, but I never drink wine, because it is forbidden me."

"Oh, you are much too scrupulous," said the other, "come, come, do as I do."

"To oblige you, then," replied Schacabac, "I will; for I observe you do not like that anything should be omitted in our feast. But as I am not in the habit of drinking wine, I am afraid of being guilty of some fault against good breeding, and even against the respect that is due to you. It is for this reason that I still entreat you to excuse my drinking any wine; I shall be well satisfied with water."

"No, no," said the Barmecide, "you must drink wine." At the same time he ordered some to be brought. But the wine, like the dinner and dessert, did not in reality appear. He, however, pretended to pour some out, and drank the first glass. After that he poured out another glass for my brother, and presenting it to him: "Come, drink my health, he cried, "and tell me if you think the wine good."

My brother took the ideal glass, and first holding it up and looking to see if it were of a good bright colour, he put it to his nose in order to examine if it had an agreeable perfume; he then, making a profound reverence to the Barmecide, to show that he took the liberty of drinking his health, drank it off: accompanied at the same time proofs of receiving great pleasure from the draught. "My lord," he said, "I find this wine excellent: but it does not seem to me quite strong enough."

"You have only to speak," replied the other, "if you wish for stronger: I have various sorts in my cellar. We will see if this will suit you better." He then pretended to pour out another for himself, and also some for my brother. He did this so frequently that Schacabac, pretending that the wine had got into his head, feigned to be drunk.

This being the case, he raised his hand and gave the Barmecide such a violent blow that he knocked him down. He was going to strike him a second time but the Barmecide, holding out his hand to avoid the blow, called out: "Are you mad?"

My brother then, recollecting himself, said: "My lord, you had the goodness to receive your slave into your house, and to make a great feast for him: you ought to have been satisfied with having made him eat, without compelling him to drink wine. I told you at first that I should be guilty of some disrespect: I am sorry for it, and ask you a thousand pardons."

He had hardly finished this speech before the Barmecide, instead of putting himself into a passion and being very angry, burst into a violent fit of laughter. "I have searched for a long time," said he, "for a person of your disposition. I not only pardon the blow you have given me, but from this moment I wish to look upon you as one of my friends, and that you shall make no other house than mine your home. You have had the complaisance to accommodate yourself to my humour, and the patience to carry on the pleasantry to the end; but we will now eat in reality." Having said this, he clapped his hands when several slaves instantly appeared, whom he ordered to set out the table, and serve dinner. His commands were quickly obeyed, and my brother was now in reality treated with the dishes he had before partaken of only in imagination. As soon as the table was cleared, they brought some wine; and a number of beautiful female slaves very richly dressed appeared, and began to sing some pleasant airs to the sound of instruments. Schacabac, in the end, had every reason to be satisfied with the kindness and civility of the Barmecide, who took a great fancy to him and treated him in the most familiar manner; he gave him also a handsome dress from his own wardrobe.

The Barmecide found my brother possessed of such varied knowledge, that in the course of a few days, he entrusted him with the care of his household and other weighty affairs: and my brother acquitted himself of his charge during the time it lasted, which was twenty years, to the complete satisfaction of his employer.

MENU:

Goose with sweet sauce,
dressed with vinegar, honey, raisins and dried figs

Lamb fattened with pistachio nuts

Cakes

(Hais)

Thirty years ago it would not have been possible to provide recipes that came even within a few centuries' range of the food described in The Arabian Nights. *The caliphs of Baghdad were proverbial for their opulent courts, but although Arabic poets and taletellers often named the elaborate dishes eaten in Baghdad, virtually nothing was known of how these foods were prepared. Then, in the 1930's an antique Arabian cookbook was unearthed. It had been written in Baghdad in 1226, just a few years before that city was sacked by the Mongols who destroyed or scattered many of its literary treasures.*

The author of the work, one Muhammad ibn al-Hasan ibn Muhammad ibn al-Karim al-Katib al-Baghdadi, was both a cook and a gastronomer. There are only six pleasures in life, Muhammad wrote: food, drink, clothes, sex, scent and sound. And of all of these, the most consequential and the noblest pleasure is that of food, for without food none of the others may be enjoyed. Ingratiatingly, he used the very authority of the Prophet to support his praise of good eating. "It is not prohibited to take delight in food," he wrote, for "whenever the Prophet was invited by any of his Companions to partake of food with him, which he had prepared to the best of his ability, according to his lights, he did not refuse."

Muhammad's recipes bear a surprising correspondence to the dishes described in the centuries-older Arabian Nights. Yet they contain detailed, step-by-step instructions and often provide exact quantities of ingredients, making his work seem far more modern than that of the even later medieval cooks of France and England.

GOOSE WITH SWEET SAUCE, DRESSED WITH VINEGAR, HONEY, RAISINS AND DRIED FIGS

FROM *Baghdad Cookery Book*, written in 1226

goose or other fat meat (2-3 pounds, cubed)

water (to barely cover)
cinnamon bark (½-1-inch piece)

salt to taste
dry coriander (a few seeds)
white onions (6-8 small pearl
 onions)
leeks (2-3)
skinned eggplant or carrots
 (1 small cutup eggplant or
 some 3-4 carrots)

saffron (a pinch, for coloring)
wine vinegar (¼-½ cup)
date juice or honey (⅜-¼ cup)
almonds, blanched and halved
 (¼ cup)
raisins, currants and chopped
 dried figs (¾ cup altogether)
rose water (a teaspoon or less)

Cut fat meat into middling pieces, place in the saucepan (brown it) and cover with water, cinnamon bark, and salt to taste. When boiling, remove the froth and cream with a ladle, and throw away. . . . Add dry coriander. Take white onions, Syrian leeks, and carrots if in season, or else eggplant. Skin, splitting (and slicing) the eggplant thoroughly, and half stew in water in a separate saucepan: then strain, and (place) in the saucepan on top of the meat. Add seasonings and salt to taste. . . . Take wine vinegar and date juice, or honey if preferred—date juice is the more suitable—and mix together so that the mixture is midway between sharp and sweet, then pour into the saucepan, and boil for an hour (or until tender). When ready to take off the fire, remove a little of the broth, bray (crush) into it saffron as required, and pour back into the saucepan. Then take sweet almonds, peel, split and place on top of the pan, together with a few raisins, currants and dried figs. Cover for an hour, to settle over the heat of the fire. (Turn off the flame and allow the liquid to settle so that the fat rises, then scoop it off with a spoon or bits of paper toweling. It isn't necessary to wait an hour as the fat will begin to accumulate on top of the liquid shortly after the heat is turned off.) Wipe the sides with a clean rag (to remove any sediment), and sprinkle rose water on top. When settled, remove.

(Serves 6-8)

LAMB FATTENED WITH PISTACHIO NUTS

FROM *Baghdad Cookery Book*, written in 1226

The Arabians often cooked lamb with pistachios and some translations of the barber's story of his sixth brother are ambiguous about whether the lamb or the lamb dish itself was stuffed or "fattened" with pistachios.

red meat (uncooked lamb), sliced
 into thin cubes (1 pound)
minced meat (lamb, 1 pound)
fresh sheep's tail (3 tablespoons melted lamb fat)*

½ *dirham* (about ¼ teaspoon) salt
a little ground coriander
water (to barely cover)
peeled pistachios (1 for each
 meat ball)

salt and pepper
rose water (just enough to wet
meat balls)
saffron (just enough to color rose
water)
1 *dirham* (about ½ teaspoon)
ground cinnamon and ginger
mixed
10 *dirhams* (about 5 teaspoons)
good vinegar
50 *dirhams* sugar (this is about

½ cup, which would make the
dish far too sweet for most
modern palates. Use considerably less. A good guide is that
Chinese sweet and sour dishes
use less sugar than vinegar.)
a handful of fresh jujube fruits
(these are datelike fruits, and
fresh or dried cut up dates
can be substituted)
½ handful peeled almonds (¼ cup)

Slice red meat into small, thin cubes; melt fresh tail,* and remove the sediment. Put the (thin cubes of) meat into the oil to fry lightly, adding half a *dirham* of salt and a little quantity of fine-brayed (crushed) dry coriander. Cover with lukewarm water. Then take (minced) red meat . . . and throw in a little of the usual seasonings. Make into cabobs the shape of jujube fruits, putting into each a peeled pistachio, and throw into the saucepan. When half boiled, make a thick mixture of saffron and rose water (go easy on the saffron—use just a pinch); take out the cabobs and put them into this, then, after they are colored, return them to the pot. When almost cooked, drop in a *dirham* of fine-brayed (crushed) cinnamon and ginger, and sprinkle with about 10 *dirhams* of good vinegar. Add 50 *dirhams* of sugar. Then throw in a handful of fresh jujube fruits, and half a handful of peeled sweet almonds. Color with saffron, and spray with a little rose water (use mixture in which meat balls were rolled). Wipe the sides of the sauce-pan with a clean rag, and leave to settle over the heat of the fire for an hour. (Turn off the light and allow the liquid to settle so that the fat rises, then scoop it off with a spoon or bits of paper toweling. It isn't necessary to wait an hour as the fat will begin to accumulate on top of the liquid shortly after the heat is turned off.) Then remove.

(Serves 4-6)

* The thirteenth-century Arabic chef used the fatty tail of a sheep to provide cooking grease. Lamb fat or ordinary vegetable oil may of course be used instead.

CAKES

Hais

FROM *Baghdad Cookery Book,* written in 1226

1 *ratl* (about 2 cups) of fine dry
bread or biscuit crumbs

3 *uqiya* (about ½ cup) of ground
almonds and pistachios

¾ *ratl* (about 1½ cups) of fresh or
   preserved stoned dates
   (coarsely chopped)
2 *uqiya* (about 6 tablespoons)
   sesame oil or melted butter

powdered sugar
(honey) *

Take fine dry bread or biscuit, and grind up well. Take a *ratl* of this, and three-quarters of a *ratl* of fresh or preserved dates with the stones removed, together with three *uqiya* of ground almonds and pistachios. Knead all together very well with the hands. Refine two *uqiya* of sesame oil, and pour over, working with the hand until it is mixed in.* Make into cabobs (little balls) and dust with fine-ground sugar. If desired, instead of sesame oil, use butter. This is excellent for travelers.

(Makes about 15 cabobs)

* You may have difficulty in shaping the crumbs into cabobs. If you do, add a little honey to the mixture, just enough to make the balls malleable.

BOCCACCIO

THE DECAMERON: FIFTH TALE ON THE FIRST DAY 1348–53

"The authority of human and divine laws almost disappeared," wrote
Boccaccio of the plague in Florence in 1348 which devastated the city.
*"Like other men the ministers and executors of the laws were all dead
or sick or shut up with their families, so that no duties were carried
out. Every man was therefore able to do as he pleased."*

*In the midst of this atmosphere of license and death, ten young
men and women join in a retreat to the country to wait out the plague*

in beauty, quiet and order. They agree upon rules: they will eat well
and rest well and, to amuse themselves, each day all ten will tell
each other tales.

The tale reprinted here is typical of the value Boccaccio placed
upon wit. The beautiful and faithful wife in this story uses her wit to
avoid being seduced by an amorous king. Thus the monarch cannot
be insulted, or seek revenge; wit can only increase his respect for her.

The marquise serves the king many different dishes, but each
one is composed in some way of chicken. And though the sauces
and flavorings differ, the king recognizes each dish is chicken. The
marquise has made her point: her recipes are delicious, but they
are all basically the same. She conveys to the king that this rule applies
to women too. All women, no matter how disguised and appealing,
are basically the same. The king would not find her so very special,
she implies, and should not then steal her away from her husband.
And the amazing marquise, by using her wit instead of cruel words,
says all this to the powerful king without offending him.

At first Dioneo's story moved the women to shame, which outwardly
manifested itself in modest blushes, but then, as they looked slyly at
one another, hardly able to contain their laughter, they listened to the
rest, smiling archly. Once ended, they chided him prettily, pretending
such naughty stories were not the sort to tell in the presence of women,
and the queen, turning to Fiammetta who was sitting next to him on
the grass, requested her to continue. With sweet grace and a blithe
face she began:

Since we're on the subject of showing the power of apt and ready
answers, it occurs to me, lovely ladies, to tell you the story of how a
noble lady retained her virtue by word and deed, and kept a man
from violating it. We all know that a man shows great good sense by
placing his affections in a woman of higher station than himself. We
also know it shows remarkable discretion in a woman to keep herself
from yielding to the passion of a man above her in rank. Here is the
story it is my turn to tell.

The Marquis of Monferrato, a man of rare courage and a standard-
bearer of the Church, had gone across the seas in an armed crusade
of the Christians. It so happened that at the court of King Philip le
Borgne, who was preparing to set out from France on the same crusade, a knight stated that there wasn't a single couple under heaven

fit to compare with the Marquis of Monferrato and his lady. For as the marquis was famed among his knights as a man of rare virtues, his wife was held among the women as incomparable for beauty and worth.

These words so struck the king's fancy that although he had never seen the lady he immediately fell deeply in love with her, and determined to sail for the crusade from no other port than Genoa, so that by journeying as far as that city by land, he might have a plausible pretext for stopping to see the marquise on the way. He thought, you see, that since the marquis was away, he might contrive to give vent to his desire.

The plan had no sooner entered his mind than he began to put it into effect. He sent all his men ahead, keeping only a small retinue of nobles about him, and set out on his journey. Then, when he was but a day's distance from the marquise's territory, he sent word to inform the lady that he would be pleased to dine with her the following morning. The marquise was a shrewd and discreet woman. Smiling, she replied she deemed the king's visit the highest possible favor, and that she would be delighted to welcome him. But privately she could not help wondering why on earth the king, of all people, should come to visit her while her husband was away. Nor was she wrong when she concluded that her beauty must have lured him there.

Nevertheless, like the gentlewoman she was, she made up her mind to receive him with due honor, and calling to her whatever men had remained behind, she managed with their help to make all the necessary preparations. The dinner alone, and the meats, she chose to decide upon for herself. As quickly as might be, she ordered all the hens the countryside contained to be brought, and commissioned her cooks to make a variety of dishes, but of such fowl only.

At last, on the day established, the king arrived, and with great honor and festivity the lady received him. He was even more impressed with her actual beauty, virtue and courtesy than he had been on hearing the knight's word, and he marveled greatly. He did nothing but shower her with praise and grew more and more inflamed with desire, the more he realized how far the woman exceeded his former conception of her.

First he rested a while in the beautifully decorated rooms that had been made ready with everything suitable to receive so great a king, and when dinnertime came, both he and the marquise took their places at table. The rest of the guests, according to their quality, were entertained at other tables.

One after another, many dishes were served the king, and wonderful, costly wines, all of which pleased him immensely, yet not so much as the delight he experienced whenever he gazed upon the ravishing marquise. And yet, as course followed course, the king could not help feeling puzzled, for in spite of the variety of the dishes, he perceived that they were all concocted of hens. Now he knew very well that the neighborhood must have abounded in all kinds of venison and game. Moreover, he had given the lady ample notice of his coming, for her to have had the leisure to send the men hunting.

Nevertheless, although it caused him much wonder, he had no wish to take exception to anything but the omnipresent hens. Turning to her merrily, he said, "Tell me, madam, are only hens born in this place, and not a single cock?"

The marquise understood his question only too well. Reflecting that God had at last offered her the opportunity she desired for speaking out her mind, she turned to the king.

"No, sire," she answered boldly. "But although females may differ in garb and dignity, they are all made the same here, as anywhere else."

On hearing these words the king was not slow to understand the reason for the dinner of hens, nor did he fail to appreciate the virtue hidden in her answer. He knew that words would be useless with such a lady, and that violence was out of place. Therefore, since he had unwisely flared up with passion for her, he could follow no other course for his honor's sake, than wisely to quench his ill-conceived ardor. Without uttering another word for fear of her retorts, he continued eating hopelessly. With the dinner over, he thought it best to take his leave as soon as possible, to cover his dishonorable visit. Thanking her for the honor she had done him and she, in turn, commending him to God, he set out for Genoa.

MENU:

One chicken course after another

Capons stwed
Giblets
Pigge or chiken in sauge
Capon brewet
Farced chickens, colored or glazed

There are only a few medieval cookbooks extant, but each one is more enticing than the last. The recipes for the marquise's chicken dinner come from Two Fifteenth Century Cookbooks, *compiled from manuscripts in England's Harleian Collection, and from Eileen Power's translation of the cookbook written by the fourteenth-century Goodman of Paris to teach his child-bride how to cook.*

CAPONS STWED

FROM *Two Fifteenth Century Cookbooks*

The seasonings should be added generously. Whatever amounts you include will hardly equal those indulged in by medieval chefs. Use a quarter- to a half-teaspoon of the herbs and spices, according to your preferences; toss in the parsley by the tablespoonful and add an abandoned handful of currants or raisins to produce an elegant dish. Salt should be used, even if the fifteenth-century cookbooks overlooked it.

1 capon (or chicken)	wine (white, about 2 cups)
parsley	currants (or raisins)
sage	sugar (to taste)
hyssop	ground ginger
rosemary	(salt)
thyme	optional: dough or batter
saffron	

Take parcelly, Sauge, Isoppe, Rose Mary and tyme, and breke hit bitwen thi hondes, and stoppe the Capon there-with; colour hym with Safferon, and couche him in a erthen potte, or of brasse, and lay splentes underneth, and al about the sides, that the Capon touche no things of the potte; strawe good herbes in the potte and put there-to a pottel of the best wyn that thou may gete, and none other licour; hele (cover) the potte with a close led, and stoppe hit aboute with dogh or bater, that no eier come oute; and set hit on the faire charcole, and lete it seethe easly and longe till hit be ynowe. And if hit be an erthen potte then set hit on the fire whan thou takest hit doune, and lete hit not touche the grounde for breking; and whan the hete is ouer past, take oute the Capon with a prik; then make a sirippe of wyne, Reysons of corance, sugur and Safferon, and boile hit a littul; medel pouder of Ginger with a litul of the same wyn, and do therto; then do awey the fatte of the sewe of the Capon and do the Sirippe to the sewe, and pure hit on the capon and serue it forth.

How to make it today:
Sprinkle the inside of your chicken or capon with parsley, sage, hyssop, rosemary and thyme, and place in a pot that has a tight lid. Sprinkle more of the same herbs on the chicken, add saffron and salt and a cupful of wine, and cover the pot tightly, sealing it with dough or batter. (Sealing the pot with dough or batter was a way of insuring that no juices would be lost in cooking; it's the manner found today in dishes cooked *en daube.* Make a paste of flour and water thick enough to handle and press it tightly all along the closure between your pot and its lid, so that no air may escape.) Put the pot on the fire and let it simmer gently until chicken is tender (about an hour), then remove chicken to a platter. In a separate saucepan make a sirup of the rest of the wine, some currants, sugar and a few grains of saffron. Simmer this briefly; add powdered ginger. Meanwhile, skim off the fat in the pot in which the chicken cooked, then combine this cooking liquid with the wine sirup. Pour the whole over your chicken and serve.

(A 4-5-pound chicken will serve 4-5)

GIBLETS

from *Two Fifteenth Century Cookbooks*

In the fifteenth century this recipe was called "Garbage." But the word did not have the connotation it has for us. It referred to the entrails and, while we don't generally eat chickens' heads these days, livers, necks, and gizzards are still a popular part of our diet. Verjuice, a common ingredient in medieval dishes, is the sour juice of crabapples or other unripe fruit. To simulate a medieval flavor, try substituting a mild cider vinegar for this rare ingredient.

chicken livers, necks, feet and
  gizzards (about 2 pounds)
beef broth (to cover)
pepper
cinnamon
cloves
mace
parsley

sage
bread (1 slice)
ginger
verjuice (substitute mild cider
  vinegar, 1/3 cup)
salt
saffron

Take faire Garbage, chikenes hedes, ffete, lyvers and gysers, and wassh hem clene; caste hem into a faire potte, and caste fressh broth of Beef, powder of peper, Canell (cinnamon), clowes, Maces, Parcely, and Sauge myced small; then take brede, stepe hit in the same brothe. Draw hit throgh a streynour, cast therto, and lete boyle ynowe; caste there-to pouder ginger, vergeous, salt and a littul Safferon, and serve hit forthe.

How to make it today:
Put chicken livers, necks, gizzards and scalded skinned feet into a pot (if you prefer, brown giblets first in a little fat) and add beef broth, pepper, cinnamon, cloves, mace and parsley. Then take bread, moisten it with some of the broth, strain it through a strainer into the broth and gizzards, and simmer for an hour. Add powdered ginger, a little vinegar, salt and saffron; heat and serve.

PIGGE OR CHICKEN IN SAUGE

FROM *Two Fifteenth Century Cookbooks*

We no longer smite off the heads of our chickens, nor use vinegar as a basic ingredient in chicken gravy. But with a few minor changes, this very popular medieval dish still tastes exceptional today: wine may be substituted for the vinegar; the salt, wine, ginger and sage may be added when the chicken is first thrust into the pot, thus giving it time to absorb their flavors. These two changes make a dish very closely resembling modern Chinese recipes for chicken.

chicken, cut in pieces
a handful or two of sage
  (1 teaspoon dried sage)
hard-cooked egg yolks (2-3)

vinegar (or wine, about 1 cup)
pepper and salt
ginger

Take a pigge or chiken, draw him, smyte of his hede, kutte him in lllj quarters, boyle him til he be ynowe; take him uppe, and lete cole, smyte him in peces; take an hondefull or ij of Sauge, wassh hit, grynde it in a morter, whit hard yokes of egges; then drawe hit uppe with goode vinegre but make hit not to thyn; then seson with powder of Peper, ginger and salt; then cowche this pigge in disshes and caste the sirippe there-upon and serue it forthe.

How to make it today:
Brown a quartered chicken. Add sage, pepper, salt, ginger, and vinegar or wine. Close pot tightly and simmer about an hour or until tender. Remove. Sprinkle chopped hard-cooked egg yolks on the chicken and serve.

(A 4-5-pound chicken will serve 4-5)

CAPON BREWET

FROM *The Goodman of Paris,* containing recipes written in the 1300's

capons (or chickens)	cloves
water and wine (to cover)	galingale (no longer available)
shortening	pepper
almonds	grain of Paradise (cardamon
ginger	seeds)
cinnamon	vinegar

Cook your capons in water and wine, then dismember them and fry them in grease,* and then bray (chop) the guts and livers of your capons with almonds, and moisten them with your sewe (the broth in which the chicken cooked) and boil; then take ginger, cinnamon, clove, galingale, long pepper and grain of Paradise and moisten them with vinegar and boil; and to serve it forth; put the solid part out into bowls and pour the pottage onto it.

(A 4-5-pound chicken will serve 4-5)

* This medieval practice was the reverse of our own. We would dismember and fry (brown) the chickens first and then cook them with the water and wine. The innards and spices would be added while the chicken simmered, not at the end.

FARCED CHICKENS, COLORED OR GLAZED

FROM *The Goodman of Paris,* containing recipes written in the 1300's

Farced meant forced, or stuffed. You may want to make a chicken this way, but first read what the Goodman thinks of it.

They first be blown up and all the flesh within taken out, then filled up with other meat, then coloured or glazed; but there is too much to do, it is not a work for a citizen's cook, nor even for a simple knight's; and therefore I leave it.

GEOFFREY CHAUCER

THE CANTERBURY TALES
c. 1387–1400

In the spring, writes Chaucer, many a man's fancy turns to thoughts of religion. What better time to make a pilgrimage to St. Thomas à Becket's tomb at Canterbury than in April, when gentle breezes awaken spring's tender shoots and small birds stay up and sing throughout the night.

On such an April day six centuries ago a motley crew of pilgrims wends its way toward Canterbury, stops at an inn and there exchanges stories drawn from the mythology of the entire medieval world. So diverse and perfectly drawn are the pilgrims that the prologue to the Canterbury Tales *has been called "the concise portrait of an entire nation." But so timeless are Chaucer's observations that his work is also a concise portrait of the vagaries of human nature in any time and country.*

Several of Chaucer's pilgrims take a great interest in food or things of the table. There is the cook, a man who could make blancmange with the best, and the prioress whose table manners were so refined that she could stick her fingers into the sauce without getting the tips too dirty. But the epicurean franklin is one of literature's greatest food lovers, a dignified, generous man who kept his house so filled with dainties "it positively snowed with meat and drink."

There was a *Franklin* . . . it appeared;
White as a daisy-petal was his beard.
A sanguine man, high-coloured and benign,
He loved a morning sop of cake in wine.
He lived for pleasure and had always done,
For he was Epicurus' very son,
In whose opinion sensual delight
Was the one true felicity in sight.
As noted as St. Julian was for bounty
He made his household free to all the County.
His bread, his ale were finest of the fine
And no one had a better stock of wine.
His house was never short of bake-meat pies,
Of fish and flesh, and these in such supplies
It positively snowed with meat and drink
And all the dainties that a man could think.
According to the seasons of the year
Changes of dish were ordered to appear.
He kept fat partridges in coops, beyond,
Many a bream and pike were in his pond.
Woe to the cook whose sauces had no sting
Or who was unprepared in anything!
And in his hall a table stood arrayed
And ready all day long, with places laid.
As Justice at the Sessions none stood higher;

He often had been Member for the Shire.
A dagger and a little purse of silk
Hung at his girdle, white as morning milk.
As Sheriff he checked audit, every entry.
He was a model among landed gentry.

MENU:

Bake meat pie of fish

Bake meat pie of flesh

Partridge

Bream

Pike

Sauces with sting

Vert sauce
Sauce Aliper

A Noble Boke of Cookry ffor a Prynce Houssolde or eny other Estately
Houssolde *is the sonorous title of the medieval manuscript from which the
Chaucerian recipes were drawn. The recipes in the* Noble Boke *seem to
have been written out sometime shortly after 1467, for they make reference
to an important feast that occurred in that year. But some of them have
been traced even further back in history to recipes found in the 1390 cookbook written by the chefs of King Richard II and to even earlier French
originals.*

BAKE MEAT PIE OF FISH

FROM *A Noble Boke of Cookry,* written circa 1467

lamprons (river lampreys; use
   eels)
water (to cover)
powder (perhaps a mixture of
   ginger, cinnamon, cloves,
   cardamon and sugar, suggested by another medieval
   cookbook)
salt
vinegar (2-3 tablespoons)
coffins (piecrusts)

thick almond milk (about 1 cup,
   made by seeping ½ cup ground
   blanched almonds in a cup of
   wine, broth, water or milk and
   forcing through a sieve)
fish broth (from cooking eels) or
   water
powdered sugar (about 1 tablespoon or to taste)
parsley

To mak bak metes on fysshe days take lamprons and strip them with a cloth till they be clene and boile them in watur, salt and venegar, and labur (work) them welle in powder (spice) and salt and lay them in coffins (pie crusts). Then make a thyk mylk of almonds and draw it up with faire watir or with the brothe of fisshe. Put there to pouder sugar and foilis (leaves) of parsley, venegar and salt and set them in the ovene and fill them up ther with and serve them.

How to make it today:
Buy skinned eels. Cut them into pieces about 3 inches long. Boil them in water, salt and vinegar. Remove the fish and reserve the broth. Salt and spice the fish well and lay them in piecrusts. Make a thick almond milk with the reserved fish broth. Add to it sugar, parsley, vinegar and salt, pour over the fish, close the pie and bake in the oven for 30-45 minutes.

(A 3-pound eel will serve 6)

BAKE MEAT PIE OF FLESH

FROM *A Noble Boke of Cookry*, written circa 1467

beef, pork, veal and venison, cut small (about ½ pound of each)
pepper (¼ teaspoon)
cloves (¼ teaspoon ground)
mace (¼ teaspoon ground)
ginger (¼ teaspoon ground)
minced dates (¼ cup)
currants (¼ cup)

malmsey wine (¾-1 cup) * or verjuice (use cider vinegar)
saffron (½ teaspoon)
salt (2 teaspoons)
coffin (piecrust)
capon, pheasant or other fowl, cut up
hard-cooked egg yolks (3-4)

To make pies of flesche of capon or of fessand tak good beef, pork, vele and venison. Hew it smalle (cut it small). Do thereto peper, clowes, maces, guinger and mynced dates and raissins of corrans (currants). Mete (mix) it with malmsey or verguis and cast in saffron and salt, and luk it be well sessoned. Then couche it in a large coffyne and couch in the capon or fessand hole if ye wille, or smyt them in peces, and colour them with saffron. And put in it other wild foule, if ye wille, and plant there in hard yolks of egges. And straw on clowes, maces, dates, mynced raissins of corrans, and quybibes (cubebs, which are no longer used in cooking). Then close them up and bak them and serve them.

* Malmsey is a sweet Madeira-like wine. At least one medieval recipe I encountered recommended substituting sauterne for malmsey, and if you prefer a less sweet wine for cooking meat and poultry, this substitution is advisable.

How to make it today:
Cut beef, pork, veal and venison (or any one or two of these) into small cubes. Add pepper, cloves, mace, ginger, minced dates and currants; mix with malmsey wine or sauterne and add saffron and salt. Add a capon or pheasant, cut into small pieces (the original recipe says that a whole or a cut-up fowl may be used, but since modern meat-pie eaters usually prefer daintier pieces, it is advisable to cut and bone the fowl). Color the dish with more saffron and add hard-cooked chopped egg yolks; strew cloves, mace, dates and minced currants on the top. Now close up the pie, bake it 1½ hours in a 350° oven and serve.

(Serves 6-8; if you use commercially prepared piecrusts, this amount of filling will make two standard pies.)

PARTRIDGE

From *A Noble Boke of Cookry*, written circa 1467

a partridge
wine (about 1 cup)

powdered ginger (about 1 teaspoon)
salt

A pertuche rost. Take a fedir and put it in to his hed and let hym dye, and pulle hym dry, and draw hym and rost hym as ye wold. . . . Then mynce hym and sauce hym with wyne, pouder of guinger and salt, and warme it on the fyere and serve it.

How to make it today:
Roast the partridge for 25-30 minutes, then cut it into small serving pieces and place in a saucepan with some wine, some powdered ginger and some salt. Add a little cornstarch dissolved in cold water to thicken sauce. Heat and serve.

(Serves 2)

BREAM

From *A Noble Boke of Cookry*, written circa 1467

a bream (or carp)
heated wine (1 cup per fish)
powdered ginger (½ teaspoon per fish)

verjuice (substitute cider vinegar to taste)
(salt and pepper)

To dight a breme in sauce tak and scale hym and drawe hym at the belly and prik hym at the cyne (jaw) and broylle him on a gredyrne till he be enoughe. Then tak wyne boiled and cast it to pouder of guinger and verguis. Then lay the breme in a dysshe and poure on the ceripe and serve it.

How to make it today:
Broil the fish, then take heated wine mixed with powdered ginger, and a little cider vinegar. Reduce sauce to desired consistency. Lay the fish in a dish, pour the sirup over it and serve.

(Serve 7-8 ounces fish per person)

PIKE

FROM A *Noble Boke of Cookry*, written circa 1467

A cooking caste system was observed at the table by medieval cooks. They served a whole pike to a lord and only a quarter of a pike to commoners. But any portion of a pike made this way tastes delicious.

a pike (any broilable fish or fillets may be used with this recipe)
chopped almonds (½ cup)
wine (white, 1 cup)
minced onions (about 2 tablespoons)
cloves (¼ teaspoon ground)

sugar (2 teaspoons or to taste)
cinnamon (¼ teaspoon)
pepper
ginger (¼ teaspoon)
vinegar (2 tablespoons)
salt

To make a pik in Brasye, tak and rost a pik. Then tak almondes and bray them in a mortair and temper them with whyne and streyne them. Then tak mynced onyons, clowes, and poudur and sugar, canelle (cinnamon), pepper, guinger, venygar and salt, and let it boile and serve it.

How to make it today:
Broil the pike, then pound almonds in a mortar, temper them with the wine and strain them (you will have made almond milk). If you tire of pounding, simply make the sauce with wine and chopped almonds. Add to them minced onions, cloves, sugar, cinnamon, pepper, ginger, vinegar and salt; let it simmer for a few minutes, then serve it on the fish.

(Broil 7-8 ounces of fish per person; this recipe will make ample sauce for 4)

SAUCES WITH STING

FROM *A Noble Boke of Cookry*, written circa 1467

Unless you are very fond of the exotic you will find Vert sauce and Sauce Aliper more of historical than culinary importance.

Vert sauce

parsley (2 tablespoons)
mint (½ teaspoon)
sorrel (1 tablespoon)
chives (1 tablespoon)
sauce alone (2 cups of thin beef
   gravy)

bread (1 slice trimmed brown
   bread)
vinegar (2 teaspoons malt
   vinegar)
pepper and salt

To make vert sauce, tak parslye, mynte, sorell, cyves and sauce alone. Then tak bred and step it in venygar. Do ther to peper and salt and grind them and temper them upe and serve it.

How to make it today:
Take parsley, mint, sorrel and chives and mix them together with 2 cups of some plain broth or gravy. Then take bread, steeped in vinegar and sprinkled with salt and pepper. Add the bread to the spices and strain the whole. (Serve over boiled beef.)

Sauce Aliper

brown bread (3-4 slices,
   trimmed)
vinegar (⅔ cup malt vinegar)

garlic (2-3 cloves, chopped)
pepper and salt

To make Sauce Aliper for rostid beef tak broun bred and stepe it in venygar and toiste it and streyne it and stampe garlik and put ther to pouder of pepper and salt and boile it a litill and serue it.

How to make it today:
Steep brown bread in vinegar, then strain it and add garlic, salt and pepper. Heat it a little, and serve. (Use as a dip for barbecued cocktail tidbits or fried fish.)

WILLIAM SHAKESPEARE
THE TAMING OF THE SHREW
c. 1594

Against everyone's advice Petruchio has married the shrew Katharine, a girl known for her wicked contemptuous manner and her temper quick to fury. But Petruchio knows how to tame her. He will rail and brawl throughout the night so that she cannot sleep, he will not let her have any new clothing on the pretext that everything looks unbecoming, he will twist her words, always interpreting them to the meanings he desires, and, especially, he will make her go hungry for "till she stoop, she must not be full-gorged."

In this scene Petruchio's servant Grumio presents food to the very hungry Kate who the night before was prevented by "kindness" from eating a roast that Petruchio termed too burnt for health. Now Kate is willing to accept almost any food and Grumio, by offering and taking away almost in the same breath, nearly gets her to acquiesce to a meal of mustard without meat. But Kate still has the strength to turn him down. She will be tamed, but she will never lose her dignity.

Scene three

A room in Petruchio's house.
Enter Katharine and Grumio.

GRUMIO

No, no forsooth, I dare not for my life.

Act four Scene three

KATHARINE

The more my wrong, the more his spite appears.
What, did he marry me to famish me?
Beggars that come unto my father's door,
Upon entreaty have a present alms;
If not, elsewhere they meet with charity.
But I, who never knew how to entreat,
Nor never needed that I should entreat,
Am starved for meat, giddy for lack of sleep;
With oaths kept waking, and with brawling fed;
And that which spites me more than all these wants,
He does it under name of perfect love;
As who should say, if I should sleep or eat,
'Twere deadly sickness or else present death.
I prithee go, and get me some repast,
I care not what, so it be wholesome food.

GRUMIO

What say you to a neat's foot?

KATHARINE
    'Tis passing good, I prithee let me have it.

GRUMIO
    I fear it is too choleric a meat.
    How say you to a fat tripe finely broiled?

KATHARINE
    I like it well, good Grumio fetch it me.

GRUMIO
    I cannot tell, I fear 'tis choleric.
    What say you to a piece of beef and mustard?

KATHARINE
    A dish that I do love to feed upon.

GRUMIO
    Ay, but the mustard is too hot a little.

KATHARINE
    Why then the beef, and let the mustard rest.

GRUMIO
    Nay then I will not, you shall have the mustard,
    Or else you get no beef of Grumio.

KATHARINE
    Then both, or one, or any thing thou wilt.

GRUMIO
    Why then the mustard without the beef.

KATHARINE
    Go get thee gone, thou false deluding slave,
                                    (Beats him.)
    That feed'st me with the very name of meat.
    Sorrow on thee, and all the pack of you
    That triumph thus upon my misery.
    Go get thee gone, I say.

Enter Petruchio and Hortensio with meat.

PETRUCHIO
> How fares my Kate? What sweeting, all amort?

HORTENSIO
> Mistress, what cheer?

KATHARINE
> Faith as cold as can be.

PETRUCHIO
> Pluck up thy spirits, look cheerfully upon me,
> Here love, thou seest how diligent I am,
> To dress thy meat myself, and bring it thee:
> I am sure sweet Kate, this kindness merits thanks.
> What, not a word? Nay then, thou lov'st it not.
> And all my pains is sorted to no proof.
> Here, take away this dish.

KATHARINE
> I pray you let it stand.

PETRUCHIO
> The poorest service is repaid with thanks,
> And so shall mine before you touch the meat.

KATHARINE
> I thank you sir.

HORTENSIO
> Signior Petruchio fie, you are to blame.
> Come Mistress Kate, I'll bear you company.

PETRUCHIO (aside to Hortensio)
> Eat it up all Hortensio, if thou lov'st me.
> (To Katharine) Much good do it unto thy gentle heart.
> Kate, eat apace. And now my honey love,
> Will we return unto thy father's house,
> And revel it as bravely as the best,

With silken coats and caps, and golden rings,
With ruffs and cuffs, and farthingales, and things;
With scarfs, and fans, and double change of bravery,
With amber bracelets, beads, and all this knavery.
What hast thou dined? The tailor stays thy leisure,
To deck thy body with his ruffling treasure.

MENU:

Neat's foot

Tripe

Beef and hot mustard

---

*The recipes for the food poor Kate never got come from Thomas Dawson's
1587* The Good Huswife's Jewell, *a minuscule book with gold-edged pages
and jewellike lettering that any housewife today or yesterday would cherish,
and from* The Closet of the Eminently Learned Sir Kenelm Digby, Opened,
*published in 1671. Digby had won fame as a naval commander and as
chancellor to Queen Henrietta Maria and was widely respected for his
knowledge both of cooking and the "secrets of physick." His book told the
seventeenth-century housewife not just how to prevent diseases by prac-
ticing good nutrition but how to cure them should anything go wrong.
His cure for the bite of a mad dog, which he guarantees to be "excellent
for Man or Beast," involved boiling together a quart of oil, a dram of treacle,
a handful of rue and a spoonful of tin shavings. This was to be drunk morning and evening until, presumably, the victim was either cured of mad-dog
bite or dead of metal shavings in his intestines.*

NEAT'S FOOT

FROM *The Good Huswifes Jewell*, 1587, Thomas Dawson

neat's (calf's) feet (about 2,
   chopped)
mutton broth (to cover)
5 or 6 onions, chopped
thyme, chopped fine
parsley, chopped fine
hyssop, chopped fine

butter (2 tablespoons)
pepper
salt
saffron
5 or 6 tablespoons vinegar
sops (chunks) of bread

Take your Neates feet out of the sawce and wash them in fayre water (use
boiling water, and scrape the feet with a knife), then put them into your
Mutton broth, and take five or six Onions chopped not smal, then take a

quantitie of Time, Parseley and Isope chopped fine: boyle altogether, and when it is half boyled or more,* then a dish or two of butter, and put to it, then season it with Pepper, Salt and Saffron, with five or sixe sponefuls of vinegar, and serve it upon soppes (of bread).

Cook for 3½ hours. Then cut the meat from the bones. Two calf's feet, served as an appetizer, will feed 6-12.

TRIPE

FROM *The Good Huswifes Jewell*, 1587, Thomas Dawson

tripe (about 2 pounds cut in
    squares and previously
    cooked)
butter or fat (about 2 table-
    spoons)

vinegar (about 2 teaspoons)
pepper
mustard

Let them be faire sodden (soaked), and take the leanst and cut it in Pieces, inch broade, frie them with butter or fats, and your sawce to be vinegar, Peper and Mustard, being put a little while in the frying panne with butter or fattes.

(Serves 6)

BEEF AND HOT MUSTARD

FROM *The Closet of the Eminently Learned Sir Kenelm Digby, Opened,*
1671, Sir Kenelm Digby

Beef

a rump of beef (5 pounds)
grated nutmeg
pepper and salt
3 pints of wine vinegar

3 pints of water
3 great onions (sliced)
a bunch of rosemary
sippets (toasted or fried bread)

Take a Rump of Beef, and season it with Nutmegs grated, and some Pepper and Salt mingled together, and season the Beef on the bony-side; lay it in a pipkin with the fat side downward. Take three pints of Elder-wine vinegar, and as much water, and three great Onions, and a bunch of Rosemary tied up together: put them all into (the) pipkin, and stew them three or four hours together with a soft fire, being covered close. Then dish it up upon sippets (toasted or fried bread), blowing off the fat from the Gravy; and some of the Gravy put onto the Beef, and serve it up.

(Serves 6-8)

Mustard

black mustard seed, a quart	a good onion, quartered
wine vinegar	a race (root) of ginger, scraped
white pepper	and bruised
a spoonful of sugar	horseradish root

The best way of making Mustard is this: Take of the best Mustard-seed [which is black] for example a quart. Dry it gently in an Oven, and beat it to a subtile powder, and searse (strain) it. Then mingle well strong Wine-vinegar with it, so much that it is pretty liquid, for it will dry with keeping. Put to this a little Pepper beaten small [white is best] at discretion, as about a good pugil (handful), and put a good spoonful of sugar to it [which is not to make it taste sweet, but rather quick, and to help with the fermentation], lay a good Onion in the bottom, quarted if you will, and a race of Ginger scraped and bruised; and stir it often with a Horseradish root cleansed, which let always lie in the pot, till it have lost its vertue, then take a new one. This will keep long, and grow better for awhile. It is not good till after a month, that it have fermented a while.

Some think it will be quicker, if the seed be ground with fair water, instead of Vinegar, putting store of Onions in it.

My Lady Holmeby makes her quick fine Mustard thus:

mustard seed	5-6 spoons of sugar to each
sherry sack	pint of mustard
	a little wine vinegar

Choose true Mustard-seed; dry it in an Oven after the bread is out. Beat and searse (strain) it to a most subtile powder. Mingle sherry-sack with it [stirring it a long time very well, so much as to have it of a fit consistency for Mustard]. Then put a good quantity of fine sugar to it, as five or six spoonfuls, or more, to a pint of mustard. Stir and incorporate all well together. This will keep good a long time. Some do like to put to it a little [but a little] of very sharp Wine Vinegar.

MIGUEL DE CERVANTES
DON QUIXOTE
1615

A terrible trick is being played on Sancho Panza. An honest laborer, he was convinced despite his sounder judgment to accompany the mad Don Quixote on chivalrous errands by that knight's promise that the first island they should conquer would be given to Sancho to govern. After many fantastic adventures, usually ending in beatings and injuries, they encounter a duke and duchess who, for the fun of it, pretend to make Sancho the governor of a town on their estate.

Sancho now discovers that being a governor is no easy matter. He must settle all sorts of disputes, put down attacks and, worst of all for a man of huge appetite, must not eat his meals. Humiliating a man by denying him food, while ever tempting him with dishes that grow increasingly less appetizing, was a popular literary device in Cervantes' time; Shakespeare used it too in Taming of the Shrew. *Sancho is forced to modify his demands from a gubernatorial dish of roast partridges to a simple peasant stew and even, finally, to a humble slice of bread and an onion, all to no avail. The physician of his court has been instructed as part of the joke to convince the "governor" that all the foods set before him would be injurious to his health. When Sancho decides to throw the physician in jail, the butler takes over and tells him that the food on the table has been poisoned. Sancho simply goes hungry; ultimately he will decide he prefers a subdued and satisfied stomach to a subdued and satisfied constituency.*

The history goes on to relate how they conducted Sancho from the court to a sumptuous palace, where, in a great hall, a royal and truly magnificent board was spread. He entered to the sound of flageolets, and four pages came forward to present him with water that he might wash his hands, which he did in a most dignified manner. As the music ceased, he took the seat at the head of the table, that being the only one there was, since no other place had been laid. An individual with a whalebone wand in his hand, who later turned out to be a physician, then stationed himself at Sancho's side, after which they lifted up a fine white cloth, revealing an assortment of fruit and many other edibles of various sorts.

One who appeared to be a student said grace as a page put a lace bib under the governor's chin and another who performed the functions of a butler set a dish of fruit in front of him. No sooner had he taken a bite, however, than the personage at his side touched the plate with the wand and it was instantly removed. The butler thereupon presented a dish containing other food, but before Sancho had had a chance to taste it—indeed, before it had so much as come within his reach—the wand had been laid upon it and a page had withdrawn it as swiftly as the other attendant had borne away the fruit. Astonished at this, the governor looked around at all the others present and demanded to know if this meal was supposed to be eaten by sleight of hand.

"Señor Governor," replied the man with the wand, "one may eat here only in accordance with the usage and custom in other islands where there are governors. I, sir, am a physician and am paid to serve the rulers of this particular island. I am far more attentive to their health than I am to my own, and study night and day to become acquainted with my patient's constitution in order to be able to cure him when he falls sick. My chief duty is to be present at his dinners and suppers and permit him to eat only what is good for him while depriving him of anything that may do harm or injury to his stomach. Thus I had them remove that dish of fruit for the reason that it contained too much moisture, and I had them do the same with the other dish because it was too hot and filled with spices that tend to increase the thirst. For he who drinks much slays and consumes that radical moisture wherein life consists."

"Well, then," said Sancho, "that dish of roast partridges over there, which appears to be very properly seasoned, surely will not hurt me."

"Ah," was the physician's answer, "so long as I live my lord the governor shall not partake of those."

"And why not?" asked Sancho.

"For the reason that our master, Hippocrates, lodestar and luminary of the science of medicine, in one of his aphorisms has stated: '*Omnis saturatio mala, perdicis autem pessima,*' which is to say, 'All surfeit is bad, but a surfeit of partridges is the worst of all.'"

"If that be true," said Sancho, "will the Señor Doctor kindly see what dishes there are on this table that will do me the most good and the least harm and then let me eat them without any more tapping; for by the life of the governor, and may God let me enjoy it, I'm dying of hunger, and in spite of the Señor Doctor and all that he may say, to deny me food is to take my life and not to prolong it."

"Your Grace is right, my Lord Governor," replied the physician. "And so, I may tell you that in my opinion you should not eat of those stewed rabbits, for it is a furry kind of food. And that veal—if it were not roasted and pickled, you might try it, but as it is, there can be no question of your doing so."

"Take that big dish," said Sancho, "that I see smoking down there —it looks to me like an olla-podrida; and, considering all the different things that go to make it up, I can't fail to hit upon something that will be tasty and at the same time good for me."

"*Absit,*" declared the doctor. "Let us put far from us any such evil thought as that. There is nothing in the world that affords less nourishment than an olla-podrida. Save them for canons, university rectors, or peasant weddings. Its presence is out of place on the tables of governors, where all should be delicacy and refinement. The reason for this is that always, everywhere and by everybody, simple medicines are more esteemed than are the compounded ones, since in the case of the former it is impossible to make a mistake whereas with the others one may readily do so by altering the proportion of the ingredients. In my opinion, what my Lord Governor should eat at the present time is a hundred wafers and a few thin slices of quince marmalade, which will be good for the stomach and an aid to digestion."

Upon hearing this, Sancho leaned back in his chair and, staring hard at the doctor, asked him what his name was and where he had studied.

"I, my Lord Governor, am Doctor Pedro Recio de Agüero, native of the village of Tirteafuera, which is on the right-hand side going from Caracuel to Almodóvar del Campo, and I hold the degree of doctor from the University of Osuna."

Sancho was greatly incensed by now. "Very well, let the Señor Doctor Pedro Recio de Mal-Agüero, graduate of Asuna and native of Tirteafuera, a village which is on the right-hand side as we come from Caracuel to Almodóvar del Campo—let him get out of here at once; for, if he does not, I swear my the sun that I will take a club and by making use of it, starting with him, will see to it that there is not a doctor left in this whole island, or, at any rate, none of those that I look upon as being ignorant. As for the wise, prudent, and learned ones, I will honor them as devine beings. And so I say once more, let Pedro Recio be gone or I will take this chair in which I am sitting and break it over his head; and if I am called into court for it, I will clear myself by saying that I did God a service by slaying a bad physician and a public executioner. Either give me something to eat or take back your government; a trade that does not feed the one who practices it is not worth two beans."

The doctor was terrified when he saw how wrathful the governor was and would have made a Tirteafuera of that room if at that moment the sound of a post horn had not been heard in the street. Going over to the window, the butler turned and said, "A courier from the duke, my lord; he must bring some message of importance." The courier entered, covered with sweat and very much agitated, and, drawing a paper from his bosom, he handed it to the major-domo, who read aloud the superscription, which ran as follows:

TO DON SANCHO PANZA, GOVERNOR OF THE ISLAND OF BARATARIA, TO
BE DELIVERED INTO HIS HANDS OR THOSE OF HIS SECRETARY.

"Who here is my Secretary?" inquired Sancho when he heard this.

"I, my lord," one of those present spoke up, "for I know how to
read and write and I am a Biscayan."

"With what you have just added," remarked Sancho, "you could
well be secretary to the emperor himself. Open that paper and see what
it says."

The newly fledged secretary did so and, having perused the contents of the letter, announced that the matter was one to be discussed
in private. Sancho thereupon ordered them to clear the hall, and when
the doctor and all the others with the exception of the major-domo
and the butler had gone, the secretary proceeded to read the communi-
cation:

It has come to my knowledge, Señor Don Sancho Panza, that
a furious assault upon it one of these nights, and it will accordingly
be necessary for you to keep a watch and be on the alert in order
not to be taken unawares. I have further learned through trust-
worthy scouts that four persons have entered your village in
disguise with the object of taking your life, for the reason that
they fear your great ability. Keep your eyes open, observe closely
all who come up to speak to you, and eat nothing that is offered
you. I will send aid to you if I see that you are in trouble. Meanwhile in all instances, you are to do the thing that is to be expected
of your good judgment.

From this village, the 16th of August, at four o'clock in the
morning. Your friend,

The Duke.

Sancho was astonished, and so, apparently, were the others. "The
thing to be done now," said the governor, "and it must be done at once,
is to throw Doctor Recio into jail; for if anybody is out to kill me, he
must be the one, and he means to do it by slow starvation, which is the
worst kind of death."

"Moreover," said the butler, "it is my opinion that your Grace
should not eat any of the food that is on this table, for it was a dona-
tion from some nuns, and, as the saying goes, behind the cross lurks
the devil."

"I do not deny it," replied Sancho, "and so for the present give me a slice of bread and three or four pounds of grapes; there can be no poison in that. The truth of the matter is, I cannot go on without eating. If we are to be ready for those battles that threaten us, we must be well nourished; for it is the tripes that carry the heart and not the other way around. As for you, my secretary, reply to my lord, the duke, and tell him that I will carry out his orders exactly as he gives them. And say to my lady the duchess that I kiss her hands and beg her to send a special messenger with the letter and bundle for my wife, Teresa Panza, as that will be a great favor to me, and I will do all in my power to serve her in any way that I can. While you are about it, you may also put in a kiss of the hands for my master, Don Quixote de la Mancha, that he may see that I am grateful for his bread which I have eaten. As a good secretary and a good Biscayan, you may add whatever you like and is most to the point. And now take away this cloth and give me something to eat and I'll be ready for all the spies, murderers, and enchanters that may descend on me or on this island of mine."

A page now came in. "There is a farmer outside who would like a word with your Lordship on a matter of business. He says it is very important."

"It is strange about these people who come to see me on business," said Sancho. "Is it possible they are so foolish as not to see that this is no time for things of that sort? We governors, we judges, are we not flesh-and-blood beings? Are we not to be allowed the time that is necessary for taking a little rest—unless they would have us made of blocks of marble? By God and upon my conscience, if this government of mine holds out (and I have a feeling that it won't), I'll have more than one of these fellows who come on business hauled up short. For the present, show this good man in, but make sure first that he is not one of those spies or killers that are after me."

"No, sir," replied the page, "I do not think he is; for he appears to be a simple soul, and either I miss my guess or he's as good as good bread."

"There is nothing to be afraid of," added the major-domo, "for we are all here."

"Butler," said Sancho, "would it be possible, now that Doctor Recio is no longer with us, for me to eat something with a little body and substance to it, even if it is only a slice of bread and an onion?"

"Tonight at supper," the butler informed him, "your Lordship will be fully compensated for what was lacking at dinner."

"God grant it may be so," was Sancho's answer.

MENU:

Roast partridges

with Sardine sauce
with Lemon and wine sauces

Stewed rabbits

Olla podrida

The partridge and the rabbit recipes come from two early Spanish cookbooks, Arte de Cocina *and* Nuevo Arte de Cocina. *Just as in English cookbooks of the same period, housewives are cautioned to keep their kitchens clean, to put all objects in predestined places and to sweep their floors often. But an entirely different reason is given for why these tasks must be performed. The English cookbook writers warned that unless women were neat and clean, they would be plagued by illness and mean-tempered husbands.* Arte de Cocina's *author, in a land where the Inquisition still reigned, said chillingly that unless women were neat and clean they would be punished by God.*

The Olla podrida comes from a book far removed in time from Cervantes' era but one that deserves attention. It is Julia C. Andrews' Breakfast, Dinner and Tea, Viewed Classically, Poetically and Practically, *a literary and learned mid-nineteenth-century cookbook that provided traditional foreign recipes still hard to come by today. "Anything that is good in itself is good for an olla," says the delightful writer of the recipe, "provided, as old Spanish books always conclude, that it contains nothing 'contrary to the holy mother church, to orthodoxy, and to good manners.'"*

ROAST PARTRIDGES

with Sardine sauce

FROM *Nuevo Arte de Cocina,* 1767, Juan Altamiras

partridges	skinned tomatoes or juice of a
2 fresh sardines (or 1 fresh	lime or orange
herring) to each partridge	salt and pepper
salt pork or bacon	parsley (chopped, about 1
	teaspoon per bird)

After your partridges are well-cleaned, put 2 sardines inside the body of each one, in a way in which they won't fall out. Roast the partridges with good salt pork or lard of bacon (laid in strips over bird). And if you have it, fry bacon, and put it on the partridges, with some skinned tomatoes. If you have no tomatoes, add the juice of a lime or an orange, with some pepper, salt and a little parsley. Roast the partridges before the fire (or on a rotisserie) and when they are done (allow about ½ hour in the oven), take out the sardines; serve the partridges. They will always retain the flavor of the sardines that were cooked in them. There are some people who crave the taste of sardines more than that of partridges, and they will not be disappointed.

(Allow 1 small bird per portion)

with Lemon and wine sauces

FROM *Arte de Cocina*, 1705, Montiño Francisco Martinez

Sauce 1:	Sauce 2:
partridges, roasted as you will	partridges, roasted as you will
lemon (sliced, ½ per bird)	lemons, peeled and sliced (½ per bird)
wine (white, 1 tablespoon or more per bird)	vinegar (1 tablespoon per bird)
pepper	pepper
nutmeg (⅛-¼ teaspoon per bird)	salt
butter (1 tablespoon per bird)	white wine (1 tablespoon per bird)
	sugar (1 teaspoon per bird)

The most usual way of cooking partridges is by roasting.* The sauce (sauce 1) is made by throwing in a little lemon and some wine, and pepper and nutmeg. Stew these a little but don't let them boil. And if you want to cast in a piece of butter or fat. *that will be good.*

Another sauce of lemons is served with partridges (sauce 2). Take lemons and peel them, cut them small, and add a little vinegar, some pepper, salt and a drop of white wine. Put this sauce on the partridges as they come from the roaster. And if you want to add some sugar to the sauce, to make it half sweet and half sour, *that won't be bad.*

* Modern chefs consider braising preferable to roasting. Brown the partridge in butter, then braise till done in either of the sauces.

STEWED RABBITS

FROM *Nuevo Arte de Cocina*, 1767, Juan Altamiras

rabbits (two 1½-pound skinned and cleaned rabbits)	garlic (1-2 cloves)
(butter)	pepper (and salt)
parsley (1-2 tablespoons chopped)	hot water
	laurel leaves (bay leaves, 2-3)
	cloves (2-3)

cinnamon (1-inch stick or   capers (1 tablespoon)
  ¼ teaspoon ground)   slices of lime

The best way to dress rabbits is in sauce. After skinning them, roast them well (sear them in butter), then cut them in pieces and place them in an earthen pot or stewing pan. Add to them parsley, garlic, pepper (and salt), and hot water (do not cover completely), and cook them on a gentle fire. When they are half cooked (after ½-¾ hour), add some laurel leaves, cloves and cinnamon. And if you add capers, it will go well, and if you add slices of lime, it will be even better. This is the most usual sauce.

(Serves 4)

OLLA PODRIDA

FROM *Breakfast, Dinner and Tea*, 1859, Julia C. Andrews

This is the *Olla en grande*, such as Don Quixote says was eaten only by canons and presidents of colleges; like turtle soup, it is so rich and satisfactory, that it is a dinner in itself. A worthy dignitary of Seville, in the good old times, told us that on feast days he used turkeys instead of chickens, and added two sharp Ronda apples, and three sweet potatoes of Malaga. In fact, anything that is good in itself, is good for an *Olla*, provided, as old Spanish books always conclude, that it contains nothing "contrary to the holy mother church, to orthodoxy, and to good manners."

garbanzos (chick peas), which
  have been soaked overnight
  (2 cups)
a good piece of beef (1-2 pounds,
  with bone)
a chicken (2-3 pounds, cut up)
a large piece of bacon (¼ pound)
water (use 3-4 cups to every
  pound of meat)
vegetables:
  lettuce
  cabbage
  a slice of gourd (squash)
  carrots
  beans

celery
endive
beets
onions
garlic
long peppers
red sausages (or *chorizos*)
½ a salted pig's face, which has
  been soaked overnight (or
  substitute smoked pork or ham)
optional: turkeys instead of
  chicken, apples, sweet
  potatoes. In fact, "anything
  that is good in itself. . . ."
(salt, pepper and herbs, to taste)

The veritable Olla is difficult to be made: a tolerable one is never to be eaten out of Spain, since it requires many Spanish things to concoct it and with care; the cook must throw his whole soul into the pan, or rather pot;

it may be made in one, but two are better. These must be of earthenware; put them on their separate stoves with water. Place into No. 1, garbanzos (chick peas), which have been soaked overnight; add a good piece of beef, a chicken, a large piece of bacon; let it boil once and quickly; then let it simmer (taste, and add seasonings); it requires four or five hours to be well done.

Meanwhile, place in No. 2, with (boiling, salted) water, whatever vegetables are to be had; lettuce, cabbage, a slice of gourd, of beet, carrots, beans, celery, endive, onions and garlic, long peppers. These must be previously well washed and cut, as if for a salad; then add red sausages, or *chorizos;* half a salted pig's face, which should have been soaked overnight. When all (in pot No. 2) is sufficiently boiled (about ¾ to 1 hour or until vegetables are tender), strain off the water and throw it away. Remember constantly to remove the scum of both saucepans. When all this is sufficiently dressed, take a large dish, lay in the bottom the vegetables, the beef in the center, flanked by the bacon, chicken and pig's face. The sausages should be arranged around *en couronne* (in a crown or circle shape); pour over some of the soup from No. 1 and serve hot.

(Serves 8 or more)

PART III

•

LA CUISINE CLASSIQUE

•

THE OLD WORLD, 1700 TO TODAY

In eighteenth-century England Gargantuan appetites were being whetted on Hannah Glasse's Good Goose Pye, a trifle that involved placing a pickled tongue inside a fowl, placing the fowl inside a goose, and the goose itself inside a giant piecrust. Mrs. Glasse, who was the century's most widely read cookbook writer, noted that this pie was meant only as "a pretty little Side-Dish for Supper." A more wholesome dish was her Christmas Pye, made of a bushel of flour, four pounds of butter and at least seven different kinds of game and birds.

So many pigs were roasting that the family dog, harnessed into a little circular cage, was drafted to turn the spits. Writers for a long while had boasted that at feasts so many dishes were laid upon the board that the "table is not thought well-furnished, except they stand one upon another." Now setting the table grew so complex that all the popular cookbooks had to include at great expense steel engravings indicating how and where the various courses should be laid out. Women argued violently with each other over whether a meat pie might stand near pickled tongue, roast chicken beside a winey pig.

But all culinary matters faded before the key issue of the era: were the French cooks who were taking over England's kitchens geniuses or boobies?

The fad for French cooking had probably begun when Charles II, long exiled in Europe, became king of England. By the eighteenth century all the fashionable homes had French chefs. At first caste-conscious Englishmen had considered that this was quite as it should be, but after a while they had regrets.

The French chefs made life miserable for all those around them. They forever complained that even the English upper classes had no taste and ran unsanitary kitchens. Lord Sefton's temperamental French chef gave notice because a dinner guest dared to put pepper into his masterpiece of a soup. Lord Hackum's French chef, William Verral, announced publicly that Hackum's expensive kitchen possessed not a single clean pot or pan. In his 1759 cookbook, A Complete System of Cookery, he humorously described his run-ins with the English cooks who assisted him. One of them, Nanny, particularly offended him. She handed him a filthy sauce strainer just as he was about to produce a chef d'oeuvre. Scolded by Verral, the wily Nanny shifted the blame to the upstairs maid, saying "Rot our Sue. She's always taking my sieve to sand her nasty dirty stairs." When the Frenchmen then begged her to clean it, she did, knocking it on the table edge and rinsing it in the pot that was simmering the family's pork and cabbage. At this point in his story Verral's indignation virtually sears the paper of his book. "She gave it to me again," he writes, "with as much of the pork fat as would poison the whole dinner." In fury, he turned his back on her and strained his sauce with a clean napkin instead, while Nanny, being a woman, got in the last word. Verral reports that he heard her say "as she flirted her tail in the scullery, 'hang these men cooks, they are so confounded nice.'"

The battle between Nanny and Verral is typical of the conflict that raged in internationally staffed kitchens. The English complained that opportunities were inequal and that their own talents were given no encouragement. The Duke of Bedford paid his French chef sixty pounds a year, tossed his English chef a measly thirty pounds. Hannah Glasse bellowed, "I have heard of a cook that used six pounds of butter to fry twelve eggs, when everybody knows that understands cooking that half a pound is enough, or more than need be used; but then it would not be *French*. So much is the blind folly of this age that they would rather be imposed on by a *French* Booby than give encouragement to a good English cook!"

But it was too late to reverse the trend. Given encouragement, France's culinary skills had grown increasingly more incredible.

In the Middle Ages they had cooked in France much the way they did in England. But their cooking surged forward in 1533 when Catherine de'Medici married France's Duke of Orleans and brought along as the best part of her dowry her renowned Italian chefs. They added zest to the French habits, devising tasty innovations to make themselves more welcome in this foreign land and creating desserts just to make the French jealous. A new cuisine began to develop, one combining all the best techniques of the time.

But it was the Bourbon kings who were chiefly responsible for turning the French into the world's most talented chefs and diners. Or rather, it was the lack of Bourbon kings.

All the Bourbons were enormous if not very refined eaters. Louis XIII, perhaps because he so much feared being poisoned, had a do-it-yourself approach to cooking rare in royalty. He both killed and prepared his own game, larding it as well as any cook in his kitchen. Louis XIV was lazier or more secure or merely a better administrator. He chose geniuses to provide for his table, including the great Béchamel, for whom one of cooking lore's most famous sauces is named. Under this Louis, chefs achieved a place of prominence not held since the time of the Romans. They wrote books, made pronouncements, even committed suicide when things went badly at their tables. The next Louis, the fifteenth, was a great drinker of champagne and set the mode for cold patés of larks. It was said of him that eating was the only serious occupation of his life. Even Louis XVIII, long after the Revolution had attempted to shock the Bourbons out of their decadent habits, proved to be as interested in elaborate eating as any of his forebears. He did not merely grill his chops but grilled them between two other chops, thus creating a magnificent cradle for their juices and perfumes.

It ran in the Bourbon family, this concern with taste and opulence. But when the French decided that God had not created kings separately, that the Bourbons were after all just another part of the family of man, they also seem to have decided that all men should share in the family trait. Indirectly, the French Revolution spread classic cuisine throughout France and the world.

Not only did it kill the king and the queen and a lot of the nobles, but it created mass unemployment among chefs. Because of their close affiliation to the nobility and because they had for so long pampered to the kind of decadence now being condemned by the republicans, the chefs themselves were in danger. Some went into hiding, taking up dubious professions like the running of casinos. Others fled to England, there introducing their new culinary arts. "There is not on the face of the globe so extravagant a people as the English," complained one French *emigré*. "In France, a dish once tasted is always known again, but in England that is not the case." Promptly he began to show the English what could be done with left-overs by a skillful man. Another refugee made his fortune in London by going from great house to great house and mixing salads before the very eyes of the vegetable-wary English. But although the French chefs thrived in England they grumbled, just as had their eighteenth-century forebears, about English extravagance, English sloppiness, English boorishness at table, even the English weather. In brief, they were homesick. As soon as the initial republican violence and rejection had worn off, a number of them returned to their homeland. They had a fantastic money-making idea. It was based on their knowledge of the human palate which, for them at least, if not for everyone else, meant a supreme knowlege of human nature.

The French nobles were gone or guillotined? All the more reason to gird up the populace to its new duty as keeper of the culture of *la belle France*. Only an irresponsible public (and an unhungry one) would fail to recognize that there was value in welcoming back the chefs of the nobility. Rather than destroying them the populace could appropriate them, as they had appropriated the tapestries and paintings and furniture of the nobles' homes. Noble dining would just have to become democratic.

This was the start of the restaurant. There were a few restaurants in France before the revolution, but as late as 1770 they offered little to intrigue the hungry stranger. Inns provided food, but it was usually bad. One or two hotels had meals, but they were sparse and had to be eaten at specified hours. Cookshops sold preroasted legs of lamb or sides of beef or big turkeys. But there the customer had to buy the whole works or nothing at all.

Finally men "of judgment" realized that if they sold a leg of chicken to one customer, a second would soon enough demand the wing, that if they sliced off a bit of lamb in the dark depths of the kitchen the rest of the roast was still not dishonored. Restaurants opened. But they only flourished when it was noised around that the very men who had catered to the refined palates of the courtiers were now available and at the service of any republican with the price of his meal.

The restaurants dished up to the populace elaborate food hitherto known by name but never tasted. It was a democratic arrangement, everybody said, although by 1830 prices had skyrocketed and financiers had become the new princes of gastronomy. A restaurant critic wrote, "One needs to be an English peer to dine at the Café Anglais, and a millionaire Parisian to try the Café de Paris. One may dine very well at Véry's, but one will ruin himself."

Nevertheless, millionaire or not, eating preoccupied the Frenchman. New taste treats came in, delicious winey matelotes and bewitching meringues, many-flavored ices and cakes in the shape of palaces. The truffled turkey was the rage, and so expensive were truffles that there is a tale of their being escorted through the streets of Paris by an armed guard.

Brillat-Savarin, a witty hungry man, wrote his *Physiology of Taste* in 1825 and became the spokesman of his era. His mission was to teach men to delight in their senses, particularly the sense of taste. A century later D. H. Lawrence, with a similar mission, was to write that perhaps the world would be better off if men wore tight red trousers instead of the shame-concealing loose-fitting ones they now wear. Brillat-Savarin, anticipating him, decreed that those who did not know how to enjoy the delicious excitements offered through the organ of taste "have long faces, and long eyes, and noses. It is they who invented trousers."

Gourmandism was what appealed to him, the "impassioned, reasoned and habitual preference for that which gratifies the organ of taste." Gourmandism was a force to be reckoned with in the world. It had been responsible for every major political decision and conspiracy since the time of Herodotus. It kept the world's economies going, causing wines, spirits, sugar, spices, pickles and provisions to cross the earth from pole to pole. And, should some horrid Puritan still hold out against his argument, he offered yet another conclusive defense of gourmandism: it maintained marriages. "For even those who sleep apart (and there are many such) eat at the same table; they have a theme of conversation which never grows stale, for they talk not only of what they are eating, but of what they are about to eat, what they have met with on the tables of their acquaintances, fashionable dishes, new inventions, etc.; and such table-talk is full of charm."

Actually, by the time Brillat-Savarin defended it, gourmandism was already fashionable. Everyone was a gastronome. The aristocratic de Goncourt brothers wrote of their many dinners with the literary greats of the nineteenth century, dinners at which Sainte-Beuve, Gautier, Taine and many other writers gathered in famous restaurants to drink twenty-two-year-old champagne and discuss, in the Greek fashion, problems of philosophy, love and art. The *Almanach des Gourmands* appeared, rating the provisions of the various Parisian food shops and wielding a critical cudgel over the restaurants. Balzac gorged himself publicly, consuming as many as one hundred oysters as the mere start of a meal. There were gastronomical contests in which prodigious eaters were challenged to consume many specified francs' worth of food, or five or six sirloins and a dozen pullets, or even an entire calf. Dumas ate and cooked magnificently and produced his *Dictionary of Cuisine* as a labor of love. It remained for Flaubert, always somewhat aloof, to remark that there was something ominous beneath France's growing concern with indulgence. "Early this week," he wrote, "I spent a day and a half in Paris to attend the ball at the Tuileries. I'm not joking when I say it was splendid. As a matter of fact, the whole trend in Paris is now toward the colossal. Everything is becoming wild and out of proportion. Perhaps we're returning to the ancient East. . . . And why not? The individual has been so negated by democracy that he will be reduced to a state of complete impotence, as under the great theocratic despotisms."

But most people called Flaubert pessimistic and continued to defend, welcome, even deify gourmandism. Suddenly French chefs were in demand everywhere. The French Urbain-Dubois was chef to the court of Germany; the French François Tanty cooked for the Imperial family of Russia; Marie-Antoine Carême baked for the rulers of England and Austria. In America Frenchmen staffed the new restaurants. At least one Connecticut family employed a French cook at the unheard of salary of three thousand dollars a year. Harsh Yankee accents struggled to pronounce the names of fashionable French equipment —the *bain-marie*, ancestor of our double boiler, and the *tamis*, cousin to our strainer. Midwesterners learned to *bard* and *purée* and make a *liaison*.

In England housewives were advised that the only really proper dishes to serve were French, "Jambon Glacé aux Epinards, Chaudfroid de Cailles à la Lucullus, Chaudfroid de Bécassines, Soufflés de Homard Glacé, Galantine de Cailles à la Périgord."

French cooking was "classic" cooking. The food of the literary and the cultured was almost exclusively French. Many of the authors represented in this section, whether they write of England or Germany or Russia, describe French meals. In the Chekhov story and the selection from Tolstoy, Russians eat *matelote* of turbot and *poulard à l'estragon*. In *The Magic Mountain* the Dutch Mynheer Peeperkorn serves his German guests a French *omelette aux fines herbes;* in Galsworthy's story an English businessman goes to an ecstatic death on St. Germain soup and rum *soufflé.*

The French had taken cooking, that long-time servitor of man, and made it into an art. Occasionally they seemed dotty to the English, like the chef in the selection by Thackeray on page 173. Occasionally they seemed unspeakably arrogant, like Louis Eustache Ude, who wrote in his 1828 *French Cook* that in England even "a scraper of catgut in an orchestra calls himself an *artist;* another, who makes pirouettes and jumps like a kangaroo on the stage, is dignified with the same title. And yet to a man who has under his sole direction those great feasts given by the nobility of England . . . who has more recently superintended the grand banquet at Crockford's on the occasion of the coronation of our amiable and beloved sovereign Victoria— and who, from the multiplicity of his engagements, has conversed with nearly all the members of the upper classes of English society— to such a man is denied that title of *artist . . .*"

But however dotty or arrogant they were, the French chefs had looked for the hidden flavor locked within a piece of meat in much the way a sculptor looks for the shape hidden within a block of wood or marble. They had approached cooking with a concern for the visual, for the arrangement of shapes and colors. Above all, they had elaborated and altered and transformed. This was the age-old technique of art. In following it, they had indeed become artists.

JANE AUSTEN

EMMA
1815

The handsome, clever and rich Emma Woodhouse has lived nearly twenty-one years in the world with very little to distress or vex her. Sorrow comes, "a gentle sorrow," when Emma's governess and substitute mother, Miss Taylor, marries, leaving Emma and her father on their own. They will have to create their own diversions and seek out new company.

The dinner party they give in the scene reprinted here is their first social venture without the guiding hand of Miss Taylor. Mr. Wood-house, a kindly hypochondriac who does not believe people should indulge heavily in food, is forever attempting not to offer things to his guests, for their own good of course. "Miss Bates," he says, "let Emma help you to a little bit of tart—a very little bit. . . . Mrs. Goddard, what say you to half a glass of wine? A small half-glass. . . ." But Emma manages to get the guests full. This is an affable, a gentle, meal, where the food is good and the partakers fond of one another.

There was no recovering Miss Taylor—nor much likelihood of ceasing to pity her; but a few weeks brought some alleviation to Mr. Wood-house. The compliments of his neighbours were over; he was no longer teased by being wished joy of so sorrowful an event; and the wedding-cake, which had been a great distress to him, was all ate up. His own stomach could bear nothing rich, and he could never believe other people to be different from himself. What was unwholesome to him he regarded as unfit for anybody; and he had, therefore earnestly tried to dissuade them from having any wedding-cake at all, and when that proved vain, as earnestly tried to prevent anybody's eating it. He had been at the pains of consulting Mr. Perry, the apothecary, on the subject. Mr. Perry was an intelligent, gentlemanlike man, whose frequent visits were one of the comforts of Mr. Woodhouse's life; and, upon being applied to, he could not but acknowledge (though it seemed rather against the bias of inclination) that wedding-cake might certainly disagree with many—perhaps with most people, unless taken moderately. With such an opinion, in confirmation of his own, Mr. Woodhouse hoped to influence every visitor of the newly married pair; but still the cake was eaten; and there was no rest for his benevolent nerves till it was all gone.

There was a strange rumour in Highbury of all the little Perrys being seen with a slice of Mrs. Weston's wedding-cake in their hands; but Mr. Woodhouse would never believe it.

•　•　•

Mr. Woodhouse was fond of society in his own way. He liked very much to have his friends come and see him; and from various united causes, from his long residence at Hartfield, and his good-nature, from his fortune, his house, and his daughter, he could command the visits of his own little circle, in a great measure as he liked. He had not much intercourse with any families beyond that circle; his horror of late hours, and large dinner-parties, made him unfit for any acquaintance but such as would visit him on his own terms. Fortunately for him, Highbury, including Randalls in the same parish, and Donwell Abbey in the parish adjoining, the seat of Mr. Knightley, comprehended many such. Not unfrequently, through Emma's persuasion, he had some of the chosen and the best to dine with him; but evening parties were what he preferred; and, unless he fancied himself at any time unequal to company, there was scarcely an evening in the week in which Emma could not make up a card-table for him.

Real, long-standing regard brought the Westons and Mr. Knightley; and by Mr. Elton, a young man living alone without liking it, the privilege of exchanging any vacant evening of his own blank solitude for the elegancies and society of Mr. Woodhouse's drawing-room, and the smiles of his lovely daughter, was in no danger of being thrown away.

After these came a second set; among the most come-at-able of whom were Mrs. and Miss Bates, and Mrs. Goddard, three ladies almost always at the service of an invitation from Hartfield, and who were fetched and carried home so often, that Mr. Woodhouse thought it no hardship for either James or the horses. Had it taken place only once a year, it would have been a grievance.

Mrs. Bates, the widow of a former vicar of Highbury, was a very old lady, almost past everything but tea and quadrille. She lived with her single daughter in a very small way, and was considered with all the regard and respect which a harmless old lady, under such untoward circumstances, can excite. Her daughter enjoyed a most uncommon degree of popularity for a woman neither young, handsome, rich, nor married. Miss Bates stood in the very worst predicament in the world for having much of the public favour; and she had no intellectual superiority to make atonement to herself, or frighten those who might hate her into outward respect. She had never boasted either beauty or cleverness. Her youth had passed without distinction and her middle of life was devoted to the care of a failing mother, and the endeavour to make a small income go as far as possible. And yet she was a happy woman, and a woman whom no one named without good-will. It was her own universal good-will and contented temper which worked such wonders. She loved everybody, was interested in everybody's happiness, quick-sighted to everybody's merits; thought herself a most fortunate creature, and surrounded with blessings in such an excellent mother, and so many good neighbours and friends, and a home that wanted for nothing. The simplicity and cheerfulness of her nature, her contented and grateful spirit, were a recommendation to everybody, and a mine of felicity to herself. She was a great talker upon little matters, which exactly suited Mr. Woodhouse, full of trivial communications and harmless gossip.

Mrs. Goddard was the mistress of a school—not of a seminary, or an establishment, or anything which professed, in long sentences of refined nonsense, to combine liberal acquirements with elegant morality, upon new principles and new systems—and where young ladies for enormous pay might be screwed out of health and into vanity —but a real, honest, old-fashioned boarding-school, where a reasonable quantity of accomplishments were sold at a reasonable price and where girls might be sent to be out of the way, and scramble themselves into a little education, without any danger of coming back prodigies. Mrs. Goddard's school was in high repute, and very deservedly; for Highbury was reckoned a particularly healthy spot: she had an ample house and garden, gave the children plenty of wholesome food, let them run about a great deal in the summer, and in winter dressed their chilblains with her own hands. It was no wonder that a train of twenty young couples now walked after her to church. She was a plain, motherly kind of woman, who had worked hard in her youth, and now thought herself entitled to the occasional holiday of a tea-visit; and having formerly owed much to Mr. Woodhouse's kindness felt his particular claim on her to leave her neat parlour, hung round with fancy work whenever she could, and win or lose a few sixpences by his fireside.

These were the ladies whom Emma found herself very frequently able to collect; and happy was she, for her father's sake, in the power; though as far as she was herself concerned, it was no remedy for the absence of Mrs. Weston [Miss Taylor]. She was delighted to see her father look comfortable, and very much pleased with herself for contriving things so well; but the quiet prosings of three such women made her feel that every evening so spent was indeed one of the evenings she had fearfully anticipated.

As she sat one morning, looking forward to exactly such a close of the present day, a note was brought from Mrs. Goddard requesting, in most respectful terms, to be allowed to bring Miss Smith with her; a most welcome request; for Miss Smith was a girl of seventeen, whom Emma knew very well by sight, and had long felt an interest in, on account of her beauty. A very gracious invitation was returned, and the evening no longer dreaded by the fair mistress of the mansion.

Harriet Smith was the natural daughter of somebody. Somebody had placed her, several years back, at Mrs. Goddard's school, and somebody had lately raised her from the condition of scholar to that of parlour boarder. This was all that was generally known of her history. She had no visible friends, but what had been acquired at Highbury, and was now just returned from a long visit in the country to some young ladies who had been at school there with her.

She was a very pretty girl, and her beauty happened to be of a sort which Emma particularly admired. She was short, plump, and fair, with a fine bloom, blue eyes, light hair, regular features, and a look of great sweetness; and, before the end of the evening, Emma was as much pleased with her manners as her person, and quite determined to continue the acquaintance.

She was not struck by anything remarkably clever in Miss Smith's conversation, but she found her altogether very engaging—not inconveniently shy, nor unwilling to talk—and yet so far from pushing, showing so proper and becoming a deference, seeming so pleasantly grateful for being admitted to Hartfield, and so artlessly impressed by the appearance in so superior a style to what she had been used to, that she must have good sense, and deserve encouragement. Encouragement should be given. Those soft blue eyes, and all those natural graces, should not be wasted on the inferior society of Highbury and its connections. The acquaintances she had already formed were unworthy of her. The friends from whom she had just parted, though very good sort of people, must be doing her harm. They were a family of the name of Martin, whom Emma well knew by character, as renting a large farm of Mr. Knightley, and residing in the parish of Donwell—very creditably, she believed; she knew Mr. Knightley thought highly of them; but they must be coarse and unpolished and very unfit to be the intimates of a girl who wanted only a little more knowledge and elegance to be quite perfect. She would notice her; she would improve her; she would detach her from her bad acquaintances, and introduce her into good society; she would form her opinions and her manners. It would be an interesting, and certainly a very kind undertaking; highly becoming her own situation in life, her leisure, and powers.

She was so busy in admiring those soft blue eyes, in talking and listening and forming all these schemes in the inbetweens that the evening flew away at a very unusual rate; and the supper-table, which always closed such parties, and for which she had been used to sit and watch the due time, was all set out and ready, and moved forwards to the fire, before she was aware. With an alacrity beyond the common impulse of a spirit which yet was never indifferent to the credit of doing everything well and attentively, with the real good-will of a mind delighted with its own ideas, did she then do all the honours of the meal, and help and recommend the minced chicken and scalloped oysters, with an urgency which she knew would be acceptable to the early hours and civil scruples of their guests.

Upon such occasions poor Mr. Woodhouse's feelings were in sad warfare. He loved to have the cloth laid, because it had been the fashion of his youth, but his conviction of suppers being very unwholesome made him rather sorry to see anything put on it; and while his hospitality would have welcomed his visitors to everything, his care for their health made him grieve that they would eat.

Such another small basin of thin gruel as his own was all that he could with thorough self-approbation, recommend; thought he might constrain himself, while the ladies were comfortably clearing the nicer things, to say—

"Mrs. Bates, let me propose your venturing on one of these eggs. An egg boiled very soft is not unwholesome. Serle understands boiling an egg better than anybody. I would not recommend an egg boiled by anybody else—but you need not be afraid, they are very small, you see—one of our small eggs will not hurt you. Miss Bates, let Emma help you to a little bit of tart—a very little bit. Ours are all apple-tarts. You need not be afraid of unwholesome preserves here. I do not advise the custard. Mrs. Goddard, what say you to half a glass of wine? A small half-glass, put into a tumbler of water? I do not think it could disagree with you."

Emma allowed her father to talk—but supplied her visitors in a much more satisfactory style; and on the present evening had particular pleasure in sending them away happy. The happiness of Miss Smith was quite equal to her intentions. Miss Woodhouse was so great a personage in Highbury, that the prospect of the introduction had given as much panic as pleasure; but the humble, grateful little girl went off with highly gratified feelings, delighted with the affability with which Miss Woodhouse had treated her all the evening, and actually shaken hands with her at last!

MENU:
Wedding cake
Minced chicken
Scalloped oysters
Thin gruel
Apple tarts
Custard

The model for the motherless Emma Woodhouse or her friend Harriet, or perhaps even Jane Austen herself, might have owned a copy of The Young Woman's Companion, *from which most of these recipes come. Being a charmer was no easy matter in 1813, as the* Companion *makes clear. You must of course know how to cook and how to carve, but you'd best, to make your husband happy, know how to brew malt liquor, how to write letters and how to draw and paint. All of this the* Companion *endeavored to teach the young nineteenth-century woman. And, should she have a little extra time for leisurely self-improvement, it also gave her an account of the kings and queens of England, of the nature of the female character and of the geography of Europe, Asia, Africa, America and all the English counties.*

Richard Briggs' 1792 New Art of Cookery, *from which the Apple tarts come, was an entirely different sort of cookbook. Briggs had been cook at a number of famous English taverns, including the White-Hart and the Globe, and he knew what men liked. Women might use his book, but clearly they were being instructed by a rough and tough, down-to-earth fellow. Seafaring men were what interested him, and he included a chapter specially designed for their well-being when far and dangerously away from their women, with such recipes as "Fish sauce to keep the whole year," and "Catchup to last 20 years," which was made with hearty, strong, stale beer.*

WEDDING CAKE

FROM *The Young Woman's Companion, 1813*

Nowadays hardly anyone makes wedding cakes at home, begging off because the procedure is so laborious. But it was in Jane Austen's time too. "Beat in your sugar a quarter of an hour," says the nonelectrically equipped author of this recipe, and "beat your yolks half an hour at least."

4 pounds flour	¼ ounce mace
4 pounds butter	¼ ounce nutmeg
2 pounds loaf sugar (granulated)	32 eggs, separated

4 pounds currants
1 pound almonds, blanched and
   slivered
1 pound citron

1 pound candied orange
1 pound candied lemon
½ pint brandy

Take 4 pounds of fine flour, well dried, 4 pounds of fresh butter, and 2 pounds of loaf sugar. Pound and sift fine ¼ ounce of mace, the same of nutmeg, and to every pound of flour put 8 eggs well beat up. Wash 4 pounds of currants, pick them well, and dry them before the fire. Blanch 1 pound of sweet almonds, and cut them lengthways very thin; take 1 pound of citron, the same of candied orange, the same of candied lemon, and ½ pint of brandy. First work the butter to a cream with your hand, then beat in your sugar a quarter of an hour, and work up the whites of your eggs to a very strong froth. Mix them with your butter and sugar, beat your yolks half an hour at least, and mix them with the other ingredients. Then put in your flour, mace, and nutmeg, and keep beating it well till the oven is ready. Put in your brandy, and beat lightly in your currants and almonds. Tie 3 sheets of paper round the bottom of your hoop (or use a steep-sided baking pan), to keep it from running out, and rub it well with butter. Then put in your cake and place your sweetmeats in three layers, with some cake between every layer. As soon as it is risen and coloured, cover it with paper, and send it to a moderate oven. Three hours will bake it.

MINCED CHICKEN

FROM *The Young Woman's Companion*, 1813

chicken, cooked and minced
   (about 3 pounds)
flour
gravy (about 2 cups)
pepper and salt
nutmeg (¼ teaspoon)

grated lemon (peel)
1 egg
cream
juice of 1 lemon
bread crumbs

Flour the chicken and put it into gravy, with white pepper, salt, nutmeg and grated lemon. When it boils (remove from fire) stir in an egg (previously beaten with a bit of cold water), and mix with it a little cream. As soon as it is throughly hot, squeeze in a little lemon juice, then put the whole into a dish; strew over it some crumbs of bread, brown them with a salamander* and then serve it up hot to the table.

(Serves 4)

* The salamander, a round flat piece of iron affixed to an iron handle, was heated in the fireplace until it was red-hot, then pressed against foods dredged in sugar or bread crumbs. This glazed the food, giving it a nice brown color. Our modern equivalent is placing a dish under the broiler to glaze.

SCALLOPED OYSTERS

FROM *The Young Woman's Companion*, 1813

oysters	(salt and pepper)
coarse bread or cracker crumbs	(milk or chicken broth)
butter	

Wash them thoroughly clean in their own liquor (chop them finely) and put them into your scallop shells (with their liquor); strew over them a few crumbs of bread (and some salt and pepper). Lay a slice of butter on the first you put in, then more oysters and bread and butter successively till the shell is full. (Pour some milk or chicken broth on top.) Put them into an oven to brown (15-20 minutes in a 400° oven), and serve them up hot in the shells.

(Use 4-6 per shell; serve 1 shell per person, as an appetizer)

THIN GRUEL

FROM *The Young Woman's Companion*, 1813

This is Emma's father's favorite dish. He finds it strange that it isn't eaten by everybody, every evening. And he is all commiseration for his daughter Isabella who can't find a cook who will make gruel properly. He and Isabella agree that it should turn out "a basin of nice, smooth gruel, thin but not too thin."

The gruel recommended by The Young Woman's Companion *seems excessively thin for our tastes, if not for Emma's father's. Most gruel is made with 3-4 tablespoons of grain to a pint of water.*

1 tablespoon oatmeal	salt
1 pint of water	butter

Put 1 large spoonful of oatmeal into a pint of water, and stir it well together, and let it boil 3 or 4 times, stirring it often; but be careful it does not boil over. Then strain it through a sieve, salt it to your palate, and put in a good piece of butter. Stir it about with a spoon till the butter is all melted, and it will be fine and smooth.

(Serves 2)

APPLE TARTS

FROM *The New Art of Cookery,* 1792, Richard Briggs

6 pippin apples
water (¼-½ cup)
lemon peel
sugar (¼-½ cup)
1 teaspoon rose water

flour for sprinkling
puff paste (below)
white of an egg
powdered sugar

Pare, quarter and core 6 pippins, put them into a saucepan with a little water and lemon-peel, and boil them gently (covered), till they are tender; then beat them up well with a spoon until they are smooth, sweeten them with fine sugar, take out the lemon-peel, and put in a tea-spoonful of rose water; sprinkle a little flour on your small tin patty-pans (muffin or tiny pie tins), lay in a thin sheet of puff paste (spoon in the filling), cut paste in as fine strings as you can, and string them across and across in what shape you please (lattice work); rub a little white of an egg on, sift a little powder sugar over, and bake them in a slow oven of a nice, light colour (350° for an hour); then slip them out into the dish.

(Makes enough filling for 15 tarts.)

Puff Paste

¼ peck flour (8 cups)
2 pounds butter

1 teaspoon salt
cold water

Take ¼ peck of fine flour (add salt), and rub in a pound of butter till it is fine, make it up in a light paste with cold water, stiff enough to work it up, but do not work it too much, as that will make it heavy: (preferably combine the flour, salt and water first, then add the butter) then roll it out about as thick as a crown piece, put a layer of butter (another pound) in lumps as big as a nutmeg all over it, and double it over (chill it), roll it out again (chill), and double it and roll it 3 or 4 times, then it will be fit for use, either for pies, tarts, or anything else that requires it. You may make a larger or smaller quantity by adding or diminishing the quantity of flour and butter.

(Makes enough dough for 24-30 tarts)

CUSTARD

FROM *The Young Woman's Companion,* 1813

1 quart of light cream (or 2 cups
   milk and 2 cups cream for a
   less rich custard)
cinnamon

½ cup sugar
8 egg yolks
1 teaspoon orange flower water

Put 1 quart of good cream over a slow fire, with a little cinnamon and the sugar. When it has boiled (scalded), take it off the fire (let it cool slightly), beat the yolks of eight eggs, and put to them a spoonful of orange flower water to prevent the cream from cracking. Stir the eggs in by degrees as your cream cools, put the pan over a very slow fire, stir it carefully one way till it is almost boiling, and then pour it into cups. (Or bake the custard: Pour it into custard cups, set these in a shallow pan filled with hot water and bake for 15 minutes in a slow oven.)

Or you may make them in this manner: Take 1 quart of new milk, sweeten to your taste, beat up the yolks of 8 eggs and the whites of 4. Stir them into the milk, and bake it in china basins. Or put them into a deep china dish and pour boiling water round them, till the water is better than half way up their sides; but take care the water does not boil too fast, lest it should get into your cups and spoil your custards.

(Serves 8)

CHARLES DICKENS

A CHRISTMAS CAROL
1843

Perhaps the most famous dinner scene in our literature is this one from A Christmas Carol. *Scrooge, the miser who thinks anyone who goes about saying "Merry Christmas" is an idiot who "should be boiled with his own pudding and buried with a stake of holly through his heart," is shown the error of his niggardly ways by a group of kindly spirits. In this scene, the Ghost of Christmas Present takes Scrooge to the home of Bob Cratchit, the clerk whom Scrooge underpays and bullies. Watching Cratchit and his family eat Christmas dinner, Scrooge is forced to realize the meanness and emptiness of his own life. The miser is rich in wealth, but the Cratchits are rich in each other.*

While the food for a Christmas dinner has changed very little since Dickens' time, manners have changed considerably. Mrs. Cratchit does the carving; the children are so well-behaved that they stuff spoons into their own mouths to prevent themselves from squealing for servings before it's their proper turn.

And perhaps it was the pleasure the good Spirit had in showing off this power of his, or else it was his own kind, generous, hearty nature, and his sympathy with all poor men, that led him straight to Scrooge's clerk's; for there he went, and took Scrooge with him, holding to his robe; and on the threshold of the door the Spirit smiled, and stopped to bless Bob Cratchit's dwelling with the sprinkling of his torch. Think of that! Bob had but fifteen "Bob" a-week himself; he pocketed on Saturdays but fifteen copies of his Christian name; and yet the Ghost of Christmas Present blessed his four-roomed house!

Then up rose Mrs. Cratchit, Cratchit's wife, dressed out but poorly in a twice-turned gown, but brave in ribbons, which are cheap and make a goodly show for sixpence; and she laid the cloth, assisted by Belinda Cratchit, second of her daughters, also brave in ribbons; while Master Peter Cratchit plunged a fork into the saucepan of potatoes, and getting the corners of his monstrous shirt collar (Bob's private property, conferred upon his son and heir in honour of the day) into his mouth, rejoiced to find himself so gallantly attired, and yearned to show his linen in the fashionable Parks. And now two smaller Cratchits, boy and girl, came tearing in, screaming that outside the baker's they had smelt the goose, and known it for their own; and basking in luxurious thoughts of sage and onion, these young Cratchits danced about the table, and exalted Master Peter Cratchit to the skies, while he (not proud, although his collars nearly choked him) blew the fire, until the slow potatoes bubbling up, knocked loudly at the saucepan lid to be let out and peeled.

"What has ever got your precious father then?" said Mrs. Cratchit. "And your brother, Tiny Tim! And Martha warn't as late last Christmas Day by half-an-hour?"

"Here's Martha, mother!" said a girl, appearing as she spoke.

"Here's Martha, mother!" cried the two young Cratchits. "Hurrah!

There's *such* a goose, Martha!"

"Why, bless your heart alive, my dear, how late you are!" said Mrs. Cratchit, kissing her a dozen times, and taking off her shawl and bonnet for her with officious zeal.

"We'd a deal of work to finish up last night," replied the girl, "and had to clear away this morning, mother!"

"Well! Never mind so long as you are come," said Mrs. Cratchit. Sit ye down before the fire, my dear, and have a warm, Lord bless ye!"

"No, no! There's father coming," cried the two young Cratchits, who were everywhere at once. "Hide, Martha, hide!"

So Martha hid herself, and in came little Bob, the father, with at least three feet of comforter exclusive of the fringe, hanging down before him; and his threadbare clothes darned up and brushed, to look seasonable; and Tiny Tim upon his shoulder. Alas for Tiny Tim, he bore a little crutch, and had his limbs supported by an iron frame!

"Why, where's our Martha?" cried Bob Cratchit, looking round.

"Not coming," said Mrs. Cratchit.

"Not coming!" said Bob, with a sudden declension in his high spirits; for he had been Tim's blood horse all the way from church, and had come home rampant. "Not coming upon Christmas Day!"

Martha didn't like to see him disappointed, if it were only in joke; so she came out prematurely from behind the closet door, and ran into his arms, while the two young Cratchits hustled Tiny Tim, and bore him off into the wash-house, that he might hear the pudding singing in the copper.

"And how did little Tim behave?" asked Mrs. Cratchit, when she had rallied Bob on his credulity, and Bob had hugged his daughter to his heart's content.

"As good as gold," said Bob, "and better. Somehow he gets thoughtful, sitting by himself so much, and thinks the strangest things you ever heard. He told me, coming home, that he hoped the people saw him in the church, because he was a cripple, and it might be pleasant to them to remember upon Christmas Day, who made lame beggars walk, and blind men see,"

Bob's voice was tremulous when he told them this, and trembled more when he said that Tiny Tim was growing strong and hearty.

His active little crutch was heard upon the floor, and back came Tiny Tim before another word was spoken, escorted by his brother and sister to his stool before the fire; and while Bob, turning up his cuffs—as if, poor fellow, they were capable of being made more shabby

—compounded some hot mixture in a jug with gin and lemons, and stirred it round and round and put it on the hob to simmer; Master Peter, and the two ubiquitous young Cratchits went to fetch the goose, with which they soon returned in high procession.

Such a bustle ensued that you might have thought a goose the rarest of all birds; a feathered phenomenon, to which a black swan was a matter of course—and in truth it was something very like it in that house. Mrs. Cratchit made the gravy (ready beforehand in a little saucepan) hissing hot; Master Peter mashed the potatoes with incredible vigour. Miss Belinda sweetened up the apple-sauce; Martha dusted the hot plates; Bob took Tiny Tim beside him in a tiny corner at the table; the two young Cratchits set chairs for everybody, not forgetting themselves, and mounting guard upon their posts, crammed spoons into their mouths, lest they should shriek for goose before their turn came to be helped. At last the dishes were set on, and grace was said. It was succeeded by a breathless pause, as Mrs. Cratchit, looking slowly all along the carving-knife, prepared to plunge it in the breast; but when she did, and when the long expected gush of stuffing issued forth, one murmur of delight arose all round the board, and even Tiny Tim, excited by the two young Cratchits, beat on the table with the handle of his knife and feebly cried Hurrah!

There never was such a goose. Bob said he didn't believe there ever was such a goose cooked. Its tenderness and flavour, size and cheapness, were the themes of universal admiration. Eked out by apple-sauce and mashed potatoes, it was a sufficient dinner for the whole family; indeed, as Mrs. Cratchit said with great delight (surveying one small atom of a bone upon the dish), they hadn't ate it all at last! Yet everyone had had enough, and the youngest Cratchits in particular, were steeped in sage and onion to the eyebrows! But now, the plates being changed by Miss Belinda, Mrs. Cratchit left the room alone—too nervous to bear witnesses—to take the pudding up and bring it in.

Suppose it should not be done enough! Suppose it should break in turning out! Suppose somebody should have got over the wall of the back-yard, and stolen it, while they were merry with the goose—a supposition at which the two young Cratchits became livid! All sorts of horrors were supposed.

Hallo! A great deal of steam! The pudding was out of the copper. A smell like a washing-day! That was the cloth. A smell like an eating-house and a pastrycook's next door to each other, with a laundress's next door to that! That was the pudding! In half a minute Mrs. Cratchit entered—flushed, but smiling proudly—with the pudding, like a speckled cannon-ball, so hard and firm, blazing in half of half-a-quartern of ignited brandy, and bedight with Christmas holly stuck into the top.

Oh, a wonderful pudding! Bob Cratchit said, and calmly too, that he regarded it as the greatest success achieved by Mrs. Cratchit since their marriage. Mrs. Cratchit said that now the weight was off her mind, she would confess she had had her doubts about the quantity of flour. Everybody had something to say about it, but nobody said or thought it was at all a small pudding for a large family. It would have been flat heresy to do so. Any Cratchit would have blushed to hint at such a thing.

At last the dinner was all done, the cloth was cleared, the hearth swept, and the fire made up. The compound in the jug being tasted, and considered perfect, apples and oranges were put upon the table, and a shovel-full of chestnuts on the fire. Then all the Cratchit family drew round the hearth, in what Bob Cratchit called a circle, meaning half a one; and at Bob Cratchit's elbow stood the family display of glass. Two tumblers, and a custard-cup without a handle.

These held the hot stuff from the jug, however, as well as golden goblets would have done; and Bob served it out with beaming looks, while the chestnuts on the fire sputtered and cracked noisily. Then Bob proposed:

"A Merry Christmas to us all, my dears. God bless us!"

Which all the family re-echoed.

"God bless us every one!" said Tiny Tim, the last of all.

MENU:
Roast goose
Sage and onion stuffing
Gravy
Applesauce
Christmas pudding

Cookbooks in Dickens' day had wonderful titles. The recipe for the gravy comes from The Frugal Housewife, Dedicated to Those Who Are Not Ashamed of Economy. *The way to roast and stuff the goose itself comes from* The Housekeeper's Guide or a Plain and Practical System of Domestic Cookery. *And the Christmas Pudding comes from the nineteen-word* Modern Cookery In All Its Branches Reduced to a System of Easy Practice for the Use of Private Families.

ROAST GOOSE

FROM *The Housekeeper's Guide,* 1838, Esther Copley

goose	flour
butter	salt

Roast it before a brisk fire (or in a moderate oven), but at considerable distance at first. It will require basting, for which purpose a little butter should be used at first, but its own fat will soon begin to drip. Dredge with flour and salt, and see that it is nicely browned all over. A green goose, i.e., one that has not attained its full growth, will take from 50 minutes to 1¼ hours; a full-grown goose will require nearly or quite 2 hours.*

(Allow 1-1½ pounds of goose per serving)

* Contemporary culinary science suggests about 25 minutes per pound for a goose, and an oven temperature of 325°.

SAGE AND ONION STUFFING

FROM *The Housekeeper's Guide,* 1838, Esther Copley

1 goose liver	1 tablespoon potato starch (or
bread or bread crumbs, twice the	2 tablespoons flour)
weight of the liver (preferably,	1 tablespoon butter
use 3-4 cups bread cubes for	1 egg yolk
an 8-pound goose)	salt
4 moderate-sized onions	pepper
sage, weighing half the weight	
of the onions (or use 1 table-	
spoon dried sage)	

Scald the liver, chop fine, and add all the ingredients. Mix them well and stuff the goose.

GRAVY

FROM *The Frugal Housewife,* 1832, Lydia Maria Child

2 tablespoons flour   salt
½ pint hot water (or stock)   pan drippings

Most people put ½ pint of flour and water into their tin-kitchen when they set meat down to roast. This does very well; but gravy is better flavored and looks darker, to shake the flour and salt upon the meat; let it brown thoroughly, put flour and salt on again, and then baste the meat with about ½ pint of hot water (or more, according to the gravy you want). When the meat is about done, pour these drippings into a skillet and let it boil. If it is not thick enough, shake in a little flour; but be sure to let it boil, and be well stirred after the flour is in. If you fear it will be too greasy, take off 1 cupful of the fat before you boil. The fat of beef, pork, turkeys and geese is as good for shortening as lard. Salt gravy to your taste. If you are very particular about dark gravies, keep your dredging box full of scorched flour for that purpose.*

*What *The Frugal Housewife* doesn't say about scorched flour, perhaps because using it is less frugal than using ordinary flour, is that it has only half as much thickening ability. So use more of it; brown it by stirring in a dry pan over low heat.

APPLESAUCE

FROM *The Housekeeper's Guide,* 1838, Esther Copley

5 or 6 juicy baking apples,   a bit of butter (1-2 tablespoons)
  peeled   1 teaspoon powdered sugar (or
the peel of the apples   more, to taste)
2 tablespoons cold water or cider   a dash of nutmeg
lemon peel (optional)

Pare, core and slice 5 or 6 juicy baking apples. Have your saucepan particularly well-tinned and clean. Two tablespoons of cold water or cider will be sufficient to keep the saucepan from burning, and more would only impoverish the sauce. Instead of putting on the lid of the saucepan, lay the longest pieces of apple peeling to keep in the steam. Some people like the flavor of a bit of lemon peel. Some apples require long stewing, others boil quickly, and all the time that they are in the saucepan beyond what is really necessary only injures the flavour; therefore calculate as near as may be the time required. The fire should be clear and slow, and the saucepan not suffered to come too near the fire, lest the fruit should burn. When done enough they will sink in the saucepan; then remove the peelings from the top; and beat up, with a small bit of butter, a teaspoonful of fine powdered sugar and a dust of nutmeg. This sauce is used with roast pork, goose and duck.

CHRISTMAS PUDDING

FROM *Modern Cookery,* 1845, Eliza Acton

½ cup flour
½ cup fine bread crumbs
¾ cup beef kidney suet, chopped
 small
¾ cup raisins
¾ cup currants
½ cup minced apples

¾ cup sugar
¼ cup candied orange rind
½ teaspoon nutmeg, mixed with
 some pounded mace
a very little salt
glass of brandy (¼ cup)
3 whole eggs

Mix and beat these ingredients well together, tie them tightly in a thickly floured cloth (or pour into a lightly greased and tightly covered pudding mold) and boil for 3½ hours. We can recommend this as a remarkably light small rich pudding. (To set pudding aflame, light heated brandy in a separate heatproof bowl and pour over pudding.)

(Serves 8-10)

ALEXANDRE DUMAS

THE VICOMTE DE BRAGELONNE 1848–50

Alexandre Dumas, besides being the world's most illustrious romancer, was one of the world's most illustrious eaters. Writing made him a fabulously rich man, and eating made him a fabulously poor one, but even to his dying days fine food was his prime love. He was a frequenter of the most magnificent and famous Parisian restaurants, and his presence was always a compliment to the chef.

Louis XIV was also a distinguished eater. He had a vast appetite and was often known to consume at a single sitting four plates of different soups, a whole pheasant, a whole partridge, a large plate of salad, a huge portion of mutton, two thick slices of ham and various side dishes and desserts! Under Louis great chefs became persons of honor in the kingdom, and the most famous story in all of cooking lore is the tale of Vatel, chef to one of Louis' lords. Vatel was preparing to serve an elaborate dinner when the fish he had ordered failed to arrive. Food, or the lack of it, was not something to be taken lightly in Louis' time. Humiliated, Vatel killed himself.

In The Vicomte de Bragelonne, *a second sequel to* The Three Musketeers, *the gastronomer Dumas expounds upon the gastronomer Louis XIV, an unbeatable combination. One of the main characters of the* Vicomte *is still the musketeer D'Artagnan, but a D'Artagnan grown wiser and more mature and holding a responsible position at court. In this scene D'Artagnan has brought Porthos to eat at the king's supper. Only too often the embarrassed Louis is the greatest consumer at his own dinners, and D'Artagnan hopes to ingratiate himself with the king by making Louis feel less gluttonous in the face of Porthos' grand appetite.*

It works. Like Shakespeare's Caesar who wants no lean and hungry men about him, Louis XIV considers a man's food consumption a mark of his loyalty. Says the king of Porthos, "It is impossible that a gentleman who eats so good a supper every day can be otherwise than the most praiseworthy man in my kingdom."

The King, meanwhile, had sat down to the supper-table, and the not very large number of guests invited for that day had taken their seats, after the usual gesture intimating the royal permission to be seated. At this period of Louis XIV's reign, although etiquette was not governed by the strict regulations which were subsequently adopted, the French Court had entirely thrown aside the traditions of good-fellowship and patriarchal affability which still existed in the time of Henry IV., and which the suspicious mind of Louis XIII. had gradually replaced by the ceremonial semblance of a grandeur which he despaired of being able fully to realize.

The king, then, was seated alone at a small separate table, which, like the desk of a president, overlooked the adjoining tables. Although we say a small table, we must not omit to add that this small table was yet the largest one there. Moreover, it was the one on which were placed the greatest number and variety of dishes—consisting of fish, game, meat, fruit, vegetables, and preserves. The king was young and vigorous, very fond of hunting, addicted to all violent exercises of the body, and possessed, besides, like all the members of the Bourbon family, a rapid digestion and an appetite speedily renewed. Louis XIV. was a formidable table-companion. He delighted to criticize his cooks; but when he honored them by praise and commendation, the honor was overwhelming. The king began by eating several kinds of soup, either mixed together or taken separately. He intermingled, or rather he isolated, the soups with glasses of old wine. He ate quickly and somewhat greedily.

Porthos, who from the beginning had out of respect been waiting for a jog of D'Artagnan's elbow, seeing the king make such rapid progress, turned to the musketeer and said in a low tone, "It seems as if one might go on now; his Majesty is very encouraging in the example he sets. Look!"

"The king eats," said D'Artagnan, "but he talks at the same time. Try to manage matters in such a manner that if he should happen to address a remark to you, he would not find you with your mouth full, for that would be very awkward."

"The best way," in that case," said Porthos, "is to eat no supper at all. And yet I am very hungry, I admit; and everything looks and smells most inviting, as if appealing to all my senses at once."

"Don't for a moment think of not eating," said D'Artagnan; "that would put his Majesty out terribly. The king has a habit of saying that he who works well eats well, and he does not like to have people eat daintily at his table."

"But how can I avoid having my mouth full if I eat?" said Porthos.

"All you have to do," replied the captain of the Musketeers, "is simply to swallow what you have in it whenever the king does you the honor to address a remark to you."

"Very good," said Porthos; and from that moment he began to eat with a well-bred enthusiasm.

The king occasionally looked at the different persons who were at table with him, and as a connoisseur could appreciate the different dispositions of his guests.

"M. du Vallon!" he said.

Porthos was enjoying a ragout of hare, and swallowed half of the back. His name pronounced in such a manner made him start, and by a vigorous effort of his gullet, he absorbed the whole mouthful.

"Sire," replied Porthos, in a stifled voice, but sufficiently intelligible, nevertheless.

"Let that fillet of lamb be handed to M. du Vallon," said the king. "Do you like browned meats, M. du Vallon?"

"Sire, I like everything," replied Porthos.

D'Artagnan whispered, "Everything your Majesty sends me."

Porthos repeated, "Everything your Majesty send me,"—an observation which the king apparently received with great satisfaction.

"People eat well who work well," replied the king, delighted to have opposite him a guest of Porthos's capacity. Porthos received the dish of lamb, and put a portion of it on his plate.

"Well?" said the king.

"Exquisite," said Porthos, calmly.

"Have you as good mutton in your part of the country, M. du Vallon?" continued the king.

"Sire," said Porthos, "I believe that from my own province, as everywhere else, the best of everything is sent to Paris for your Majesty's use; but, on the other hand, I do not eat mutton in the same way your Majesty does."

"Ah! and how do you eat it?"

"Generally I have a lamb dressed quite whole."

"Quite whole?"

"Yes, Sire."

"In what manner, then?"

"In this, Sire: my cook, who is a German, first stuffs the lamb in question with small sausages which he procures from Strasburg, force-meat-balls which he procures from Troyes, and larks which he procures from Pithiviers; by some means or other, with which I am not acquainted, he bones the lamb as he would bone a fowl, leaving the skin on, however, which forms a brown crust all over the animal. When it is cut in beautiful slices, in the same way that one would cut an enormous sausage, a rose-colored gravy issues forth, which is as agreeable to the eye as it is exquisite to the palate;" and Porthos finished by smacking his lips.

The king opened his eyes with delight, and, while cutting some of the *faisan en daube*, which was handed to him, he said, "That is a dish I should very much like to taste, M. du Vallon. Is it possible?—a whole lamb!"

"Yes, Sire."

"Pass those pheasants to M. du Vallon; I perceive that he is a connoisseur."

The order was obeyed. Then, continuing the conversation, he said, "And do you not find the lamb too fat?"

"No, Sire; the fat falls down at the same time that the gravy does, and swims on the surface; then the servant who carves removes the fat with a silver spoon, which I have had made expressly for that purpose."

"Where do you reside?" inquired the king.

"At Pierrefonds, Sire."

"At Pierrefonds; where is that, M. du Vallon,—near Belle-Isle?"

"Oh, no, Sire; Pierrefonds is in the Soissonnais."

"I thought that you alluded to the mutton on account of the salt marshes."

"No, Sire; I have marshes which are not salt, it is true, but which are not the less valuable on that account."

The king had now arrived at the *entrées,* but without losing sight of Porthos, who continued to play his part in the best manner.

"You have an excellent appetite, M. du Vallon," said the king, "and you make an admirable table-companion."

"Ah, Sire, if your Majesty were ever to pay a visit to Pierrefonds, we would both of us eat our lamb together; for your appetite is not an indifferent one, by any means."

D'Artagnan gave Porthos a severe kick under the table, which made Porthos color up.

"At your Majesty's present happy age," said Porthos, in order to repair the mistake he had made, "I was in the Musketeers, and nothing could ever satisfy me then. Your Majesty has an excellent appetite, as I have already had the honor of mentioning, but you select what you eat with too much refinement to be called a great eater."

The king seemed charmed at his guest's politeness.

"Will you try some of these creams?" he said to Porthos.

"Sire, your Majesty treats me with far too much kindness to prevent me from speaking the whole truth."

"Pray do so, M. du Vallon."

"Well, Sire, with regard to sweet dishes, I recognize only pastry, and even that should be rather solid; all these frothy substances swell my stomach, and occupy a space which seems to me to be too precious to be so badly tenanted."

"Ah, Messieurs," said the king, indicating Porthos by a gesture, "here is indeed a perfect model of gastronomy. It was in such a manner that our fathers, who so well knew what good living was, used to eat; while we," added his Majesty, "can do nothing but trifle with our food;" and as he spoke he took a fresh plate of chicken, with ham, while Porthos attacked a ragout of partridges and landrails.

The cup-bearer filled his Majesty's glass to the brim. "Give M. du Vallon some of my wine," said the king. This was one of the greatest honors of the royal table.

D'Artagnan pressed his friend's knee. "If you can only manage to swallow the half of that boar's head I see yonder," said he to Porthos, "I shall believe that you will be a duke and a peer within the next twelvemonth."

"Presently," said Porthos, phlegmatically; "I shall come to it by and by."

In fact it was not long before it came to the boar's turn, for the king seemed to take pleasure in urging on this famous guest. He did not pass any of the dishes to Porthos until he had tasted them himself, and he accordingly took some of the boar's head. Porthos showed that he could keep pace with his sovereign; and instead of eating the half, as D'Artagnan had told him, he ate three-fourths of it. "It is impossible," said the king in an undertone, "that a gentleman who eats so good a supper every day and who has such beautiful teeth can be otherwise than the most praiseworthy man in my kingdom."

"Do you hear?" said D'Artagnan in his friend's ear.

"Yes; I think I am rather in favor," said Porthos, balancing himself on his chair.

"Oh, you are in luck's way."

The king and Porthos continued to eat in the same manner, to the great satisfaction of the other guests, some of whom from emulation had attempted to follow them, but had been obliged to give up on the way. The king soon began to get flushed, and the reaction of the blood to his face announced that the moment of repletion had arrived. It was then that Louis XIV., instead of becoming gay and cheerful, as most good livers generally do, became dull, melancholy and taciturn. Porthos, on the contrary, was lively and communicative. D'Artagnan's foot had more than once to remind him of this peculiarity of the king. The dessert now made its appearance. The king had ceased to think anything further of Porthos; he turned his eyes anxiously towards the entrance-door, and was heard occasionally to inquire how it happened that M. de Saint-Aignan was so long in arriving. At last, at the moment when his Majesty was finishing a pot of preserved plums with a deep sigh, M. de Saint-Aignan appeared. The king's eyes, which had become somewhat dull, immediately began to sparkle. The count advanced towards the king's table, and Louis rose at his approach. Everybody rose at the same time,—even Porthos, who was just finishing an almond cake which might have made the jaws of a crocodile stick together. The supper was over.

MENU:

Several kinds of soup

Veal soup
Herb soup à la Dauphine
Onion soup

Ragout of hare

(Young rabbit fricassee)

Fillet of lamb

(*Ratonnet* of lamb)

Faisan en daube

(Braised pheasant à l'Angoumoise)

Creams

(Crème au chocolat iced cream)

Chicken with ham
Almond cakes

Most of the recipes are Dumas' own. His ardent interest in cooking resulted in Le Grand Dictionnaire de Cuisine, *a majestic cookbook filled with anecdote, historical color, and so much enthusiasm that the larding of a bird or the stewing of a piece of beef become as exciting as a rendezvous with Constance or the queen in* The Three Musketeers. *Both common and extraordinary foods—items like sautéed fillets of kangaroo and the meat of panthers—are considered, and the recipes are made even more interesting by Dumas' references to his own friends and personal experiences. There is the twelve-item dinner he cooked in an hour and a half; there is his hunting trip with the Abbé Fortier who said Mass, Low Mass, High Mass and Vespers at five thirty in the morning so that by six thirty he had finished all his services and had the whole beautiful day in which to shoot.*

There is his delightful description of the life of the chef Carême which begins, in the very manner of the fairy tale it was, "Like Theseus and Romulus, like all founders of empires, Carême was a sort of lost child."

Dumas lavished much care on the Dictionary. *He had undertaken it in the hope that it would be a diversion to him and instead it turned out to be exhausting, laborious work. Shortly before it was published he died, and the* Dictionary *lived on as the final crown of a lifetime's literary activity.*

SEVERAL KINDS OF SOUP

Veal Soup

FROM *Le Grand Dictionnaire de Cuisine,* 1873, Alexandre Dumas

butter	bouillon to cover
a few slices of ham	parsley
4-5 pounds veal (cut in pieces)	scallions
2-3 carrots	½ clove garlic
2-3 onions	1 clove
1 tablespoon fine bouillon	(salt and pepper)

Butter the bottom of a pot. Put into it a few slices of ham, 4 or 5 pounds of good-quality veal, 2 or 3 carrots, the same number of onions. Pour over it 1 tablespoonful (or a bit more) of fine bouillon and let it stew on a low fire until the liquid is reduced to a glaze and has turned a fine yellow color. Remove from the stove, cut the meat with the point of a knife to let the juices flow. Cover. Let it stew another 15 minutes. Then cover with good bouillon, add a bouquet of parsley and scallions with ½ clove of garlic and 1 clove stuck into them. Bring to a boil. Skim. Let it simmer until the meat is done (1-1½ hours). Skim off fat, strain (taste and add seasoning), and serve with rice or vermicelli, or use the broth to make your sauces.

(Serves 8-10)

Herb Soup à la Dauphine

FROM *Le Grand Dictionnaire de Cuisine,* 1873, Alexandre Dumas

4 handfuls spinach	2 handfuls chard
3 hearts of lettuce	a good pinch of chervil
the white of 1 leek	a few tansy leaves
2 onions	a few stalks purslane
2 handfuls sorrel	(petrouchka)
2 handfuls garden orach	marigold petals

butter	bouillon (to cover vegetables)
hot water, root vegetable	(salt and pepper)
water, rice water or fish	bread without crust

Chop together 4 handfuls of spinach, 3 hearts of lettuce, the white of 1 leek, 2 onions, 2 handfuls of sorrel, 2 of garden orach, 2 of chard, a good pinch of chervil, a few tansy leaves, a few stalks of purslane, and finally some marigold petals—be sure to use only the petals; the ovaries and calyx are very bitter. Heat with butter until all is wilted. Add hot water, or water in which root vegetables have cooked, or rice water, or fish bouillon, and bring to a boil. (Season to taste.) Put bread without crust in the bottom of the tureen. The flavor of the crust would spoil the fine, simple delicacy of this vegetable combination.

Onion Soup

ADAPTED FROM *Le Grand Dictionnaire de Cuisine*, 1873, Alexandre Dumas

It is unlikely that King Louis would have been served so robust a peasant soup as this one, but commoners will revel in it.

10-12 big white onions, chopped	½ cup water
½ pound of butter	6 raw egg yolks
2½ quarts of milk	salt and pepper
1½ quarts chicken stock	toasted bread crusts
2 tablespoons cornstarch	

There are two types of onions, the big white Spanish and the little red Italian. The Spanish has more food value and is therefore chosen to make soup for huntsmen and drunkards, two classes of people who require fast recuperation.

Chop fine big Spanish onions. Put onions into a blender and make a purée. Simmer the purée in ½ pound of butter. Add 1½ quarts scalded milk and 1½ quarts boiling stock and cook for 20 minutes. Bind with 2 tablespoons cornstarch dissolved in ½ cup water. Remove from fire and let cool. Beat 6 egg yolks into 1 quart of cold milk and add to the soup, stirring through. Heat, add salt and pepper to taste and pieces of toasted bread crust. And there you have it.

(Serves 12 or more)

RAGOUT OF HARE

Young Rabbit Fricassee

FROM *Le Grand Dictionnaire de Cuisine,* 1873, Alexandre Dumas

2 young tender rabbits, cut in
  pieces
water
onion slices
a bay leaf
a sprig of parsley
a few scallions
a little salt
butter

flour
mushrooms and morels
4 egg yolks mixed with butter,
  cream or some of the sauce,
  chilled
juice of a lemon, or a dash of
  verjuice or white vinegar
  (1-2 tablespoons)

Cut 2 very young, tender rabbits into pieces, wipe off the blood. Put into a pot with water, a few slices of onion, a bay leaf, a sprig of parsley, a few scallions, and a little salt. Bring to a boil. Drain. Wipe dry. Trim.

In another pot, sauté the pieces in butter, sprinkle lightly with flour, add some of the water in which they were boiled, being careful to stir so that no lumps are formed. Bring to a boil. Add mushrooms and morels, cook (for 1-1½ hours). Reduce the sauce. (Remove from fire.) Thicken it with 4 egg yolks, mixed with butter or cream or with some of the sauce, chilled. Finish with the juice of a lemon, or a dash of verjuice, or a dash of white vinegar, and serve.

(Serves 4)

FILLET OF LAMB

Ratonnet of Lamb or Mutton

FROM *Le Grand Dictionnaire de Cuisine,* 1873, Alexandre Dumas

a leg of lamb, sliced
salt and pepper
chopped *fines herbes*
  (chives, tarragon and chervil)
parsley
scallions
garlic

1 glass of oil (about ¼ cup)
the juice of 1 lemon
chopped chicken (cooked)
bacon slices
1 glass white wine
a little cullis * and meat broth

Slice a leg of lamb. Flatten the slices, season with salt, pepper, chopped *fines herbes,* parsley, scallions, garlic, 1 glass of oil, the juice of 1 lemon, all mixed together. Let them marinate 2 hours. Cover each slice with a layer of chopped chicken. Roll, fasten with a skewer, with a slice of bacon over each end to prevent the stuffing from spilling. Attach to a spit and broil, basting with the marinade mixed with 1 glass of white wine. Arrange on a platter. Add a little cullis * and meat broth to the drippings, skim off the fat, and sauce your *ratonnets,* or serve with an Italienne sauce. You can do the same with well-hung veal or beef.

* Cullis, an elaborate preparation made of meat or poultry, vegetables, flour and bouillon, was used for thickening and enhancing sauces and every good. chef always had some cullis at hand. But times have changed, so if you have no cullis, dilute your pan drippings as you would to make a gravy, with humble flour and broth.

FAISAN EN DAUBE

Braised Pheasant à l'Angoumoise

FROM *Le Grand Dictionnaire de Cuisine,* 1873, Alexandre Dumas

truffles	thin slices beef, veal and
pheasant	(blanched) bacon
4 ounces (¼ pound) grated bacon	1 glass Malaga or white wine
4 ounces (¼ pound) butter	2 tablespoons caramel
salt and pepper	chestnut purée
25-30 roasted chestnuts	

Peel some truffles and cut them into cloves, which stick into all the fleshy parts of the pheasant. Put into a pot 4 ounces of grated bacon and a similar amount of butter. In it heat some truffles cut into pieces and the chopped skins and scraps of those you used for larding. Season with a little salt and pepper. Let it simmer a few minutes, then add 25 to 30 roasted chestnuts. Stuff the pheasant with this mixture. Wrap it in thin slices of beef, veal and bacon. Tie it up with string and put into a heavy pot lined with sliced bacon. (Brown pheasant in the bacon fat.) Add 1 glass of Malaga or white wine and 2 tablespoonfuls of caramel. Cook (closely covered) over a very slow fire. When it is cooked (1½ hours or until tender) remove the bird, take off the string. Skim the fat off the liquid, add some chopped truffles, let it boil a few moments. Thicken the sauce with chestnut purée. Pour it into the platter and place the pheasant on top.

CREAMS

Crème au Chocolat Iced Cream

FROM *The French Cook*, 1828, Louis Eustache Ude

¼ pound chocolate, melted
1 quart of cream, scalded
salt
8 eggs

melted isinglass (use 2 tablespoons gelatine, softened in
water)
(1 cup sugar)

For a second course dish, take ¼ pound of vanilla chocolate, rasp it very fine, and throw it into a pan to melt with a little water (in top of a double-boiler). When melted, mix and beat it with some cream, which you have boiled (scalded), and a little salt (and the sugar). Except in *crème* of fruit, as pineapple, apricots, raspberries, etc., a little salt is always requisite, but very little, however. If you wish to make iced cream, instead of 16 eggs for 1 quart of cream, only put 8, which set on the fire to thicken (in the chocolate cream mixture), but take particular care to prevent its curdling: as soon as you take it from the fire, mix it with a little melted isinglass, and rub the whole through a tammy (fine sieve). Now try a little of the preparation in a small mold over ice. If you should find that the cream has not substance enough to allow of being turned upside down, you must add a little more isinglass.

It is to be observed that the isinglass must previously be melted in a little water.

(Serves 10-12)

CHICKEN WITH HAM

FROM *Le Grand Dictionnaire de Cuisine*, 1873, Alexandre Dumas

¾ pound butter
a little salt
juice of a lemon
a little nutmeg
2 fat pullets
bacon slices (blanched)
1 carrot
1 onion
2 cloves

parsley
scallions
½ bay leaf
½ garlic clove
a slice of ham
veal scraps
a peeled lemon, sliced
a ladleful of bouillon
½ glass white wine

Put about ¾ pound of butter (½ pound will be sufficient), a little salt, the juice of a lemon, and a little nutmeg in a bowl and mix thoroughly with a wooden spoon. Use this mixture to stuff 2 fat pullets previously prepared for the oven. Truss and tie. Line the bottom of a roasting pan (which has a lid) with slices of bacon. Put your pullets on these. Add 1 carrot, 1 onion with 2 cloves stuck in it, a bouquet of parsley and scallions, ½ bay leaf, ½ clove of garlic, a slice of ham, and a few scraps of veal. Peel a lemon to the flesh. Slice it thin, remove the seeds, put the slices on your pullets, which should lie breast up. Cover with slices of bacon. Add a ladleful of bouillon and ½ glass of white wine. Cover. Roast in a moderate oven (for 30-40 minutes per pound). When the pullets are done, untruss them, drain off the fat, and serve, on a platter, on truffle, highly-spiced espagnole, tomato, or any other sauce you prefer. (It has a fine delicate flavor of its own, and may be served without any other sauce.)

(½-¾ pound of a pullet per portion)

ALMOND CAKES

FROM *Le Grand Dictionnaire de Cuisine*, 1873, Alexandre Dumas

butter (1 cup)
2-3 egg yolks
flour (2½ cups)
sugar (¾ cup)
125 grams (about ¾ cup) crushed
  almonds

a good pinch of salt
a little orange-flower water
  (¼ teaspoon)
2 additional egg yolks for
  glazing

Make dough in the usual way, with some butter, 2 or 3 egg yolks and flour; add some sugar, 125 grams of crushed almonds, a good pinch of salt, and a little orange-flower water. Mix the ingredients well together, make a smooth paste, roll out with a rolling pin on greased paper (chill for an hour), glaze with egg-yolk (cut into small round shapes), and bake in the oven. (Moderate 375° oven for 10-15 minutes or until lightly browned.)

(Makes 2-3 dozen small almond cookies)

WILLIAM MAKEPEACE THACKERAY

PENDENNIS
1850

After a stay abroad the Clavering family returns to England, bringing with them the incredible cook Alcide Mirobolant, formerly chef to His Highness the Duc de Borodino and to His Eminence Cardinal Becca-fico. The Claverings, Papa, Mama and romantic daughter Blanche, like to be conspicuously rich and Alcide is a perfect possession for them. He wears long ringlets, a red velvet waistcoat and a gold-embroidered cap, and disdains the English as "carnivorous insularies,"

unable to appreciate the "poesy" of cooking. In the character of Alcide,
Thackeray parodies the actual French chefs who came to England in
the mid-nineteenth century and so elevated cooking that they de-
manded to be known not as chefs but as artists—men like Louis Eu-
stache Ude who insisted that, if ballet dancers and musicians were to
be called artists, cooks deserved that title too; or like the great Carême,
with his flowing painter's cravat and delicate, beringed fingers.

But like them, and despite his pretensions, Alcide really is an
artist, able to use cooking to express inner emotion. In this scene he
tells the only friend he has made in England, the elderly milliner
Madame Fribsby, about a meal he created to honor his beloved Blanche.
An absolute tour de force of cookery, virtually everything in the de-
licious meal was white to celebrate the maiden innocence of Blanche.

And there was another person connected with the Clavering estab-
lishment who became a constant guest of our friend, the milliner.
This was the chief of the kitchen, Monsieur Mirobolant, with whom
Madame Fribsby soon formed an intimacy.

Not having been accustomed to the appearance or society of persons of the French nation, the rustic inhabitants of Clavering were
not so favorably impressed by Monsieur Alcide's manners and appearance, as that gentleman might have desired that they should be. He
walked among them quite unsuspiciously upon the afternoon of a
summer day, when his services were not required at the House, in his
usual favourite costume, namely, his light-green frock or paletot, his
crimson velvet waistcoat with blue glass buttons, his *pantalon Ecossais*
of a very large and decided check pattern, his orange satin neckcloth,
and his jean-boots, with tips of shiny leather,—these, with a gold
embroidered cap, and a richly-gilt cane, or other varieties of ornament
of a similar tendency, formed his usual holiday costume, in which he
flattered himself there was nothing remarkable (unless, indeed, the
beauty of his person should attract observation), and in which he
considered that he exhibited the appearance of a gentleman of good
Parisian *ton.*

He walked then down the street, grinning and ogling every
woman he met with glances, which he meant should kill them out-
right, and peered over the railings, and in at the windows, where
females were, in the tranquil summer evening. But Betsy, Mrs. Pybus's
maid, shrank back with a "Lor bless us!" as Alcide ogled her over

the laurel bush; the Misses Baker and their mamma stared with wonder; and presently a crowd began to follow the interesting foreigner, of ragged urchins and children, who left their dirt-pies in the street to pursue him.

For some time he thought that admiration was the cause which led these persons in his wake, and walked on, pleased himself that he could so easily confer on others so much harmless pleasure. But the little children and dirt-pie manufacturers were presently succeeded by followers of a larger growth, and a number of lads and girls from the factory being let loose at this hour, joined the mob, and began laughing, jeering, hooting, and calling out opprobrious names at the Frenchman. Some cried out, "Frenchy! Frenchy!" some exclaimed "Frogs!" one asked for a lock of his hair, which was long and in richly-flowing ringlets; and at length the poor artist began to perceive that he was an object of derision rather than of respect to the rude grinning mob.

It was at this juncture that Madame Fribsby spied the unlucky gentleman with the train at his heels, and heard the scornful shouts with which they assailed him. She ran out of her room, and across the street to the persecuted foreigner; she held out her hand, and, addressing him in his own language, invited him into her abode; and when she had housed him fairly within her door, she stood bravely at the threshold before the gibing factory girls and boys, and said they were a pack of cowards to insult a poor man who could not speak their language, and was alone, and without protection. The little crowd, with some ironical cheers and hootings, nevertheless felt the force of Madame Fribsby's vigorous allocution, and retreated before her; for the old lady was rather respected in the place, and her oddity and her kindness had made her many friends there.

Poor Mirobolant was grateful indeed to hear the language of his country ever so ill spoken. Frenchmen pardon our faults in their language much more readily than we excuse their bad English; and will face our blunders throughout a long conversation, without the least propensity to grin. The rescued artist vowed that Madame Fribsby was his guardian angel, and that he had not as yet met with such suavity and politeness among *les Anglaises*. He was as courteous and complimentary to her as if it was the fairest and noblest of ladies whom he was addressing: for Alcide Mirobolant paid homage after his fashion to all womankind, and never dreamed of a distinction of rank in the realms of beauty, as his phrase was.

A cream, flavoured with pine-apple—a mayonnaise of lobster, which he flattered himself was not unworthy of his hand, or of her to whom he had the honour to offer it as an homage, and a box of preserved fruits of Provence, were brought by one of the chef's aides-de-camp, in a basket, the next day to the milliner's, and were accompanied with a gallant note to the amiable Madame Fribsby. "Her kindness," Alcide said, "had made a green place in the desert of his existence,—her suavity would ever contrast in memory with the *grossièreté* of the rustic population, who were not worthy to possess such a jewel." An intimacy of the most confidential nature thus sprang up between the milliner and the chief of the kitchen; but I do not know whether it was with pleasure or mortification that Madame received the declarations of friendship which the young Alcide proffered to her, for he persisted in calling her, "*La respectable Fribsbi*," "*La vertueuse Fribsbi*,"—and in stating that he should consider her as his mother, while he hoped she would regard him as her son. Ah! it was not very long ago, Fribsby thought, that words had been addressed to her in that dear French language indicating a different sort of attachment. And she sighed as she looked up at the picture of her Carabineer. For it is surprising how young some people's hearts remain when their heads have need of a front or a little hair-dye—and, at this moment, Madame Fribsby, as she told young Alcide, felt as romantic as a girl of eighteen.

When the conversation took this turn—and at their first intimacy Madame Fribsby was rather inclined so to lead it—Alcide always politely diverged to another subject: it was as his mother that he persisted in considering the good milliner. He would recognize her in no other capacity, and with that relationship the gentle lady was forced to content herself, when she found how deeply the artist's heart was engaged elsewhere.

He was not long before he described to her the subject and origin of his passion.

"I declared myself to her," said Alcide, laying his hand on his heart, "in a manner which was as novel as I am charmed to think it was agreeable. Where cannot Love penetrate, respectable Madame Fribsbi? Cupid is the father of invention!—I inquired of the domestics what were the *plats* of which Mademoiselle partook with most pleasure; and built up my little battery accordingly. On a day when her parents had gone to dine in the world (and I am grieved to say that a *grossier* dinner at a restaurant, on the Boulevard, or in the Palais Royal, seemed to form the delights of these unrefined persons), the charming Miss entertained some comrades of the pension; and I advised myself to send up a little repast suitable to so delicate young palates. Her lovely name is Blanche. The veil of the maiden is white; the wreath of roses which she wears is white. I determined that my dinner should be as spotless as the snow. At her accustomed hour, and instead of the rude *gigot à l'eau* which was ordinarily served at her too simple table, I sent her up a little *potage à la Reine—à la Reine Blanche* I called it,—as white as her own tint—and confectioned with the most fragrant cream and almonds. I then offered up at her shrine a *filet de merlan à l'Agnès*, and a delicate *plat*, which I have designated as *Eperlan à la Sainte Thérèse*, and of which my charming Miss partook with pleasure. I followed this by two little *entrées* of sweetbread and chicken; and the only brown thing which I permitted myself in the entertainment was a little roast of lamb, which I laid in a meadow of spinaches, surrounded with croustillons, representing sheep, and ornamented with daisies and other savage flowers. After this came my second service: a pudding *à la Reine Elizabeth* (who, Madame Fribsbi knows, was a maiden princess); a dish of opal-coloured plovers' eggs, which I called *Nid de tourtereaux à la Roucoule;* placing in the midst of them two of those tender volatiles, billing each other, and confectioned with butter; a basket containing little *gateaux* of apricots, which, I know, all young ladies adore; and a jelly of marasquin, bland, insinuating, intoxicating as the glance of beauty. This I designated *Ambroisie de Calypso à la Souveraine de mon Coeur*. And when the ice was brought in—an ice of *plombière* and cherries—how do you think I had shaped them, Madame Fribsbi? In the form of two hearts united with an arrow, on which I had laid, before it entered, a bridal veil in cut paper, surmounted by a wreath of virginal orange-flowers. I stood at the door to watch the effect of this entry. It was but one cry of admiration. The three young ladies filled their glasses with the sparkling Ay, and carried me in a toast. I heard it—I heard Miss speak of me— I heard her say, 'Tell Monsieur Mirobolant that we thank him—we admire him—we love him!' My feet almost failed as as she spoke.

"Since that, can I have any reason to doubt that the young artist has made some progress in the heart of the English Miss? I am modest, but my glass informs me that I am not ill-looking. Other victories have convinced me of the fact."

"Dangerous man!" cried the milliner.

"The blonde misses of Albion see nothing in the dull inhabitants of their brumous isle which can compare with the ardour and vivacity of the children of the South. We bring our sunshine with us; we are Frenchmen, and accustomed to conquer. Were it not for this affair of the heart, and my determination to marry an Anglaise, do you think I would stop in this island (which is not altogether ungrateful, since I have found here a tender mother in the respectable Madame Fribsbi), in this island, in this family? My genius would use itself in the company of these rustics—the poesy of my art cannot be understood by these carnivorous insularies. No—the men are odious, but the women—the women! I own, dear Fribsbi, are seducing! I have vowed to marry one; and as I cannot go into your markets and purchase, according to the custom of the country, I am resolved to adopt another custom, and fly with one to Gretna Grin. The blonde Miss will go. She is fascinated. Her eyes have told me so. The white dove wants but the signal to fly."

"Have you any correspondence with her?" asked Fribsby, in amazement, and not knowing whether the young lady or the lover might be labouring under a romantic delusion.

"I correspond with her by means of my art. She partakes of dishes which I make expressly for her. I insinuate to her thus a thousand hints, which, as she is perfectly spiritual, she receives. But I want other intelligences near her."

"There is Pincott, her maid," said Madame Fribsby, who, by aptitude or education, seemed to have some knowledge of affairs of the heart; but the great artist's brow darkened at this suggestion.

"Madame," he said, "there are points upon which a gallant man ought to silence himself; though, if he break the secret, he may do so with the least impropriety to his best friend—his adopted mother. Know then, that there is a cause why Miss Pincott should be hostile to me—a cause not uncommon with your sex—jealousy."

"Perfidious monster!" said the confidante.

"Ah, no," said the artist, with a deep bass voice, and a tragic accent worthy of the Porte St. Martin, and his favorite *melodrames*, "Not perfidious, but fatal. Yes, I am a fatal man, Madame Fribsbi. To inspire hopeless passion is my destiny. I cannot help it that women love me. Is it my fault that that young woman deperishes and languishes to the view of the eye, consumed by a flame which I cannot return? Listen! There are others in this family who are similarly unhappy. The governess of the young Milor has encountered me in my walks, and looked at me in a way which can bear but one interpretation. And Milady herself, who is of mature age, but who has oriental blood, has once or twice addressed compliments to the lonely artist which can admit of no mistake.

I avoid the household, I seek solitude, I undergo my destiny. I can marry but one, and am resolved it shall be to a lady of your nation. And, if her fortune is sufficient, I think Miss would be the person who would be most suitable. I wish to ascertain what her means are before I lead her to Gretna Grin."

Whether Alcide was as irresistible a conqueror as his namesake, or whether he was simply crazy, is a point which must be left to the reader's judgment. But the latter, if he has had the benefit of much French acquaintance, has perhaps met with men amongst them who fancied themselves almost as invincible; and who, if you credit them, have made equal havoc in the hearts of *les Anglaises*.

MENU:

Potage à la Reine

Sweetbread

Chicken

(à la Reine, Sauce suprême)

Roast lamb in a meadow of spinaches

Pudding à la Reine

(Chicken croquettes)

Opal-colored plovers' eggs

Gateau of apricots

(Apricot tart)

Jelly of marasquin

Ice of plombière and cherries

The flamboyant Alcide Mirobolant must have been modeled on several French chefs living in England in Thackeray's time, but he is most reminiscent of Louis Eustache Ude, from whose The French Cook *a number of these recipes come. Ude's father had been chef to Louis XVI, had perhaps baked for the king and Marie Antoinette the very cakes the queen wanted the starving populace to eat. Ude, a handsome ambitious youth, wanted desperately to carve a distinguished future for himself. He seems to have attempted success in every field except cooking, perhaps because he felt that all the glory in the culinary world had already been culled by his father. But chefdom was in his stars. When his father died the support of the family fell upon young Ude. He had failed at one career after another; his father's old job in the royal kitchens was offered to him; he made up his mind to become a cook.*

Quickly he learned all his father had known and more. But Louis XVI was not long to enjoy the delights provided by Ude, Jr. The revolution abruptly severed, along with the king's head, their new-found relationship and Ude was once more foiled in his quest for fame. He went into obscurity, surviving the revolution by managing a gambling house, and emerged some years later as chef to Madame Letitia Bonaparte. She, however, proved parsimonious when compared to a grande dame like Marie Antoinette. By now Ude could not bear to have his cooking skills hampered, especially by something so prosaic as a budget, and he determined to flee to the extravagant England.

There, at last, his boyhood wishes came true. He was a huge success, rubbed shoulders with the nobility and not only made their food but ran their entertainments. Ultimately he became so vain that when news was brought him of the death of the Duke of York, one of his former employers, he whimsically exclaimed, "Ah, mon pauvre Duc. How you will miss me where you are gone!"

POTAGE À LA REINE

FROM *The French Cook*, 1828, Louis Eustache Ude

3 chickens (2-3 pounds each)
parsley
broth (2-3 quarts per chicken)
soaked bread (about 10 slices
   of trimmed white bread)

3 or 4 hard-cooked egg yolks
1 quart of cream
optional: barley, rice or
   vermicelli

For twelve people take 3 fat chickens or pullets, which are generally cheaper and better than fowls: skin them, take out the lungs, wash them clean, and put them in a pan with a bunch of parsley only; moisten the whole with good broiling broth: let it stew for 1 hour, then take out the chickens: soak the crumb of 2 penny loaves in the broth; take off the flesh of the chickens, and pound it with the yolks of 3 or 4 eggs boiled hard, and the crumb of bread which has been sufficiently soaked in the broth.

Rub the whole through a tammy (fine sieve); then put 1 quart of cream on the fire, and keep stirring it continually till it comes to a boil. Pour it into the soup.

It is not so liable to curdle as when the other method is used,* and it tastes more of the chickens. If you think proper to add either barley, rice or vermicelli, let it be stewed in broth beforehand, and pour it into the soup only when quite done. When you have a great dinner, and fowls are very dear, use the fillets for the first-course dishes, and make the soup with the legs only; the soup is as good, but not quite so white, as when made with the fillets.

(Serves 12 or more)

* Ude is referring here to the fact that this Potage à la Reine is an entirely new recipe. He writes, "Formerly I used roasted chicken to make this potage, but I have found this new method cheaper, and not so subject to curdle as the other method."

SWEETBREAD

FROM *The Franco-American Cookery Book*, 1884, Felix J. Déliée

8 heart sweetbreads	a few aromatics (thyme, bay leaf,
cold water	sage or what you will)
shreds of fat salt pork	pork trimmings
sliced onions (2-3)	white broth to half cover
carrots (2-3)	buttered brown paper (or foil)

There are two kinds of veal sweetbreads, and housekeepers should be able to select the better—that is, the heart sweetbread, which is round, generally white and thick; the irregular and long throat sweetbread is inferior and is mostly cut up for garnishing, croquettes, etc. Trim 8 heart sweetbreads of equal size and steep them in cold water for 3 hours (remove their membraneous covering); parboil in water for a few minutes (about 15) till they are firm; cool (by plunging into cold water for 5 minutes) and press them between two tin sheets with a weight on top till cold; lard the best side with small shreds of fat salt pork; put them in a *sautoir* (sauté pan) with sliced onions and carrots, a few aromatics, and pork trimmings, half covering with white broth; put a buttered paper over; heat on a quick fire and afterward let simmer occasionally with the liquid to glaze of a bright yellow color; transfer to another *sautoir;* strain and free the gravy from its fat, reduce to a demiglaze sauce (you may add here a little white wine and basil-flavored tomato paste to enhance the flavor), pour over the sweetbreads and keep warm.

(Serves 8)

CHICKEN

à la Reine, Sauce Suprême

FROM *The Franco-American Cookery Book*, 1884, Felix J. Déliée

3 small chickens (about 2 pounds each)
butter (1-2 tablespoons per chicken)
slices of peeled lemon
thin bardes (slices) of fat pork (or bacon, blanched)

rich white broth
sliced vegetables (celery, onions)
small bunch of parsley
(salt, pepper and herbs to taste)
triangular piece of fried bread *
large fresh mushrooms (8-10)
sauce suprême (below)

Prepare 3 small and well-fed spring chickens; put a piece of butter into each one, truss nicely, put slices of peeled lemon on the breasts and tie over them thin bardes of fat pork; cook in rich white broth (to half cover the chickens), with sliced vegetables and a small bunch of parsley (and seasonings); then untruss, drain well, and dish them, the small ends up against a triangular piece of bread fried pretty hard and make fast on the centre of a dish with some thick sauce; garnish the top with a few large fresh mushrooms; pour a sauce suprême made with the broth, over all, and serve.

* This should be made from unsliced bread cut thick enough to support the chickens.

Sauce Suprême

7 tablespoons butter
5 tablespoons flour
1 quart (or use just 3 cups for a more substantial sauce) of broth chicken cooked in

lemon juice (about 1 tablespoon)
1 cup thick cream
optional: heart-shaped slices of corned beef tongue

Melt in a very clean saucepan 5 tablespoons of butter, with the same of flour; stir and fry a little; dilute with 1 quart (or 3 cups for a thicker sauce) of the chicken broth; boil (simmer) 15 minutes; skim, add rest of table butter, lemon juice, and a cup of boiled (scalded) cream; mix well, boil no longer, and press through a napkin (or fine sieve); drain, remove the fat and dish up the chickens; pour the sauce over, surround with heart-shaped hot slices of red corned beef tongue, to make the whiteness of the sauce more apparent.

(Serves 6-8)

ROAST LAMB IN A MEADOW OF SPINACHES

FROM *The Franco-American Cookery Book,* 1884, Felix J. Déliée

leg of lamb	salt and pepper
salt	nutmeg
spinach	garnish: croutons
½ cup of butter	

Choose a thick and fat leg of lamb; pare the knucklebone; salt and roast rather well for about an hour (or 20 minutes per pound in a 350° oven). Pick and wash enough spinach (1 pound will serve 2-3); cook uncovered, and at the last moment (before dinner), in plenty of salted boiling water (¾ cups water and ½ teaspoon salt to each pound of spinach; it will be cooked in 5-10 minutes); drain thoroughly without cooling; chop it a little, season it with the surface of the lamb drippings; put the lamb on a dish, surround with the spinach, put a white-paper ruffle on the bone, and serve the rest of the drippings in a sauce bowl. Add croutons, for garnish.

PUDDING À LA REINE

FROM *The French Cook,* 1828, Louis Eustache Ude

This titled dish is the humble chicken croquette.

cooked cold chicken, diced	eggs
Béchamel sauce (see Tolstoy,	salt
p. 149)	fat for frying
bread crumbs (fine and dry)	

This dish is made out of cold fowls. Take the breast and fleshy parts of several fowls, which you cut into small dice, all of an equal size. Throw these dice into some Béchamel boiled down thick, and season them well; next put them into a dish that they may cool, and give them good form with your knife. When quite cold, cut them into two equal parts, which you make into boudins (long thin shapes) of the size of the dish: roll them into crumbs of bread; then dip them into an omelet (Ude's "omelet" consists of uncooked eggs beaten together with a little salt), and roll them again in bread. You must take care that the extremities are well covered with the crumbs, otherwise they would break in the frying pan. When they are fried to a good color, drain them, wipe off the grease with a thin towel, and serve with a thin Béchamel sauce.

OPAL-COLORED PLOVERS' EGGS

FROM *The Household Cookery Book,* 1871, Urbain-Dubois

salt	water cress
18 or 20 plovers' eggs	butter
cold water to cover	

Choose a fine damask napkin, fold it on the wrong side, roll it up (into) a ring, and fasten it with two pins; place it on a dish, and fill the central hollow with pulverized white salt. Place in a stewpan 18 or 20 fresh plovers' eggs; cover them over with cold water; let the water boil for 8 or 10 minutes; drain the eggs, wipe them, break the shell on the pointed side, and range them in a pyramid on the salt contained in the cavity of the napkin; surround the base of the latter with water cresses, serve separately good and fresh butter.

(Serves 8)

GATEAU OF APRICOTS

Apricot Tart

FROM *The Franco-American Cookery Book,* 1884, Felix J. Déliée

1 pound flour	sirup *
1 teaspoon sugar	marmalade
salt (1 teaspoon)	well-drained preserved apricots
2 egg yolks	(5-6 cups)
½-¾ pound butter (kneaded)	1 glass maraschino liqueur
cold water (2/3-1 1/3 cups)	(¼-½ cup)
buttered brown paper (or foil)	
plum or cherry pits or dry corn	
(or rice or beans; the object	
is to shape the dough)	

Sift 1 pound of flour on the table; make a hole in the center; put in 1 teaspoonful of sugar, a little salt and 2 egg yolks; knead the whole together while adding gradually sufficient cold water to make a smooth, pretty stiff dough; roll in a moist cloth (and keep in a cool place for half an hour. Then roll it out, place the kneaded butter in its center; fold over and let stand. Roll out, fold over, chill again, then roll and fold again. Repeat 3 or 4 times.)

Butter and line a 10-inch pastry circle with tart paste; place the circle on a baking sheet; line the paste with a buttered strip of paper; fill with plum or cherry pits, or dry corn, and bake as you would a pie (bake at 400° for 15–20 minutes until light brown); remove the pits and paper, baste the paste all over with thick sirup * and dry in the oven; let cool, then spread some marmalade on the bottom, cover with well-drained preserved apricots, reduce the sirup with a little more sugar and a glass of maraschino liqueur; let cool, pour this over the apricots and serve cold.

(Serves 8)

* What kind of sirup Déliée had in mind here is best illustrated by his similar recipe for gooseberry tarts. He explicitly recommends stewing a quart of the berries with a half-pound of sugar, then removing the berries and reducing the liquid to the consistency of thick sirup. Do the same here with the juice of canned apricots. Add sugar to taste, and boil till the mixture is reduced to a thick sirup.

JELLY OF MARASQUIN

FROM *The Franco-American Cookery Book,* 1884, Felix J. Déliée

3 tablespoons gelatin
1 quart warm water
1½ cups sugar
juice of 2 lemons

2 egg whites
a few drops of cold water
a gill (½ cup) of maraschino liqueur

Melt gelatin in 1 quart of warm water, add white sugar, and the juice of 2 lemons; mingle in a saucepan with the whites of 2 eggs, well beaten; heat on a slow fire, stirring occasionally; as soon as it boils, throw in a few drops of cold water, skim off the white froth, and strain through a wet napkin or jelly bag; cool a little and add a gill of maraschino liqueur; pour in a jelly mold, cool thoroughly and serve.

(Serves 8)

ICE OF PLOMBIÈRE AND CHERRIES

FROM *The Franco-American Cookery Book,* 1884, Felix J. Déliée

lady fingers
1 quart (soft) vanilla ice cream
1 pint of cream à la Chantilly
(thick whipped cream, flavored with a bit of vanilla)

1 wineglass (¼ cup) kirschwasser
1 pint of candied fruits (use cherries soaked in their sirup)
preserved fruits for decoration

Wet and put a round paper on the bottom of a plain charlotte mold, and line the sides with lady fingers; mix with 1 quart of vanilla ice cream, 1 pint of cream à la Chantilly, 1 wineglassful of kirschwasser, and 1 pint of candied fruits soaked in sirup; pour into the prepared mold, cover hermetically, and put into a freezer or a pail of salted ice; at serving time, turn upon a folded napkin, remove the paper, ornament the top with a variety of preserved fruits and serve.

(Serves 8)

GUSTAVE FLAUBERT

MADAME BOVARY
1857

Emma Bovary's outward femininity is undeniable; she has grace of language, a relaxed dovelike posture, and excellent taste in dainty slippers, clothes and curtains. But within her soul Emma harbors a dread dissatisfaction with her womanly state. She longs to give birth only to a son, not a daughter, for "this idea of having a male child was like a promise of compensation for all her past frustrations. A man is free, at least—free to range the passions and the world, to surmount obstacles, to taste the rarest pleasures. Whereas a woman is continually thwarted. Inert, compliant, she has to struggle against her physical weakness and legal subjection. Her will, like the veil tied to her hat, quivers with every breeze: there is always a desire that entices, always a convention that restrains."

Emma's first confrontation with the desires that entice and the conventions that restrain occurs here at the ball of the Marquis of Vaubyessard, one of the most seductive dinner parties in literature. Emma and her husband Charles encounter a new world of elegance: silver dishes, cut crystals, lobsters, quails in their plumage—a far cry from the Bovarys' normal dinner, which Flaubert takes care to mention, of onion soup and veal with sorrel. The men Emma meets at the ball have the complexion of wealth, and not just their clothing but even their hair seems consequently more beautiful. Wealth and the sophisticated world make an indelible impression upon her and from this time forward she can no longer be content with her husband.

The chateau, a modern building in Italian style, with two projecting wings and three flights of steps, lay at the foot of an immense greensward, on which some cows were grazing among groups of large trees set out at regular intervals, while large beds of arbutus, rhododendron, syringas, and guelder roses bulged out their irregular clusters of green along the curve of the gravel path. A river flowed under a bridge; through the mist one could distinguish buildings with thatched roofs scattered over the field bordered by two gently sloping well-timbered hillocks, and in the background amid the trees rose in two parallel lines the coach houses and stables, all that was left of the ruined old chateau.

Charles's dogcart pulled up before the middle flight of steps; servants appeared; the Marquis came forward, and offering his arm to the doctor's wife, conducted her to the vestibule.

It was paved with marble slabs, was very lofty, and the sound of footsteps and that of voices reechoed through it as in a church. Opposite rose a straight staircase, and on the left a gallery overlooking the garden led to the billiard room, through whose door one could hear the click of the ivory balls. As she crossed it to go to the drawing room, Emma saw standing around the table men with grave faces, their chins resting on high cravats. They all wore orders, and smiled silently as they made their strokes. On the dark wainscoting of the walls large gold frames bore at the bottom names written in black letters. She read: "Jean-Antoine d'Andervilliers d'Yverbonville, Count de la Vaubyessard and Baron de la Fresnaye, killed at the battle of Coutras on the 20th of October 1587." And on another: "Jean-Antoine-Henry-Guy d'Andervilliers de la Vaubyessard, Admiral of France and Chevalier of the Order of St. Michael, wounded at the battle of the Hougue-Saint-Vaast on the 29th of May 1692; died at Vaubyessard on the 23rd of January 1693." One could hardly make out those that followed, for the light of the lamps lowered over the green cloth threw a dim shadow around the room. Burnishing the horizontal pictures, it broke up against these in delicate lines where there were cracks in the varnish, and from all these great black squares framed in with gold stood out here and there some lighter portion of the painting— a pale brow, two eyes that looked at you, perukes flowing over and powdering red-coated shoulders, or the buckle of a garter above a well-rounded calf.

The Marquis opened the drawing-room door; one of the ladies, the Marchioness herself, came to meet Emma. She made her sit down by her on an ottoman, and began talking to her as amicably as if she had known her a long time. She was a woman of about forty, with fine shoulders, a hook nose, a drawling voice, and on this evening she wore over her brown hair a simple guipure fichu that fell in a point at the back. A fair young woman was by her side in a high-backed chair, and gentlemen with flowers in their buttonholes were talking to ladies around the fire.

At seven dinner was served. The men, who were in the majority, sat down at the first table in the vestibule; the ladies at the second in the dining room with the Marquis and Marchioness.

Emma, on entering felt herself wrapped around by the warm air, a blending of the perfume of flowers and of the fine linen, of the fumes of the viands, and the odor of the truffles. The silver dish covers reflected the lighted wax candles in the candelabra, the cut crystal covered with light steam reflected from one to the other pale rays; bouquets were placed in a row the whole length of the table; and in the large bordered plates each napkin, arranged after the fashion of a bishop's miter, held between its two gaping folds a small oval-shaped roll. The red claws of lobsters hung over the dishes; rich fruit in open baskets was piled up on moss; there were quails in their plumage; smoke was rising; and in silk stockings, knee breeches, white cravat, and frilled shirt, the steward, grave as a judge, offering ready carved dishes between the shoulders of the guests, with a touch of the spoon gave you the piece chosen. On the large stove of porcelain inlaid with copper baguettes the statue of a woman, draped to the chin, gazed motionless on the room full of life.

Madame Bovary noticed that many ladies had not put their gloves in their glasses.

But at the upper end of the table, alone among all these women, bent over his full plate, and his napkin tied around his neck like a child, an old man sat eating, letting drops of gravy drip from his mouth. His eyes were bloodshot, and he wore a little queue tied with a black ribbon. He was the Marquis's father-in-law, the old Duke de Laverdiere, once on a time favorite of the Count d'Artois, in the days of the Vaudreuil hunting parties at the Marquis de Conflans', and had been, it was said, the lover of Queen Marie Antoinette, between Monsieur de Coigny and Monsieur de Lauzun. He had lived a life of noisy debauch, full of duels, bets, elopements; he had squandered his fortune and frightened all his family. A servant behind his chair named aloud to him in his ear the dishes that he pointed to stammering, and constantly Emma's eyes turned involuntarily to this old man with hanging lips, as to something extraordinary. He had lived at court and slept in the bed of queens!

Iced champagne was poured out. Emma shivered all over as she felt it cold in her mouth. She had never seen pomegranates nor tasted pineapples. The powdered sugar even seemed to her whiter and finer than elsewhere.

The ladies afterwards went to their rooms to prepare for the ball.

Emma made her toilet with the fastidious care of an actress on her debut. She did her hair according to the directions of the hairdresser, and put on the barege dress spread out upon the bed. Charles's trousers were tight across the belly.

"My trouser-straps will be rather awkward for dancing," he said.

"Dancing?" repeated Emma.

"Yes!"

"Why, you must be mad! They would make fun of you; keep your place. Besides, it is more becoming for a doctor," she added.

Charles was silent. He walked up and down waiting for Emma to finish dressing.

He saw her from behind in the glass between two lights. Her black eyes seemed blacker than ever. Her hair, undulating towards the ears, shone with a blue luster; a rose in her chignon trembled on its mobile stalk, with artificial dew-drops on the tip of the leaves. She wore a gown of pale saffron trimmed with three bouquets of pompon roses mixed with green.

Charles came and kissed her on her shoulder.

"Let me alone!" she said; "you are tumbling me."

One could hear the flourish of the violin and the notes of a horn. She went downstairs restraining herself from running.

Dancing had begun. Guests were arriving. There was some crushing. She sat down on a form near the door.

The quadrille over, the floor was occupied by groups of men standing up and talking and servants in livery bearing large trays. Along the line of seated women painted fans were fluttering, bouquets half hid smiling faces, and gold stoppered scent bottles were turned in partly closed hands, whose white gloves outlined the nails and tightened on the flesh at the wrists. Lace trimmings, diamond brooches, medallion bracelets trembled on bodices, gleamed on breasts, clinked on bare arms. The hair, well smoothed over the temples and knotted at the nape, bore crowns, or bunches, or sprays of myosotis, jasmine, pomegranate blossoms, ears of corn, and cornflowers. Calmly seated in their places, mothers with forbidding countenances were wearing red turbans.

Emma's heart beat rather faster when, her partner holding her by the tips of the fingers, she took her place in a line with the dancers, and waited for the first note to start. But her emotion soon vanished, and, swaying to the rhythm of the orchestra, she glided forward with slight movements of the neck. A smile rose to her lips at certain delicate phrases of the violin, that sometimes played alone while the other instruments were silent; one could hear the clear clink of the louis d'or that were being thrown down upon the card tables in the next room; then all struck in again, the cornet-a-piston uttered its sonorous note, feet marked time, skirts swelled and rustled, hands touched and parted; the same eyes falling before you met yours again.

A few men (some fifteen or so) of twenty-five to forty, scattered here and there among the dancers or talking at the doorways, distinguished themselves from the crowd by a certain air of breeding, whatever their differences in age, dress or face.

Their clothes, better made, seemed of finer cloth, and their hair, brought forward in curls towards the temples, glossy with more delicate pomades. They had the complexion of wealth—that clear complexion that is heightened by the pallor of porcelain, the shimmer of satin, the veneer of old furniture, and that an ordered regimen of exquisite nurture maintains at its best. Their necks moved easily in their cravats, their long whiskers fell over their turned-down collars, they wiped their lips upon handkerchiefs with embroidered initials that gave forth a subtle perfume. Those who were beginning to grow old had an air of youth, while there was something mature in the faces of the young. In their unconcerned looks was the calm of passions daily satiated, and through all their gentleness of manner pierced that peculiar brutality, the result of a command of half easy things, in which force is exercised and vanity amused—the management of thorough-bred horses and the society of loose women.

A few steps from Emma a gentleman in a blue coat was talking of Italy with a pale young woman wearing a parure of pearls.

They were praising the breadth of the columns of St. Peter's, Tivoli, Vesuvius, Castellamare, and Cassines, the roses of Genoa, the Coliseum by moonlight. With her other ear Emma was listening to a conversation full of words she did not understand. A circle gathered round a very young man who the week before had beaten "Miss Arabells" and "Romolus," and won two thousand louis jumping a ditch in England. One complained that his race horses were growing fat; another of the printers' errors that had disfigured the name of his horse.

The atmosphere of the ball was heavy; the lamps were growing dim. Guests were flocking to the billiard room. A servant got upon a chair and broke the window panes. At the crash of the glass Madame Bovary turned her head and saw in the garden the faces of peasants pressed against the window looking in at them. Then the memory of the Bertaux came back to her. She saw the farm again, the muddy pond, her father in a blouse under the apple trees, and she saw herself again as formerly, skimming with her finger the cream off the milk pans in the dairy. But in the refulgence of the present hour her past life, so distinct until then, faded away completely, and she almost doubted having lived it. She was there; beyond the ball was only shadow overspreading all the rest. She was just eating a maraschino ice that she held with her left hand in a silver gilt cup, her eyes half closed, and the spoon between her teeth.

A lady near her dropped her fan. A gentleman was passing.

"Would you be so good," said the lady, "as to pick up my fan that has fallen behind the sofa?"

The gentleman bowed, and as he moved to stretch out his arm,

Emma saw the hand of the young woman throw something white, folded in a triangle, into his hat. The gentleman picking up the fan, offered it to the lady respectfully; she thanked him with an inclination of the head, and began smelling her bouquet.

After supper, where were plenty of Spanish and Rhine wines, soups a la bisque and au lait d'amandes, puddings a la Trafalgar, and all sorts of cold meats with jellies that trembled in the dishes, the carriages one after the other began to drive off. Raising the corners of the muslin curtain, one could see the light of their lanterns glimmering through the darkness. The seats began to empty, some card players were still left; the musicians were cooling the tips of their fingers on their tongues. Charles was half asleep, his back propped against a door.

At three o'clock the cotillion began. Emma did not know how to waltz. Everyone was waltzing, Mademoiselle d'Andervilliers herself and the Marquis; only the guests staying at the castle were still there, about a dozen persons.

One of the waltzers, however, who was familiarly called Viscount, and whose low cut waistcoat seemed molded to his chest, came a second time to ask Madame Bovary to dance, assuring her that he would guide her, and that she would get through it very well.

They began slowly, then more rapidly. They turned; all around them was turning—the lamps, the furniture, the wainscoting, the floor, like a disc on a pivot. On passing near the doors the bottom of Emma's dress caught against his trousers. Their legs commingled; he looked down at her; she raised her eyes to his. A torpor seized her; she stopped. They started again, and with a more rapid movement; the Viscount, dragging her along, disappeared with her to the end of the gallery, where, panting, she almost fell, and for a moment rested her head upon his breast. And then, still turning, but more slowly, he guided her back to her seat. She leaned back against the wall and covered her eyes with her hands.

When she opened them again, in the middle of the drawing-room three waltzers were kneeling before a lady sitting on a stool. She chose the Viscount, and the violin struck up once more.

Everyone looked at them. They passed and repassed, she with rigid body, her chin bent downward, and he always in the same pose, his figure curved, his elbow rounded, his chin thrown forward. That woman knew how to waltz! They kept up a long time, and tired out all the others.

Then they talked a few moments longer, and after the good nights, or rather good mornings, the guests of the chateau retired to bed.

Charles dragged himself up by the balusters. His "knees were going up into his body." He had spent five consecutive hours standing bolt upright at the card tables, watching them play whist, without understanding anything about it, and it was with a deep sigh of relief that he pulled off his boots.

Emma threw a shawl over her shoulders, opened the window, and leaned out.

The night was dark; some drops of rain were falling. She breathed in the damp wind that refreshed her eyelids. The music of the ball was still murmuring in her ears, and she tried to keep herself awake in order to prolong the illusion of this luxurious life that she would soon have to give up.

Day began to break. She looked long at the windows of the chateau, trying to guess which were the rooms of all those she had noticed the evening before. She would fain have known their lives, have penetrated, blended with them. But she was shivering with cold. She undressed, and cowered down between the sheets against Charles, who was asleep.

There were a great many people to luncheon. The repast lasted ten minutes; no liquors were served, which astonished the doctor. Next, Mademoiselle d'Andervilliers collected some pieces of roll in a small basket to take them to the swans on the ornamental waters, and they went to walk in the hot houses, where strange plants, bristling with hairs, rose in pyramids under hanging vases, where, as from overfilled nests of serpents, fell long green cords interlacing. The orangery, which was at the other end, led by a covered way to the outhouses of the chateau. The Marquis, to amuse the young woman, took her to see the stables. Above the basket-shaped racks porcelain slabs bore the names of the horses in black letters. Each animal in its stall whisked its tail when anyone went near and said "Tchk! tchk!" The boards of the harness room shone like the flooring of a drawing-room. The carriage harness was piled up in the middle against two twisted columns, and the bits, the whips, the spurs, the curbs, were ranged in a line all along the wall.

Charles, meanwhile, went to ask a groom to put his horse to. The dogcart was brought to the foot of the steps, and all the parcels being crammed in, the Bovarys paid their respects to the Marquis and Marchioness and set out again for Tostes.

Emma watched the turning wheels in silence. Charles, on the

extreme edge of the seat, held the reins with his two arms wide apart, and the little horse ambled along in the shafts that were too big for him. The loose reins hanging over his crupper were wet with foam, and the box fastened on behind the chaise gave great regular bumps against it.

They were on the heights of Thibourville when suddenly some horsemen with cigars between their lips passed laughing. Emma thought she recognized the Viscount, turned back, and caught on the horizon only the movement of the heads rising or falling with the unequal cadence of the trot or gallop.

A mile farther on they had to stop to mend with string the traces that had broken.

But Charles, giving a last look to the harness, saw something on the ground between his horse's legs, and he picked up a cigar case with a green silk border and emblazoned in the center like the door of a carriage.

"There are even two cigars in it," said he; "they'll do for this evening after dinner."

"Why, do you smoke?" she asked.

"Sometimes, when I get a chance."

He put his find in his pocket and whipped up the nag.

When they reached home the dinner was not ready. Madame lost her temper. Natasie answered rudely.

"Leave the room!" said Emma. "You are forgetting yourself. I give you warning."

For dinner there was onion soup and a piece of veal with sorrel. Charles, seated opposite Emma, rubbed his hands gleefully.

"How good it is to be at home again!"

Natasie could be heard crying. He was rather fond of the poor girl. She had formerly, during the wearisome time of his widowhood, kept him company many an evening. She had been his first patient, his oldest acquaintance in the place.

"Have you given her warning for good?" he asked at last.

"Yes. Who is to prevent me?" she replied.

Then they warmed themselves in the kitchen while their room was being made ready. Charles began to smoke. He smoked with lips protruding, spitting every moment, recoiling at every puff.

"You'll make yourself ill," she said scornfully.

He put down his cigar and ran to swallow a glass of cold water at the pump. Emma seizing hold of the cigar case threw it quickly to the back of the cupboard.

The next day was a long one. She walked about her little garden, up and down the same walks, stopping before the beds, before the espalier, before the plaster curate, looking with amazement at all these things of once-on-a-time that she knew so well. How far off the ball seemed already! What was it that thus set so far asunder the morning of the day before yesterday and the evening of to-day? Her journey to Vaubyessard had made a hole in her life, like one of those great crevasses that a storm will sometimes make in one night in mountains. Still she was resigned. She devoutly put away in her drawers her beautiful dress, down to the satin shoes whose soles were yellowed with the slippery wax of the dancing floor. Her heart was like these. In its friction against wealth something had come over it that could not be effaced.

The memory of this ball, then, became an occupation for Emma. Whenever the Wednesday came round she said to herself as she awoke, "Ah! I was there a week—a fortnight—three weeks ago." And little by little the faces grew confused in her remembrance. She forgot the tune of the quadrilles; she no longer saw the liveries and appointments so distinctly; some details escaped her, but the regret remained with her.

MENU:

Truffles

Quails

(Compote of quails)

Soup à la bisque

(Bisque of clams)

Soup au lait d'amandes

TRUFFLES

FROM *The French Cook*, 1828, Louis Eustache Ude

Brillat-Savarin loved truffles, and wrote, "Who says truffle *pronounces a great word, charged with toothsome and amorous memories for the skirted sex, and for the bearded sex with memories amorous and toothsome. . . . The truffle is not a positive aphrodisiac, but it can upon occasion make women tenderer and men more apt to love."*

truffles, washed and cleaned (and sliced)
slices of (blanched) bacon (to line a small pan)
a bunch of parsley
green onions (2-3, sliced)
thyme (½ teaspoon)
bay leaves (1-2)

cloves (5-6)
basil (½ teaspoon)
a spoonful (or more, as needed) of good consommé
2 glasses of champagne (1-1¼ cups)
salt and pepper
poêlé (below, optional)

After having selected the best truffles, and washed and cleaned them from the sand which is apt to accumulate in their cavities, trim a stewpan with slices of bacon; put the truffles into it, with a bunch of parsley and green onions, well seasoned with thyme, bay leaves, cloves, basil, and the like; moisten with 1 spoonful of good consommé, 2 glasses of champagne, some salt and pepper, and if you have a good poêlé, put in some of it, fat and liquid together; set them to boil gently for one hour; let this cool in the stewpan, after tossing those which are at the bottom up to the top, to give them an equal flavor. When you wish to serve up, warm them again, and drain them in a very clean towel. Serve them up in a beautiful napkin, so perfectly white that it may contrast as strongly as possible with the black of the truffles; and be particular to save the bacon and the liquor in which they have been braized, which will serve well for either fowl or turkey, or to moisten a *salmis*, and, in fact, improve a great many dishes.

Poêlé

1 pound of beef suet
1 pound of very fresh butter
1 pound of very fat bacon (blanched)
2 pounds of veal
3 pints of clear boiling water
1 handful of salt

1 bay leaf
a few sprigs of thyme (or ¼ teaspoon dried thyme)
1 onion stuck with 3 cloves
a bundle of parsley and green onions

Take 1 pound of beef suet, 1 pound of very fresh butter, and 1 pound of very fat bacon; cut the suet and the bacon into very large dice, put them into a stewpan with 2 pounds of veal cut in the same manner, fry till the veal becomes very white, and then moisten with about 3 pints of clear boiling water, 1 handful of salt, one bay leaf, a few sprigs of thyme, 1 onion stuck with three cloves, and a great bundle of parsley and green onions:

let the whole boil gently till the onion is done, then strain it through a hair sieve, and use it for anything that may want poêlé. The use of poêlé is to make everything boiled in it very white and tasty: in the winter it keeps for a week, and is very useful in the larder, particularly if you do not put in any of the fleshy part of the bacon; otherwise the meat that you boil in it will turn quite red, on account of the saltpeter used in curing the bacon.

QUAILS

Compote of Quails

FROM *The French Cook,* 1828, Louis Eustache Ude

Ude had a low opinion of quails; he objected to the enormous price charged for them in England, felt they had no flavor, and wrote that "from the circumstances of confinement and bad breeding they are never very fat; it is only their rarity that makes them fashionable."

6 or 8 quails
1 dozen pieces of bacon or salt
   pork, cut in the shape of corks
   and blanched
butter (about 1 tablespoon)
a roux (equal parts of flour and
   melted butter; about 1 tablespoon of each)

a ladleful of veal gravy (1 cup
   veal stock)
a bunch of parsley
green onions (minced, 3-4)
optional: white onions
mushrooms
seasoning

Take 6 or 8 quails, according to the size of your dish. Cut the claws off, empty the birds, without making too large an opening. Truss them *en poul,* that is to say, with the legs inward. Have a dozen pieces of bacon cut in the shape of corks, blanch them in order to draw the salt out; then let them fry in butter till they are of a light brown; next take them out of the stewpan to make room for the quails, which stew (fry) till they begin to be of a light brown also, and then take them out. Make a roux, which moisten with a ladleful of gravy of veal; add a bunch of parsley and green onions, (the bacon), some small white onions if approved of, mushrooms, and so on.

(Put the quails into this and simmer about 10 minutes, turning twice.) As soon as the quails are done, take them out of the stewpan, and let the bacon stew till thoroughly done. Skim the sauce well, and strain it through a tammy (fine sieve) over the quails: then dish the bacon, mushrooms, and small onions and send up quite hot and well seasoned. This dish will not do for an English dinner.

(Serves 6-8)

SOUP À LA BISQUE

Bisque of Clams

FROM *French Dishes for American Tables,* 1886, Pierre Caron

50 shucked clams and their juice
   (or a 20-ounce can minced
   clams)
½ cup butter
¼ cup flour

2 pinches of salt
a pinch of pepper (2 pinches)
a pinch of cayenne (2 pinches)
2½ pints milk

Boil the clams in their juice for about 5 minutes, drain them (reserve liquor), chop them fine, then pound them. Put in a saucepan on the fire the butter and flour (melt butter and stir in flour), add your clams with their juice, 2 pinches of salt, 1 of pepper, 1 of cayenne, and 2½ pints of milk. Stir constantly, and, just before beginning to boil, remove from the fire, strain, heat again over the fire and serve.

Bisque of oysters is prepared in the same manner.

(Serves 4-5)

SOUP AU LAIT D'AMANDES

FROM *The French Cook,* 1828, Louis Eustache Ude

1 quart of milk
a leaf of almond laurel (bay leaf)
some sugar (about 1 tablespoon)
salt (about ¼ teaspoon)
¼ pound sweet almonds
1 dozen bitter almonds

hot water (for blanching)
milk (about ¼ cup, for moisten-
   ing the almonds)
bread
fine pounded sugar

Boil in 1 quart of milk a leaf of almond laurel, some sugar, and a little salt. Put ¼ pound of sweet almonds and 1 dozen bitter ones into hot water, peel and pound them in a mortar: moisten with a little milk to prevent their turning into oil.° When sufficiently fine, rub them through a tammy (fine sieve), and throw them into the soup. They must not boil.

Have a tin cutter, and cut some slices of bread the size of a penny. The crumb only—not the crust—must be used. Cut a great many pieces, and put them on a baking sheet near one another; then pour over them some fine pounded sugar, and place them in the oven. Then put the salamander over, to give them a good color (or brown them quickly under broiler).

Just as you are going to serve up, throw the pieces of bread into the soup tureen, and pour the soup over them. Serve quick. This soup is intended for Lent, when neither meat nor butter are permitted to Catholics.

(Serves 4)

° It is far simpler to use commercial almond paste instead of making your own. Mash 1½ tablespoons of almond paste with a little milk. When the paste is dissolved, add the rest of 1 quart of milk, the bay leaf and salt. Omit the sugar and proceed as above.

LEO TOLSTOY
ANNA KARENINA
1875–76

Levin has come to Moscow from the country to court Oblonsky's pretty young sister-in-law, Kitty. He and Oblonsky have dinner in a restaurant, and in that one scene, very early in the novel, Tolstoy conveys the essential difference between these two men and sets up what will be an underlying theme of the novel: Is the aim of refinement and civilization to make everything a source of enjoyment? Might we not then be better off as savages?

Tolstoy had two distinct methods of revealing personality. His most frequent method, and the one which least beguiles the modern reader, was a direct, blunt reportage of the inner thoughts of his characters. His second method, less frequent but always tremendously exciting, was to convey the nuances of character through a description of actual physical traits and objects: thus a fat man who undergoes a change in ethics appears thinner, more vigorous; a woman who is frigid and corrupt remains, despite the encroachment of age, always whitely beautiful, untouched; and thus, on the basis of what foods Oblonsky and Levin desire, we know immediately what their personalities are. "Show me what a man eats," said Brillat-Savarin, "and I will tell you what he is." This Tolstoy does. Oblonsky, a sensualist, untormented by guilt and conscience, wants the refined cuisine of the restaurant— oysters, turbot with thick sauce, roast beef, capons. Levin, forever seeking a right, ascetic and spiritual life, a life deriving its guidance from what is essentially Russian and simple, not foreign and false, would have liked porridge, Russian cabbage soup, bread and cheese.

When Levin went into the restaurant with Oblonsky, he could not help noticing a certain peculiarity of expression, as it were, a restrained radiance, about the face and whole figure of Stepan Arkadyevitch. Oblonsky took off his overcoat, and with his hat over one ear walked into the dining-room, giving directions to the Tatar waiters, who were clustered about him in evening coats, bearing napkins. Bowing to right and left to the people he met, and here as everywhere joyously greeting acquaintances, he went up to the sideboard for a preliminary appetizer of fish and vodka, and said to the painted Frenchwoman decked in ribbons, lace, and ringlets, behind the counter, something so amusing that even the Frenchwoman was moved to genuine laughter. Levin for his part refrained from taking any vodka simply because he felt such a loathing of that Frenchwoman, all made up, it seemed, of false hair, *poudre de riz*, and *vinaigre de toilette*. He made haste to move away from her, as from a dirty place. His whole soul was filled with memories of Kitty, and there was a smile of triumph and happiness shining in his eyes.

"This way, your excellency, please. Your excellency won't be disturbed here," said a particularly pertinacious, white-headed old Tatar with immense hips and coat-tails gaping widely behind. "Walk in, your excellency," he said to Levin; by way of showing his respect to Stepan

Arkadyevitch, being attentive to his guest as well.

Instantly flinging a fresh cloth over the round table under the bronze chandelier, though it already had a table-cloth on it, he pushed up velvet chairs, and came to a standstill before Stepan Arkadyevitch with a napkin and a bill of fare in his hands, awaiting his commands.

"If you prefer it, your excellency, a private room will be free directly; Prince Golitsin with a lady. Fresh oysters have come in."

"Ah! Oysters."

Stepan Arkadyevitch became thoughtful.

"How if we change our program, Levin?" he said, keeping his finger on the bill of fare. And his face expressed serious hesitation. "Are the oysters good? Mind now."

"They're Flensburg, your excellency. We've no Ostend."

"Flensburg will do, but are they fresh?"

"Only arrived yesterday."

"Well, then, how if we were to begin with oysters, and so change the whole program? Eh?"

"It's all the same to me. I should like cabbage soup and porridge better than anything; but of course there's nothing like that here."

"*Porridge à la Russe*, your honor would like?" said the Tatar, bending down to Levin, like a nurse speaking to a child.

"No, joking apart, whatever you choose is sure to be good. I've been skating, and I'm hungry. And don't imagine," he added, detecting a look of dissatisfaction on Oblonsky's face, "that I shan't appreciate your choice. I am fond of good things."

"I should hope so! After all, it's one of the pleasures of life," said Stepan Arkadyevitch. "Well then, my friend, you give us two—or better say three—dozen oysters, clear soup with vegetables . . ."

"*Printanière*," prompted the Tatar. But Stepan Arkadyevitch apparently did not care to allow him the satisfaction of giving the French names of the dishes.

"With vegetables in it, you know. Then turbot with thick sauce, then . . . roast beef; and mind it's good. Yes, and capons, perhaps, and then sweets."

The Tatar, recollecting that it was Stepan Arkadyevitch's way not to call the dishes by the names in the French bill of fare, did not repeat them after him, but could not resist rehearsing the whole menu to himself according to the bill:—"*Soupe printanière, turbot, sauce Beaumarchais, poulard à l'estragon, macédoine de fruits . . . etc.*," and then instantly, as though worked by springs, laying down one bound bill of fare, he took up another, the list of wines, and submitted it to Stepan Arkadyevitch.

"What shall we drink?"

"What you like, only not too much. Champagne," said Levin.

"What! To start with? You're right though, I dare say. Do you like the white seal?"

"Cachet blanc," prompted the Tatar.

"Very well, then, give us that brand with the oysters, and then we'll see."

"Yes, sir. And what table wine?"

"You can give us Nuits. Oh, no, better the classic Chablis."

"Yes, sir. And *your* cheese, your excellency?"

"Oh, yes, Parmesan. Or would you like another?"

"No, it's all the same to me," said Levin, unable to suppress a smile.

And the Tatar ran off with flying coat-tails, and in five minutes darted in with a dish of opened oysters on mother-of-pearl shells, and a bottle between his fingers.

Stepan Arkadyevitch crushed the starchy napkin, tucked it into his waistcoat, and settling his arms comfortably, started on the oysters.

"Not bad," he said, stripping the oysters from the pearly shell with a silver fork, and swallowing them one after another. "Not bad," he repeated, turning his dewy, brilliant eyes from Levin to the Tatar.

Levin ate the oysters indeed, though white bread and cheese would have pleased him better. But he was admiring Oblonsky. Even the Tatar, uncorking the bottle and pouring the sparkling wine into the delicate glasses, glanced at Stepan Arkadyevitch, and settled his white cravat with a perceptible smile of satisfaction.

"You don't care much for oysters, do you?" said Stepan Arkadye-vitch, emptying his wine-glass. "Or you're worried about something. Eh?"

He wanted Levin to be in good spirits. But it was not that Levin was not in good spirits; he was ill at ease. With what he had in his soul, he felt sore and uncomfortable in the restaurant, in the midst of private rooms where men were dining with ladies, in all this fuss and bustle; the surroundings of bronzes, looking-glasses, gas, and waiters— all of it was offensive to him. He was afraid of sullying what his soul was brimful of.

"I? Yes, I am; but besides, all this bothers me," he said. "You can't conceive how queer it all seems to a country person like me, as queer as that gentleman's nails I saw at your place . . . ."

"Yes, I saw how much interested you were in poor Grinevitch's nails," said Stepan Arkadyevitch, laughing.

"It's too much for me," responded Levin. "Do try, now, and put yourself in my place, take the point of view of a country person. We in the country try to bring our hands into such a state as will be most convenient for working with. So we cut our nails; sometimes we turn up our sleeves. And here people purposely let their nails grow as long as they will, and link on small saucers by way of studs, so that they can do nothing with their hands."

Stepan Arkadyevitch smiled gaily.

"Oh, yes, that's just a sign that he has no need to do coarse work. His work is with the mind . . . ."

"Maybe. But still it's queer to me, just as at this moment it seems queer to me that we country folks try to get our meals over as soon as we can, so as to be ready for our work, while here are we trying to drag out our meal as long as possible, and with that object eating oysters . . . ."

"Why, of course," objected Stepan Arkadyevitch. "But that's just the aim of civilization—to make everything a source of enjoyment."

"Well, if that's its aim, I'd rather be a savage."

"And so you are a savage. All you Levins are savages."

MENU:

Oysters

Potage à la printanière

Turbot with thick sauce

Roast beef

Poulard a l'Estragon

Macédoine de fruits

The recipes for the meal Oblonsky orders come principally from the work of Pierre Blot, editor of one of Paris' powerful nineteenth-century culinary almanacs. But the turbot is the recipe of an even more prominent cook, Urbain-Dubois, chef to the court of Germany.

OYSTERS

FROM *What To Eat and How To Cook It*, 1863, Pierre Blot

Raw

oysters   lemon juice
salt and pepper

When well washed, open them, detaching the upper shell, then detach them from the under shell, but leave them on it; place on a dish and leave the upper shell on every oyster and serve thus.
To eat them you remove the upper shell, sprinkle salt, pepper and lemon juice on, and eat.

Broiled

oysters   butter
oyster liquor   chopped parsley
bread crumbs

When well washed, open and detach from both shells, save the water, and put it on a sharp fire in a kettle; when it boils, throw the oysters in, boil one minute, take off and drain them. Put each oyster on a shell, dust them a little with fine bread crumbs, put on each a little butter and chopped parsley, kneaded together, and place on a gridiron; set it on a good fire, watch carefully, and as soon as you see any of them beginning to boil, take off and serve.

POTAGE À LA PRINTANIÈRE

FROM *What To Eat and How To Cook It*, 1863, Pierre Blot

12 leaves of sorrel	2 onions
6 sprigs of chervil	1 tablespoon green beans
1 lettuce	1 tablespoon green peas
2 leeks	1 tablespoon tops of asparagus
1 middling-sized parsnip	½ dozen small spring radishes
1 middling-sized carrot	boiling salted water
1 turnip	¼ pound butter
1 head of soup celery (celery	salt and pepper
leaves)	broth (6-7 cups)

Chop the vegetables (preferably omit the radishes, which tend to make soup bitter), throw them into boiling water and a little salt for one minute;

drain, put in a stewpan with butter, salt and pepper. Set on fire, stir now and then until about half cooked (about 5-10 minutes), when, cover with broth, simmer till well cooked (about 20-25 minutes more) and serve.

(Serves 6)

TURBOT WITH THICK SAUCE

FROM *The Household Cookery Book*, 1871, Urbain-Dubois

Levin and Oblonsky eat their turbot with a thick sauce named Beaumar-chais. But no sauce Beaumarchais turned up in the cookbooks of the period and we have substituted Urbain-Dubois' thick Béchamel.

half a small turbot, raw or
  cooked (or substitute halibut
  or flounder)
Béchamel sauce (below) reduced
  with mushroom juice and
  cream

a handful of bread crumbs
melted butter
butter or crayfish butter
  (see p. 144)

Take half of a small turbot, raw or cooked; if it is raw, boil it (simmer it very gently on a greased rack placed above 2 inches of boiling water or court bouillon) in salted water; if cooked, warm it in its own cooking stock; in either case, it must be warm and well-drained. While the turbot boils prepare a little Béchamel sauce, let it reduce without leaving it, mixing into it the liquor of some fresh mushrooms, as well as a little good raw cream, so as to get it succulent and consistent; take it off the fire and thus introduce into it a piece either of fresh butter or else of crayfish butter. Drain the turbot, remove all the bones and skin; divide the flesh in pieces, which range on the bottom of a flat, long dish, alternating the layers with a little of the previously prepared sauce. Mask its surface with the remainder of the sauce, on which sprinkle a handful of fresh bread crumbs, pour over a little butter, give it a fine color, with the aid of the salamander (or place briefly under the broiler); serve the fish immediately.

(If you use a whole fish allow 1 pound per serving;
if you use fillets, allow 1 pound for three servings)

Béchamel sauce

¼ pound butter
¼ pound flour
3 ounces raw ham, diced
warm milk (about 2 quarts)

(½ teaspoon salt)
a bunch of parsley (chopped)
a bay leaf
2 small onions (chopped)

some peppercorns (5 or 6,   spoonfuls of raw cream (about
  bruised)   1 cup)
(salt)

Melt the butter in a stewpan; add to it a ¼ pound of flour, and 3 ounces of raw ham, cut in dice; fry the flour for 10 minutes (a minute or 2 will do) on a moderate fire, stirring it, and without allowing it to take color; take it off the fire, gradually dilute it with warm milk (and salt), but avoiding to make it grainy; remove it back to the side of the fire; add to it a bunch of parsley mixed with a bay leaf, some peppercorns (and salt) and two small onions. Boil (simmer) the sauce for 20 minutes; pass it then through a sieve into another stewpan; let it reduce on a brisk fire, stirring it, and gradually introducing into it some spoonfuls of raw cream (one spoonful at a time, until it achieves the consistency you prefer). When the sauce is of good taste and creamy, take it off the fire.

(Makes 8 cups of sauce)

ROAST BEEF

FROM *What To Eat and How To Cook It*, 1863, Pierre Blot

3 pounds fillet of beef   salt and pepper
½ pound bacon (preferably use   1 teaspoon vinegar
  ½ pound salt pork)   1 saltspoonful (tablespoon)
buttered brown paper (or foil)   chopped shallots
pan gravy   2-3 sliced pickled cucumbers

Take 3 pounds of fillet, cut off part of the fat, and the thin skin on the top, lard it with about ½ pound of bacon (or salt pork), envelop it with buttered paper (or foil), and place upon the spit before a sharp fire (or roast in the oven, 25-30 minutes per pound); take the paper off 5 minutes before taking from the fire; baste often during the process (baste with pan drippings and, if necessary, add a little water mixed with beef broth), and serve with the gravy, to which you add salt, pepper, 1 teaspoonful of vinegar, 1 saltspoonful of chopped shallots, and 2 or 3 pickled cucumbers, cut in slices.

POULARD À L'ESTRAGON

FROM *Little French Dinners*, 1900, Eveleen De Rivaz

a good-sized chicken, cut up   a rasher of bacon, diced (and
  (3-4 pounds)   blanched)
pepper and salt   tarragon stalks (¼ cup fresh or
butter (½ cup)   2 tablespoons dried tarragon)

| tarragon leaves, blanched and chopped | a tumblerful of clear gravy or stock |

Cut up a good-sized raw chicken as neatly and as skilfully as possible. The leg bones should be cut off short, the flesh being first pushed back, the sinews round it having been cut, and when the bone is chopped off, the flesh should be drawn forward again so as not to leave the leg bone sticking out when the piece of leg is cooked. When the pieces of fowl have all been neatly trimmed, sprinkle them with (salt and pepper and simmer them in the) butter and a rasher of bacon cut in dice, till they are quite cooked. In the meantime put some tarragon stalks into a saucepan with a tumblerful of clear gravy or of very good stock. When it has boiled for ½ hour, dish up the pieces of fowl, pour the gravy over them strained, and sprinkle on the surface some tarragon leaves, previously blanched and roughly chopped.

(If you use dried tarragon it too must cook in the broth, but don't strain it out when you pour the broth over the chicken.)

(Serves 3-4)

MACÉDOINE DE FRUITS

FROM *What To Eat and How To Cook It,* 1863, Pierre Blot

| apricots, peaches, pears, straw- berries, raspberries, black- berries, currants and/or like berries | powdered sugar a pinch of grated nutmeg brandy or rum to suit your taste |

Dust the bottom of a dish with powdered sugar, put a layer of slices of apricots, oranges, peaches or pears, or a layer of the others entire, and dust again; repeat the same till the whole is in, then add over the whole a pinch of grated nutmeg and French brandy or rum to suit your taste, and serve.

EMILE ZOLA

L'ASSOMMOIR
1877

Degraded by the men who have formed liaisons with her, Gervaise has always had a hard life. She is very pretty, but she is crippled in one leg; when she was little more than a child herself she had her first baby and now, in her early twenties, she is burdened with three; her first man, Lantier, was good to her until the influence of drink made him brutal; her present husband, Coupeau, was a vigorous workman until, injured on his job one day and forced to remain inactive for many months, he too became debased by drink. Despite Gervaise's efforts to maintain the family through the successful laundry she has opened, things go badly. Still, on her birthday, Gervaise decides to throw a dinner party and invite all her neighbors and friends. For one brief moment she wants excess and gaiety. "When a man drinks all you have," she feels, "it is fools' labour to let everything run away in drink, and not fill your own stomach."

The dinner party, one of the highlights of the novel, is like a Breughel painting, filled with movement, color, broad humor. Pot-au-feu, the great French peasant soup, and a huge roast goose and plates upon plates of vegetables and salad are all devoured; everyone eats too much, but who knows when they will eat again?

Meanwhile Gervaise served the soup, the *pâtes d'Italie*, and the guests had taken up their spoons, when Virginie cried out that Coupeau had disappeared. Very likely he had gone back to old Colombe's. There was a general murmur of disapproval. This time, anyway, no one was going to run after him, he could stay in the street if he wasn't hungry. And as the spoons were scraping up the last drops of the soup, Coupeau reappeared, with two flower-pots, one under each arm, a stock and balsamine. The whole table applauded. He placed the pots one on each side of Gervaise's glass with a flourish; then he bent down and kissed her.

"I had forgotten you, ducky. No matter, we love each other just the same, especially on a day like this!"

"Monsieur Coupeau's in good form tonight," whispered Clemence in Boche's ear. "He has had just enough to put him in a good temper."

The master's agreeable way had restored the good spirits of the company, which, but just before, had been endangered. Gervaise, now herself again, was as smiling as ever. The guests had finished their soup, and the bottles were passed round; the first glass of wine was drunk, a thimbleful of neat wine, to settle the *pâtes d'Italie*. In the next room, the children were heard quarrelling. There was Etienne, Nana, Pauline, and little Victor Fauconnier. A table had been put there for the four of them, and they had been told they must be very good. The cross-eyed Augustine, who was looking after the fires, had to hold her plate on her knees.

"Mamma! mamma!" cried Nana, all of a sudden, "Augustine is dropping her bread in the roaster."

The laundress rushed in, and surprised her swallowing a piece of bread and butter dipped in the boiling fat, nearly scalding her throat in her hurry. She boxed her ears, for the mischievous imp declared she was doing nothing of the sort.

After the beef came the *blanquette,* in a salad-bowl, the household not having a dish big enough; and it was received with a shout of laughter.

"This is becoming serious," said Poisson, who rarely spoke.

It was half-past seven. They had closed the door of the shop, so as not to have all the neighbours spying upon them; the little watchmaker every mouthful with so greedy a look that they couldn't go on eating. The curtains hung over the windows gave a clear white light without a shadow, bathing the white table, with its knives and forks still in neat order, its flower-pots in their paper frills; and this pale, lingering twilight gave to the company a sort of air of distinction. Virginie found the right word. She looked all round the room, closed in and hung with muslin, and declared that it was quite cosy. When a cart passed in the street, the glasses clattered on the table, and the women had to shout as loud as the men. But there was not much talking, everyone was on his best behaviour, a little formal. Coupeau alone wore his blouse, "because," said he, "one doesn't mind with friends, and besides the blouse is the workman's garb of honour." The women were all tightly laced, and their hair was plastered down with pomade so that it shone like mirrors, whilst the men, sitting well out from the table, held themselves erect, and kept their elbows square, for fear of soiling their frock-coats.

Heavens! what a hole they made in the *blanquette!* If there was not much talking, there was plenty of eating. The salad bowl was emptying; it had a spoon planted in the midst of the thick sauce, a fine yellow sauce which quivered like jelly. Everyone fished out bits of veal, and the salad bowl went travelling continuously from hand to hand, all eyes bent over it, looking for mushrooms. The great rolls of bread standing against the wall behind the guests seemed to melt away. Between the mouthfuls one could hear the sound of glasses as they were put down on the table. The sauce was a little too salt, it required four bottles to drown the blessed *blanquette,* which melted in your mouth like cream, and felt like a fire in your insides. And there was no breathing-space, for the crackling, laid out on a soup plate, and

surrounded by potatoes, arrived in a cloud of steam. There was a shout.
The devil! it was the very thing! It was just what everybody liked.
Now for a good appetite; and all followed the dish with longing eyes,
wiping their knives on their bread in order to be ready. When they
were served, they jogged one another's elbows, talking with their mouths
full. Eh! isn't the crackling just nobby? it's soft and it's solid all at once,
and it trickles down your inside, down to your very heels. The potatoes
were stunning. No, not at all too salt, though, on their account one did
have to rinse out one's mouth every minute or so. So they had to wet
their whistles with four more bottles. The plates were so thoroughly
cleaned that they did not need to be changed for the peas with bacon.
Oh! vegetables were a mere nothing; one could swallow them by the
spoonful, without thinking anything of it. It was a delicacy, certainly,
the sort of thing, in short, "that pleases the ladies". What was best in
the peas were the bits of bacon, which were done to a turn, till they
stank like a horse's hoof. This time two bottles were enough.

"Mamma! mamma!" cried Nana suddenly, "Augustine is putting
her hands in my plate."

"Don't bother me; give her a slap!" replied Gervaise, gobbling
down her peas.

At the children's table in the next room, Nana was acting as the
lady of the house. She was sitting beside Victor, and she had put her
brother Étienne to sit by little Pauline; they played at keeping house;
they were like newly-married people on a pleasure party. At first Nana
had served her guests quite prettily, with the little airs and graces of
a grown-up person; but now she had given way to her fondness for
bacon, and kept all the bits for herself. The cross-eyed Augustine, who
prowled about the children's table, seized the excuse for taking them
away from her bodily, under the pretext of dividing them round more
fairly. Nana was furious, and bit her wrist.

"All right!" muttered Augustine, "I'll tell your mother that after
the *blanquette* you told Victor to give you a kiss."

But quiet was restored as Gervaise and old Madame Coupeau
made their appearance to get out the goose. The guests at the large
table, took deep breaths, lying back in their chairs. The men unbut-
toned their waistcoats, the women wiped their faces with their servi-
ettes. The feast was momentarily interrupted; but a few of them, their
jaws working unconsciously, went on swallowing great mouthfuls of
bread. They waited, letting the food settle. Night had gradually come
on; a dull ashen light now made its way through the curtains. When

Augustine placed two lamps on the table, one at each end, the disorder of things was plainly visible, the greasy plates and knives, the
table-cloth stained with wine and covered with bread-crumbs. A sti-
fling odour rose all around. However, at certain hot whiffs, all sniffed
in the direction of the kitchen.

"Shall I help you?" cried Virginie.

She left her seat and went into the next room. All the women
followed her, one by one. They stood around the roaster, gazing with
profound curiosity at Gervaise and old Madame Coupeau, who were
extricating the goose. Then a general shout arose, through which
pierced the shrill voices of the children, jumping for joy. And there
was a triumphal entry: Gervaise carried the goose with outstretched
arms, her face covered with sweat and beaming with smiles; the wom-
en followed her, smiling as well; whilst Nana, at the very end, her
eyes staring their widest, stood on tip-toe to have a look. When the
goose was on the table, huge and golden and running with gravy, it
was not begun upon all at once. A sort of respectful wonderment had
silenced every tongue. There were winks and nods, as everybody
pointed it out to everybody. What a devilish fine fat beast it was! what
legs! what a breast!

"That didn't fatten itself by licking the walls, I should say," said
Boche.

Thereupon there were endless details about the creature. Gervaise
stated the facts; it was the best that was to be found at the poulterer's
in the Faubourg Poissonniere; it weighed twelve pounds and a half
by the coal-dealer's scales; it had taken a bushel of coals to cook; and
it had made three bowlfuls of dripping.

Virginie interrupted her to boast of having seen the creature before it was cooked.

"You could have eaten it as it was," she said; "its skin was so fine
and white, a regular blonde's skin."

All the men laughed, and smacked their lips with a knowing air.
Meanwhile, Lorilleux and his wife drew a long face, filled with envy
at seeing such a goose on Clop-clop's table.

"Well, come now!" said the laundress at last, "we can't eat it as it
is. Who is going to carve? No, no, not me! It is too big; it frightens me."

Coupeau offered. Lord! it was simple enough; you take it limb by
limb, you pull, it turns out all right. But they cried out, and took the
carving-knife out of his hands by force; when he carved, he turned the
dish into a perfect cemetery. For a moment they looked round to see

who would be willing. Then Madame Lerat said in an amiable tone:

"It is Monsieur Poisson's job, certainly, Monsieur Poisson's."

And as the company did not seem to see the point, she added, more conciliatory than ever:

"Monsieur Poisson, of course; he is accustomed to the use of weapons."

And she passed him the carving-knife which she held in her hands. The whole company laughed approvingly, and Poisson bowed with military stiffness, and set the goose before him. His neighbours, Gervaise and Madame Boche, moved away a little, so as to leave him elbow-room. He carved deliberately, with great sweeping movements, his eyes fixed on the creature as if to nail it to the bottom of the dish. When he stuck his knife into the carcase, which crackled, Lorilleux was seized with an access of patriotism. He cried:

"Ah! if it were only a Cossack!"

"Have you ever fought with Cossacks, Monsieur Poisson?" asked Madame Boche.

"No, with Bedouins," replied the policeman, as he separated a wing. "There are no more Cossacks."

Then there was a profound silence. Necks were craned out, all eyes following the movements of the knife. Poisson was preparing a little surprise. Suddenly he gave a last stroke; the hind-quarters split open and stood erect, the rump in the air; it was "the parson's nose". There was a burst of admiration. It was only old soldiers who could make themelves so agreeable in company. Meanwhile the goose had let a flood of gravy run out of the gaping orifice; and Boche began to laugh.

"I'll stand in," he murmured, "if anyone'll do it into my mouth like that."

"Oh! the dirty beast!" cried the women. "He is a dirty beast!"

"I never met such a disgusting man!" said Madame Boche, more furious than the rest. "Will you be quiet! You would make a trooper blush. You know he sticks at nothing."

At this moment Clemence was heard crying out emphatically:

"Monsieur Poisson, listen! Monsieur Poisson, you will keep the rump for me, won't you?"

"My dear, the rump is yours by right," said Madame Lerat, in her discreetly venturesome manner.

Meanwhile the goose was all carved. The policeman, after having allowed the company to admire the parson's nose for several minutes, had cut up the bits, and ranged them all round the dish. Now they could help themselves. But the women, beginning to unbutton their bodices, complained of the heat. Coupeau declared that his house was his own, and he didn't care a damn for the neighbours; and he threw the door wide open. The feast went on to the accompaniment of the rumbling of vehicles and the trampling of feet on the pavements. Now their jaws were rested, they had more room inside, and they set-to once more on the dinner, falling furiously to work on the goose. Merely to see the creature being carved, said that inveterate joker Boche, all the *blanquette* and crackling had gone down into his calves.

And now there was a fine set-to indeed; and no one of all the company remembered to have ever had such an indigestion on his conscience. Gervaise stuffed mightily, eating great chunks of the white meat, not saying a word for fear of losing a mouthful; she was a little ashamed for Goujet to see her like that, as greedy as a cat. Goujet, however, was too busy eating away on his own account to notice that she was getting redder with cramming. Then, *gourmande* as she was, she was so nice and good all the same! She never spoke a word, but she interrupted herself at every moment to look after old Bru, and to put something dainty on his plate. It was quite touching to see her pick out a bit of the wing, halfway to her mouth, and give it to the old man, who seemed unable to distinguish between one piece and another, and who swallowed everything, his head bowed, dazed with so much eating, he whose palate had lost the taste of food. The Lorilleux vented all their rage on the roast; they ate enough to last three days; they would have swallowed up dish and plate and laundry if they could, to have ruined Clop-clop straight away. All the women wanted some of the breast; it was the ladies' part. Madame Lerat, Madame Boche, and Madame Putois scraped the bones, whilst old Madame Coupeau, who adored the neck, picked at the meat with her two last teeth. Virginie loved the skin when it was brown, and all the men passed her their skin in the most gallant manner, till Poisson cast severe looks at her, telling her to give over, that was quite enough; once already she had eaten too much roast goose, and was laid up in bed for a fortnight, her stomach all in disorder. But Coupeau was quite angry and passed Virginie a part of the leg, crying out that if she didn't scrape it clean—blast it all!—she wasn't worth her salt. As if goose had ever hurt anyone! On the contrary, goose was good for the liver. You could eat it by itself, like dessert. He could stuff all night, without being a penny the worse; and by way of boast, he thrust a whole chunk into his mouth. Meanwhile Clémence finished her rump, sucking it with a gurgle of the lips, and screwing about on her chair in a paroxysm of laughter at the smutty stories that Boche whispered in her ear. Oh Lord! it was a tightener, sure enough! When you're at it, you're at it, eh? and if you only get a good tuck-in now and again, you would be a sap not to stuff yourself up to the ears when you got a chance. Why, you could see the corporation getting larger every minute! The women were big enough to burst—damned lot of gluttons that they were!—with their open mouths, their chins bedabbled with grease; they had faces for all the world like backsides, and so red too, that you would say they were rich people's belongings, rich people bursting with prosperity.

And the wine too, my friends, the wine flowed round about the table as the water flows in the Seine. It was like a stream after the rain, when the soil is athirst. Coupeau lifted the bottle up when he poured it out, to see the red stream foam; and when a bottle was empty, he would wring its neck, for a joke, with the movement of a woman who is milking a cow. They had cracked another black girl's neck! And in a corner of the laundry the heap of black girls grew larger and larger, a very cemetery of bottles, on the top of which they threw the leavings on the cloth. Madame Putois, having asked for some water, the tinsmith indignantly got up and removed the water bottles from the table. Rightminded people didn't drink water! No Adam's ale to be had there! And the glasses were drained at a gulp; one heard the sound of the liquid as it was gulped down, like the noise of rain water down a water-pipe on a pouring day. It rained wine, a thin wine which tasted a bit of the cask at first; but you soon get jolly well used to it, and then you found it nutty enough. Devil take it all! the Jesuits might say what they like, the fruit of the vine was a famous find all the same! The company laughed approval; for the workman, sure enough, could never have lived without wine, and Father Noah, without a doubt, planted the vine on purpose for tinsmiths, tailors, and blacksmiths. Wine brightened you up, and rested you after your work; it stirred you up if you weren't inclined to work; and if the joker did you now and then, well, Lord! the king wasn't your uncle, you had all Paris before you. As if, too, the workman, penniless and downtrodden and despised as he was, had so much fun in his life that anyone had a right to complain if he got a bit boozed now and again, and all just for the sake of seeing things look rosy for once in a while. Why, now, for example, who cared a twopenny damn for the Emperor? Very likely the Emperor himself was tight; that was all very well. Who cared a twopenny damn for the Emperor? Let him get more tight still, and he'd have more of a spree. *That* for the swells! Coupeau sent everybody to the deuce. Women for him, he said; and he slapped his pocket, in which three sous jingled, laughing as if he had five-franc pieces in his purse. Goujet himself, usually so sober, was a bit screwed. Boche's eyes seemed to shrink up, and Lorilleux's went paler than ever, whilst Poisson's bronzed soldierly face looked more and more severe every moment. They were all perfectly drunk. And the women, too, were a trifle elevated; oh! a mere bit of breeziness, cheeks flushed and a sort of necessity of taking off things; only Clemence began to be not quite decent. All at once Gervaise remembered the six bottles of better wine; she had forgotten to serve them with the goose. She went and fetched them, and the glasses were filled. Then Poisson rose, glass in hand, and said:

"I drink to the health of the lady of the house."

There was a scraping of chairs, and the whole company rose to their feet; they clinked glasses in the midst of a regular uproar.

"Fifty years from now," cried Virginie.

"No, no," cried Gervaise, smiling, and half overcome, "I should be too old. A time is sure to come when one is glad enough to be taken."

Meanwhile, through the open door, the whole neighborhood gazed at the feast, shared in it almost. Passers-by stopped as the light from the open door came across their path, and laughed good-naturedly, to see these people eat so heartily. The cabmen bowed on their seats, whipping up their nags, looked in and made jokes: "I say, how much do you pay? Mother, shall I fetch the midwife?" And the smell of the goose was a delight to the whole street; the grocer's boys opposite felt that they were actually eating it; the fruiterer and the tripeseller, every other minute, came and stood outside the shop, sniffing and licking their lips. The whole street was positively in a state of indigestion. Madame Cudorge and her daughter, the umbrella-sellers near by, who were never seen outside, crossed the road, one behind the other, looking out of the corners of their eyes, as red as if they had been making pancakes. The little watchmaker, sitting at his workboard, could work no longer, drunk with the bottles he had counted, quite off his head in the midst of all his gay clocks. "The neighbours are full of it!" cried Coupeau. What was the good of hiding out of sight? The company were no longer ashamed to be seen at table; on the contrary, they gloated over all this greedy crowd which had gathered in their honour; they would gladly have taken down the shopfront, and shoved the table out into the street, and so had their dessert out there, under the very nose of the public, in the very crush of the pavement. They weren't such a sight, eh? Besides, they needn't be selfish enough to shut themselves away. Coupeau, taking pity on the poor thirsting watchmaker across the way, held up to him a bottle from a distance; and as the other nodded vigorously, he took him the bottle and a glass. They were all on friendly terms now, the street and they. They drank to the health of the passers-by. They called out to those who seemed good fellows. The feasting spread and spread, till the whole quarter of the Goutte-d'Or scented the grub, and held their sides in a very hell of a racket.

MENU:

Pot-au-feu

Blanquette de veau

Peas with bacon

Roast goose

(with Pork and onion stuffing)

The pot-au-feu, *one of the sovereigns of French cooking, comes from the work of a man who was a true scholar of soup. Felix J. Déliée felt that soup had been slighted by most of the cookbooks of his time. To make up for this, he provided over 350 different soup recipes in his 1884* Franco-American Cookery Book, *including the following varieties of consommé:*

> *Consommé à l'Andalouse*
> *à l'Bourdaloue*
> *à la Brisse*
> *à la Carême*
> *à la Célestine*
> *à la Châtelaine*
> *à la Crécy*
> *à la Cussy*
> *à la Deslignac*
> *à la D'Orléans*

à la D'Orsay
à l'impériale
à la MacDonald
à la Magenta
à la Médicis
à la Montmorency
à la Napolitaine
à la Piémontaise
à la Rachel
à la Rivoli
à la Roqueplan
à la Sevigné
à la Talma
à la Xavier
aux laitues
aux profiterolles
aux quenelles
with bread crusts
with poached eggs

POT-AU-FEU

FROM *The Franco-American Cookery Book*, 1884, Felix J. Déliée

Pot-au-feu has three elements: beef, vegetables and broth. The broth is eaten first, with the beef and vegetables which flavored it served on a separate platter, with mustard, horseradish, tomato or other sauce. Long slow cooking is the key to its success. Alexandre Dumas said of pot-au-feu that it reaches its peak only after eight hours of cooking, and he or she who has nothing better to do with time than allow a pot-au-feu to develop according to its lights will undoubtedly eat superior soup. His concierge, he wrote, whose only responsibility was to open the door all day, "eats better soup than any Rothschild."

Gervaise was entertaining many greedy guests, and clearly a vast pot-au-feu would have served her purposes magnificently. But to suit today's smaller dinner parties and smaller families, Déliée's original recipe, made with 10 pounds of beef, has been adapted to feed 6.

3-4 pounds round of beef	1 tablespoon salt
(1 marrow bone, browned	1-2 large carrots
in oven)	1 turnip
2 quarts of cold water	1-2 onions

1 parsnip
2-3 leeks
½ stalk celery
(seasoning)

beef extract
¼ of a large cabbage
½ pound French bread

Put in a stock pot a piece of the round of beef (and a marrow bone which
has been browned in the oven) with cold water and salt; boil slowly, scum
well, add a little water to stop the boiling, and scum again; then add (cut
up) large carrots, turnip, onion, a parsnip, leeks, and celery (add seasoning
to taste); cook slowly for 3 hours, take out the beef (and the marrow bone);
trim the beef neatly and put it in a saucepan with a ladleful of the surface
of the broth; with a pastry brush spread some beef extract on the fatty part,
let it glaze slowly for an hour in a moderately hot oven; boil the cabbage
for 5 minutes in salted water to take away the strong odor; cool, drain,
and put in the broth after the beef has been taken out; boil (the broth)
1 hour longer and skim off the fat. When the beef is of a nice brown color
set it in a dish, trim neatly the carrots and turnips, and with the cabbage
(and the marrow bone) range them alternately around the beef, and serve;
a bowl of tomato sauce passed at the same time improves the dish.

Cut ½ pound of French bread in thin sippets;* put it in a soup tureen; strain
and pour over it 3 quarts of the well-skimmed beef broth . . . and serve (at
the same time as the beef and vegetables but in a separate bowl).

* Gervaise's soup contained *pâtes d'Italie,* Italian pastes like macaroni or spaghetti.
These can be precooked and put into the soup instead of the bread that Déliée recommends.

BLANQUETTE DE VEAU

FROM *The Franco-American Cookery Book,* 1884, Felix J. Déliée

a short breast of veal (about
   4 pounds)
water
¾ cup butter
¼ cup flour
salt and pepper
nutmeg (about ½ teaspoon)*
parsley with aromatic herbs
   (bay leaf, parsley, thyme)

a carrot
an onion
3 cloves *
4 egg yolks
(½ pint cream)
lemon juice

Procure a short breast of white veal; cut it in pieces (2-inch cubes) and
steep in water for 1 hour; drain, put in a saucepan with fresh water (to
cover) and boil 5 minutes (remove scum); turn in a colander and save the

* For today's tastes, omit nutmeg and cloves.

broth; wash the meat well, drain on a cloth, trim a little, return to a clean saucepan with ½ cup of the butter; put this on a brisk fire and stir until the butter turns clear, sprinkle the flour over, mix well, dilute with the broth; add salt, pepper, nutmeg, a bunch of parsley with aromatics, a carrot, and an onion with 3 cloves in it; cover and boil slowly for about 40 minutes (to 1½ hours, until tender); skim the fat, remove the parsley, carrot and onion; remove from fire and add a liaison of 4 egg yolks (mixed with ½ pint cream), the rest of the butter, and lemon juice; dish up.

(Serves 8)

PEAS WITH BACON

FROM *French Dishes for American Tables,* 1886, Pierre Caron

¼ pound bacon, diced
1 tablespoon flour
pepper (and salt)
nutmeg

10 branches of parsley
1 glass water
6 cups green peas

Cut the rind from a ¼ pound of bacon, cut the bacon in small pieces and place in a saucepan on the fire; when beginning to color add 1 table-spoonful of flour, a little pepper (salt), and nutmeg, add 10 branches of parsley tied together; moisten with a glass of water; add green peas and boil (simmer) about 30 minutes (20-30); (add more water if necessary), if sufficiently done, remove the bunch of parsley and serve.

(Serves 8-10)

ROAST GOOSE

with Pork and Onion Stuffing

FROM *The Household Cookery Book,* 1871, Urbain-Dubois

a goose (about 8 pounds)
minced fresh pork (roasted;
    2 cups)
2 chopped onions, fried slightly
softened bread cubes (4 cups)
a pinch of chopped parsley or
    sage

2 whole (beaten) eggs
salt and pepper
cut goose fat
hot water

Only young and tender geese must be roasted on the spit; as soon as they are advanced in age, it is preferable to roast them in the oven; in this case, one must take care not to keep the meat underdone, else it would be tough; it must be thoroughly done.

Singe a goose, draw it, keeping the fat and giblets by; carefully wipe the interior.—Prepare a mince of fresh pork, add to it 2 chopped onions fried slightly, a piece of softened bread crumbs (cubes of bread), a pinch of chopped parsley or sage, and 2 whole eggs; season it; with this stuffing, fill the body of the goose; sew up its apertures, truss it, place it in a roasting pan, of enameled cast iron, of proportionate size, the bottom of which is masked with the cut fat of the goose; add to it some tablespoonfuls of hot water; salt the goose, cover it with a sheet of buttered paper (or foil), let it roast in a slack oven, basting it repeatedly (with pan juice), and turning it; when it is done (roast it 25-30 minutes per pound in a 325-350° oven), drain it, untruss it, dish it up; pour a little gravy into a roasting pan, let it boil, skim off its fat; pass it through a sieve, serve it separately.

(Allow 1-1½ pounds per serving)

GUY DE MAUPASSANT
FORBIDDEN FRUIT
c. 1880

Paul and Henrietta, a most modern couple, marry but soon tire of each other. Their love had been an impassioned thing, "all their looks signified something impure, and all their gestures recalled to them the ardent intimacy of the night." But though they are experimental in their love-making, inventing new endearments and new caresses every day, their desire for each other begins to wane.

Henrietta thinks of one more experiment: perhaps passion would be rekindled if Paul made love to her while pretending she was not his wife but, rather, a mistress. Paul agrees to this and they go to an inn where he has in the past taken his mistresses. Henrietta is veiled, they sit in a private room lit only by candles, and they eat a luxurious meal designed to stimulate their appetite—appetite for both food and sensuality. But, while the experiment is momentarily satisfying, it only seems to make Henrietta aware of her desire for even more forbidden experiences.

Before marriage they had loved each other chastely in the starlight. At first there was a charming meeting on the shore of the ocean. He found her delicious, the rosy young girl who passed him with her bright umbrellas and fresh costumes on the marine background. He loved this blonde, fragile creature in her setting of blue waves and immense skies. And he confounded the tenderness which this scarcely fledged woman caused to be born in him with the vague and powerful emotion awakened in his soul, in his heart, and in his veins by the lovely salt air and the great seascape full of sun and waves.

She loved him because he paid her attention, because he was young and rich enough, genteel and delicate. She loved him because it is natural for young ladies to love young men who say tender words to them.

Then for three months they lived side by side, eye to eye and hand to hand. The greeting which they exchanged in the morning before the bath, in the freshness of the new day, and the adieu of the evening upon the sand under the stars, in the warmth of the calm night, murmured low and still lower, had already the taste of kisses, although their lips had never met.

They dreamed of each other as soon as they were asleep, thought of each other as soon as they awoke and, without yet saying so, called for and desired each other with their whole soul and body.

After marriage they adored each other above everything on earth. It was at first a kind of sensual, indefatigable rage, then an exalted tenderness made of palpable poesy, of caresses already refined and of inventions both genteel and ungenteel. All their looks signified something impure, and all their gestures recalled to them the ardent intimacy of the night.

Now, without confessing it, without realizing it, perhaps, they commenced to weary of one another. They loved each other, it is true, but there was nothing more to reveal, nothing more to do that had not often been done, nothing more to learn from each other, not even a new word of love, an unforeseen motion or an intonation, which sometimes is more expressive than a known word too often repeated.

They forced themselves, however, to relight the flame, enfeebled from the first embraces. They invented some new and tender artifice each day, some simple or complicated ruse, in the vain attempt to renew in their hearts the unappeasable ardor of the first days and in their veins the flame of the nuptial month.

From time to time, by dint of whipping their desire, they again found an hour of factitious excitement which was immediately followed by a disgusting lassitude.

They tried moonlight walks under the leaves in the sweetness of the night, the poesy of the cliffs bathed in mist, the excitement of public festivals.

Then one morning Henrietta said to Paul:

"Will you take me to dine at an inn?"

"Why, yes, my dearie."

"In a very well-known inn?"

"Yes."

He looked at her, questioning with his eye, understanding well that she had something in mind which she had not spoken.

She continued: "You know, an inn—how shall I explain it?—in a gallant inn, where people make appointments to meet each other?"

He smiled. "Yes. I understand, a private room in a large cafe?"

"That is it. But in a large cafe where you are known, where you have already taken supper—no, dinner—that is—I mean—I want—no, I do not dare say it!"

"Speak out, *chérie;* between us what can it matter? We are not like those who have little secrets from each other."

"No, I dare not."

"Oh! Come now! Don't be so innocent. Say it."

"Well—oh! Well—I wish—I wish to be taken for your mistress—and that the waiters, who do not know that you are married, may look upon me as your mistress, and you, too—that for an hour you believe me your mistress in that very place where you have remembrances of—That's all! And I myself will believe that I am your mistress. I want to commit a great sin—to deceive you—with yourself—

there! It is very bad, but that is what I want to do. Do not make me blush—I feel that I am blushing—imagine—my wanting to take the trouble to dine with you in a place not quite the thing—in a private room where people devote themselves to love every evening—every evening. It is very bad. I am as red as a peony! Don't look at me!"

He laughed, very much amused, and responded:

"Yes, we will go this evening to a very chic place where I am known."

Toward seven o'clock they mounted the staircase of a large cafe on the boulevard, he smiling, with the air of a conqueror, she timid, veiled, but delighted. When they were in a little room furnished with armchairs and a large sofa covered with red velvet, the steward, in black clothes, entered and presented the bill of fare. Paul passed it to his wife.

"What do you wish to eat?" he said.

"I don't know; what do they have that is good here?"

Then he read off the list of dishes while taking off his overcoat, which he handed to a waiter. Then he said:

"Serve this menu: Bisque soup, deviled chicken, sides of hare, duck, American style, vegetable salad and dessert. We will drink champagne."

The steward smiled and looked at the young lady. He took the card, murmuring, "Will Monsieur Paul have a cordial or some champagne?"

"Champagne, very dry."

Henrietta was happy to find that this man knew her husband's name. They sat down side by side upon the sofa and began to eat.

Ten candles lighted the room, reflected in a great mirror, mutilated by the thousands of names traced on it with a diamond, making on the clear crystal a kind of huge cobweb.

Henrietta drank glass after glass to animate her, although she felt giddy from the first one. Paul, excited by certain memories, kissed his wife's hand repeatedly. Her eyes were brilliant.

She felt strangely moved by this suspicious situation; she was excited and happy, although she felt a little defiled. Two grave waiters, mute, accustomed to seeing everything and forgetting all, entered only when it was necessary and went out in the moments of overflow, going and coming quickly and softly.

Toward the middle of the dinner Henrietta was tipsy, completely tipsy, and Paul, in his gaiety, pressed her knee with all his force. She prattled now, boldly, her cheeks red, her look lively and dizzy.

"Oh, come, Paul," she said, "confess now, won't you? I want to know all.'"

"What do you mean, *chérie?*"

"I dare not say it."

"But you must always—"

"Have you had mistresses—many of them—before me?"

He hesitated, a little perplexed, not knowing whether he ought to conceal his good fortunes or boast of them.

She continued: "Oh! I beg you to tell me; have you had many?"

"Why, some."

"How many?"

"I don't know. How can one know such things?"

"You cannot count them?"

"Why, no!"

"Oh! Then you have had very many?"

"Yes."

"How many, do you suppose?—somewhere near—"

"I don't know at all, my dear. Some years I had many and some only a few."

"How many a year, should you say?"

"Sometimes twenty or thirty, sometimes four or five only."

"Oh! That makes more than a hundred women in all."

"Yes, somewhere near."

"Oh! How disgusting!"

"Why disgusting?"

"Because it is disgusting—when one thinks of all those women—bare—and always—always the same thing. Oh! It is disgusting all the same—more than a hundred women."

He was shocked that she thought it disgusting and responded with that superior air which men assume to make women understand that they have said something foolish:

"Well, that is curious! If it is disgusting to have a hundred women, it is equally disgusting to have one."

"Oh, no, not at all!"

"Why not?"

"Because with one woman there is intrigue, there is a love that attaches you to her, while with a hundred women there is filthiness, misconduct. I cannot understand how a man can meddle with all those girls who are so foul."

"No, they are very neat."

"One cannot be neat, carrying on a trade like that."

"On the contrary, it is because of their trade that they are neat."

"Oh, pshaw! When one thinks of the nights they pass with others! It is ignoble!"

"It is no more ignoble than drinking from a glass from which I know not who drank this morning, and that has been less thoroughly washed—you may be certain of it."

"Oh, be still; you are revolting."

"But why ask me then if I have had mistresses?"

"Then tell me, were your mistresses all girls, all of them—the whole hundred?"

"Why, no—no. Some were actresses—some little working girls—and some women of the world."

"How many of them were women of the world?"

"Six."

"Only six?"

"Yes."

"Were they pretty?"

"Yes, of course."

"Prettier than the girls?"

"No."

"Which did you prefer, girls or women of the world?"

"Women of the world."

"Oh! How filthy! Why?"

"Because I do not care much for amateur talent."

"Oh! Horror! You are abominable, do you know it? But tell me, is it very amusing to pass from one to another like that?"

"Yes, rather."

"Very?"

"Very."

"What is there amusing about it? Is it because they do not resemble each other?"

"They do not."

"Ah! The women do not resemble each other?"

"Not at all."

"In nothing?"

"In nothing."

"That is strange! In what respect do they differ?"

"In every respect."

"In body?"

"Yes, in body."

"In the whole body?"

"Yes, in the whole body."

"And in what else?"

"Why, in the manner of—of embracing, of speaking, of saying the least thing."

"Ah! And it is very amusing, this changing?"

"Yes."

"And are men different too?"

"That I do not know."

"You do not know?"

"No."

"They must be different."

"Yes, without doubt."

She remained pensive, her glass of champagne in her hand. It was full, and she drank it at a draught; then placing the glass upon the table, she threw both arms around her husband's neck and murmured in his mouth:

"Oh, my dear, how I love you!" He seized her in a passionate embrace.

A waiter, who was entering, drew back, closing the door, and the service was interrupted for about five minutes.

When the steward again appeared, with a grave, dignified air, bringing in the fruits for the dessert, she was holding another glassful between her fingers and, looking to the bottom of the yellow, transparent liquid, as if to see there things unknown and dreamed of, she murmured with a thoughtful voice:

"Oh yes! It must be very amusing, all the same!"

MENU:

Bisque soup
(Crawfish and lobster bisques)

Deviled chicken

Sides of hare
Fillets of hare sautées
Hare à la bourgeoisie

Duck, American style

Vegetable salad
à la Baron Brisse
à la Pierre Blot

Fruits for dessert
Macédoine of fruits in jelly
Broiled apricots à la Breteuil

Several famous nineteenth-century chefs provided the recipes for Paul and Henrietta's surreptitious dinner, but the most delightful of them all was certainly the Baron Brisse. The baron was so fat that when he traveled from his home in Fontenay-aux-Roses to Paris he had to purchase two seats in the coach just to have enough room to sit. It never discouraged him. He not only loved to eat but, a trait rare in nobility, loved to cook. His friends, to whom he was exceedingly generous, fondly called him "Baron Falstaff" and popularized his aristocratic mottoes like, "A host whose guest has had to ask for anything is a dishonored man."

BISQUE SOUP

FROM *French Dishes for American Tables,* 1886, *Pierre Caron*

Bisque of Crawfish

4 dozen crawfish, washed and cleaned	1 tablespoon vinegar
water to cover	4 tablespoons butter
1 carrot	2 tablespoons flour
1 onion	3½ cups cream
3 cloves garlic, sliced	1 quart consommé
2 cloves	¾ cup tomatoes
parsley	salt and pepper
	cayenne

Wash crawfish and put them in sufficient water to cover them, cut a carrot, an onion, and three cloves of garlic in slices; add cloves, a few branches of parsley, a little salt, and the vinegar, and boil for 15 minutes. Drain them (discarding the garlic and vegetables) and then pound to a paste (or chop very finely). Melt 2 tablespoons of butter in a saucepan, add the flour, which mix well with the butter. Then add the paste of crawfish, the cream, the consommé, the tomatoes, salt and pepper, and a little cayenne. Boil and stir with a spoon, press through a sieve, and put back on the fire, with 2 more tablespoons of butter; as soon as it boils (heats) up again, serve.

Bisque of lobster is prepared in the same manner. Use half a pound of boiled lobster from which you have removed the shell and add half instead of three-quarters of a cupful of tomatoes.

(Serves 6-8)

DEVILED CHICKEN

FROM *The Hostess of To-day,* 1899, Linda Hull Larned

6 small, raw fillets of chicken (white meat), boned	3 tablespoons vinegar
2 tablespoons butter, melted	1 teaspoon mustard
2 tablespoons Worcestershire sauce	¼ teaspoon salt
	¼ teaspoon chili pepper or paprika

Dip the chicken in melted butter and broil 10 to 15 minutes. Mix the rest of the ingredients together and pour them on the chicken when it is done. Serve.

(Serves 3-6, depending on size of fillets and appetites)

SIDES OF HARE

FROM *French Dishes for American Tables*, 1886, Pierre Caron

Fillets of Hare Sautées

2 hares, filleted (2½-3 pounds skinned and cleaned rabbit)	¼ teaspoon thyme
	1 tablespoon flour
¼ cup butter	½ cup consommé
1 onion, sliced	½ cup red wine
1 clove garlic, chopped	salt and pepper
2 bay leaves	1 tablespoon vinegar
2 cloves	

Take the fillets of 2 hares and cut them in medium-sized pieces. Put them in a saucepan with the butter, an onion, a clove of garlic, two bay leaves, cloves and thyme. (Brown the fillets on all sides.) After having been on a good fire 10 minutes, add the flour to your fillets; moisten with consommé and red wine. Add a pinch of salt and pepper and boil (simmer, covered) on a good fire for 40 minutes (to an hour or until tender). Remove your fillets, strain the liquid, put it back on the fire with your fillets, add the vinegar, boil 5 minutes, and serve.

(Serves 4)

Hare à la Bourgeoisie

1 hare, cut up (2½-3 pounds skinned, cleaned rabbit)	3 peppercorns
	¼ teaspoon thyme
¼ pound bacon, cut in pieces (and blanched)	2 cloves garlic
	1 cup consommé
parsley (a few sprigs)	1 cup white wine
3 cloves	5 turnips, quartered

When your hare is uncased and cleaned, cut it in pieces and put it in a saucepan, with the bacon cut in small pieces, parsley, cloves, peppercorns, thyme and garlic. (Brown it first in 2 tablespoons of butter.) Moisten the hare with half a pint of consommé and the same of white wine, and add the turnips cut into small quarters; reduce the fire (cook on a low flame for about 1 hour or until tender) and serve.

(Serves 4)

DUCK, AMERICAN STYLE

FROM *The Franco-American Cookery Book*, 1884, Felix J. Déliée

2 or more mallard ducks
½ pint broth
2 shallots
1 bay leaf
a sprig of thyme (or ½ teaspoon
   dried thyme)

2 cloves
2 ladlefuls of thick brown
   gravy (½ cup)
2 glasses (about ½ cup) port wine
melted currant jelly (2 tablespoons)
quartered lemon

Roast rare 2 or more mallard ducks; carve the legs in two, and the fillets in 3 or more slices, keep warm in a covered plate; crack the carcasses, put them in a saucepan with ½ pint of broth, 2 shallots, a bay leaf, a sprig of thyme, 2 cloves and 2 ladlefuls of thick brown gravy; boil ½ hour, strain through a colander, add 2 glasses of port wine and some melted currant jelly; reduce to the desired consistency, skim and press through a napkin; dish up the ducks in a pyramid form, pour the sauce over, and serve with quartered lemon on a plate.

(Serves 4-6)

VEGETABLE SALAD

NUMBER ONE

FROM *366 Menus and 1200 Recipes*, 1882, Baron Brisse

equal quantities of carrots, peas,
   asparagus heads, French beans,
   potatoes

half that quantity of turnips
1 boiled cauliflower

Boil the vegetables in separate saucepans; when done, drain carefully and place in a salad bowl in separate groups, with a fine head of boiled cauliflower in the center. Cover with the following sauce:

12 tablespoons (¾ cup) olive oil
2 tablespoons vinegar
½ teaspoon anchovy paste

salt and pepper
a pinch of cayenne
1 head of garlic

Stir the sauce well and remove the garlic before pouring over salad.

VEGETABLE SALAD

NUMBER TWO

FROM *What To Eat and How To Cook It,* 1863, Pierre Blot

fish (herring, sprats, anchovies, etc.)
meat (any bits of left-over meat
 or cold cuts)
green vegetables (peas, string beans,
 salad greens, asparagus, artichoke
 hearts, etc., cooked and cold)

parsley
sweet oil
vinegar
salt and pepper

This salad ought to be called a "compound salad," as it is made of a little of everything that can be served in a salad, *i.e.,* fish, meat, green vegetables, etc. When the whole is mixed, you add chopped parsley, sweet oil, vinegar, salt and pepper; you move till your arms are sore, and you have a salad *macédoine.* Everyone has a right to try it.

FRUITS FOR DESSERT

FROM *366 Menus and 1200 Recipes,* 1882, Baron Brisse

Macédoine of Fruit in Jelly

2½ tablespoons gelatin
1 pound sugar
3 whipped whites of egg
juice of a lemon

1 pint of water
½ bottle champagne
apples, pears, plums, cherries, apricots, stewed and cut in pieces

Take gelatin, sugar, egg whites, juice of lemon and 1 pint water; warm in a preserving pan, stir until it boils, and pass through a jelly-bag or cheesecloth; if necessary, pass it a second time, as the jelly must be perfectly clear (no lumps); when cold, add half a bottle of champagne to it. Stew some pieces of apple, pear, plums, cherries and apricots in sirup, leave until cold. Fill a mold with alternate layers of the fruit and jelly mixture until within half an inch from the top; let the last layer be of jelly, place in the refrigerator until set; turn out of mold and serve.

(Serves 6-8)

Broiled Apricots à la Breteuil

apricots, halved and stoned

candied sugar (confectioners' sugar)
raspberries

Cut the apricots into halves, remove the stones, sprinkle with candied sugar, and broil them on the gridiron over hot cinders; when done, place in a glass dish. Pound some apricots, raspberries, and sugar together, boil, and pour over the broiled fruit. Serve very hot.

ANTON CHEKHOV
A WOMAN'S KINGDOM
1894

The new industrial middle class in Chekhov's time, with its roots among the peasants and its aspirations among the professionals, provides the background for the painful story of Anna Akimovna, who has inherited the wealth and responsibilities of her peasant-turned-factory-owner father. Anna wishes she could marry a man as warm and simple as her father was, but her upbringing has placed her almost exclusively

*among men who are vacuous, licentious and decadent, like the lawyer
Lysevich and the civil councilor Krylin. On the day this story takes
place, however, she has just met Pimenov, a sensitive worker who is
one of her own employees, and has decided that this is the kind of man
she would like to marry.*

*It is Christmas. Krylin and Lysevich have come to dinner and
throughout the evening Anna finds herself caught between her own
idealism and their cynicism. They tell her she ought to take a lover,
in fact, "one for each day of the week," and when she explains to them,
"For myself personally, I can't conceive of love without family life,"
they reply, "No, frivolity, frivolity! . . . it's your duty to be frivolous
and depraved!" The meal itself parallels this schism in Anna's kingdom
and soul: two meals are served at Christmas, the Russian meal, traditional and wholesome, and the French meal, flamboyant and frivolous.*

*During dinner Anna manages to maintain her hopes of marrying
without class considerations. But afterwards she imagines Pimenov
dining with the lawyer and civil councilor and finds herself repelled
by the thought of the worker's timid, unintellectual figure. She cannot
move backward in class, despite the attraction of warmth and understanding. And tearfully she realizes "that all she had said and thought
about Pimenov and marrying a workman was nonsense, folly and wil-
fulness. . . . It was too late to dream of happiness . . . and it was impossible to go back to the life when she had slept under the same quilt
with her mother. . . ."*

Just as the year before, the last to pay her visits were Krylin, an actual
civil councilor, and Lysevich, a well-known barrister. It was already
dark when they arrived. Krylin, a man of sixty, with a wide mouth and
with grey whiskers close to his ears, with a face like a lynx, was wearing a uniform with an Anna ribbon, and white trousers. He held Anna
Akimovna's hand in both of his for a long while, looked intently in her
face, moved his lips, and at last said, drawling upon one note:

"I used to respect your uncle . . . and your father, and enjoyed the
privilege of their friendship. Now I feel it an agreeable duty, as you
see, to present my Christmas wishes to their honoured heiress . . . in
spite of my infirmities and the distance I have to come . . . . And I am
very glad to see you in good health."

The lawyer Lysevich, a tall, handsome, fair man, with a slight
sprinkling of grey on his temples and beard, was distinguished by ex-

ceptionally elegant manners; he walked with a swaying step, bowed as it were reluctantly, and shrugged his shoulders as he talked, and all this with an indolent grace, like a spoiled horse fresh from the stable. He was well fed, extremely healthy, and very well off; on one occasion he had won forty thousand roubles, but concealed the fact from his friends. He was fond of good fare, especially cheese, truffles, and grated radish with hemp oil; while in Paris he had eaten, so he said, baked but unwashed guts. He spoke smoothly, fluently, without hesitation, and only occasionally, for the sake of effect, permitted himself to hesitate and snap his fingers as if picking up a word. He had long ceased to believe in anything he had to say in the law courts, or perhaps he did believe in it, but attached no kind of significance to it; it had all so long been familiar, stale, ordinary. . . . He believed in nothing but what was original and unusual. A copybook moral in an original form would move him to tears. Both his notebooks were filled with extraordinary expressions which he had read in various authors; and when he needed to look up any expression, he would search nervously in both books and usually failed to find it. Anna Akimovna's father had in a good-humoured moment ostentatiously appointed him legal advisor in matters concerning the factory and had assigned him a salary of twelve thousand roubles. The legal business of the factory had been confined to two or three trivial actions for recovering debts, which Lysevich handed to his assistants.

Anna Akimovna knew that he had nothing to do at the factory, but she could not dismiss him—she had not the moral courage; and besides, she was used to him. He used to call himself her legal advisor, and his salary, which he invariably sent for on the first of the month punctually, he used to call "stern prose." Anna Akimovna knew that when, after her father's death, the timber of her forest was sold for railway sleepers, Lysevich had made more than fifteen thousand out of the transaction and had shared it with Nazarich. When first she found out they had cheated her she had wept bitterly, but afterwards she had grown used to it.

Wishing her a happy Christmas, and kissing both her hands, he looked her up and down and frowned.

"You mustn't," he said with genuine disappointment. "I have told you, my dear, you mustn't!"

"What do you mean, Viktor Nikolaitch?"

"I have told you you mustn't get fat. All your family have an unfortunate tendency to grow fat. You mustn't," he repeated in an imploring voice, and kissed her hand. "You are so handsome! You are so splendid! Here, Your Excellency, let me introduce the one woman in the world whom I have ever seriously loved."

"There is nothing surprising in that. To know Anna Akimovna at your age and not to be in love with her, that would be impossible."

"I adore her," the lawyer continued with perfect sincerity, but with his usual indolent grace. "I love her, but not because I am a man and she is a woman. When I am with her I always feel as though she belongs to some third sex, and I to a fourth, and we float away together into the domain of the subtlest shades, and there we blend into the spectrum. Leconte de Lisle defines such relations better than anyone. He has a superb passage, a marvellous passage. . . ."

Lysevich rummaged in one notebook, then in the other, and, not finding the quotation, subsided. They began talking of Duse. Anna Akimovna remembered that the year before Lysevich and, she fancied, Krylin had dined with her, and now when they were getting ready to go away, she began with perfect sincerity pointing out to them in an imploring voice that, as they had no more visits to pay, they ought to remain to dinner with her. After some hesitation the visitors agreed.

In addition to the family dinner, consisting of cabbage soup, suckling pig, goose with apples, and so on, a so-called "French" or "chef's" dinner used to be prepared in the kitchen on great holidays, in case any visitor in the upper storey wanted a meal. When they heard the clatter of crockery in the dining room, Lysevich began to betray a noticeable excitement; he rubbed his hands, shrugged his shoulders, screwed up his eyes, and described with feeling what dinners her father and uncle used to give at one time, and a marvelous *matelote* of turbots the cook here could make; it was not a *matelote*, but a veritable revelation! He was already gloating over the dinner, already eating it in imagination and enjoying it. When Anna Akimovna took his arm and led him to the dining-room, he tossed off a glass of vodka and put a piece of salmon in his mouth; he positively purred with pleasure. He munched loudly, disgustingly, emitting sounds from his nose, while his eyes grew oily and rapacious.

The *hors d'oeuvres* were superb; among other things, there were fresh white mushrooms stewed in cream, and *sauce provençale* made of fried oysters and crayfish, strongly flavoured with some bitter pickles. The dinner, consisting of elaborate holiday dishes, was excellent, and so were the wines. Mishenka waited at table with enthusiasm. When he laid some new dish on the table and lifted the shining cover, or poured out the wine, he did it with the solemnity of a professor of black magic, and, looking at his face and his movements suggesting the first figure of a quadrille, the lawyer thought several times, "What a fool!"

After the third course Lysevich said, turning to Anna Akimovna:

"The *fin de siècle* woman—I mean when she is young, and of course, wealthy—must be independent, clever, elegant, intellectual, bold, and a little depraved. Depraved within limits, a little; for excess, you know, is wearisome. You ought not to vegetate, my dear; you ought not to live like everyone else, but to get the full savour of life, and a slight flavor of depravity is the sauce of life. Revel among flowers of intoxicating fragrance, breathe the perfume of musk, eat hashish, and best of all, love, love, love. . . . To begin with, in your place I would set up seven lovers—one for each day of the week; and one I would call Monday, one Tuesday, the third Wednesday, and so on, so that each might know his day."

This conversation troubled Anna Akimovna; she ate nothing and only drank a glass of wine.

"Let me speak at last," she said. "For myself personally, I can't conceive of love without family life, I am lonely, lonely as the moon in the sky, and a waning moon, too; and whatever you may say, I am convinced, I feel that this waning can only be restored by love in its ordinary sense. It seems to me that such love would define my duties, my work, make clear my conception of life. I want from love peace of soul, tranquillity; I want the very opposite of musk, and spiritualism, and *fin de siècle* . . . in short"—she grew embarrassed—"a husband and children."

"You want to be married? Well, you can do that, too," Lysevich assented. "You ought to have all experiences: marriage, jealousy, and the sweetness of the first infidelity, and even children. . . . But make haste and live—make haste, my dear; time is passing; it won't wait."

"Yes, I'll go and get married!" she said, looking angrily at his well-fed, satisfied face. "I will marry in the simplest, most ordinary way and be radiant with happiness. And, would you believe it, I will marry some plain workingman, some mechanic or draughtsman."

"There is no harm in that, either. The Duchess Josiana loved Gwinplin, and that was permissible for her because she was a grand duchess. Everything is permissible for you, too, because you are an exceptional woman: if, my dear, you want to love a Negro or an Arab, don't scruple; send for a Negro. Don't deny yourself anything. You ought to be as bold as your desires; don't fall short of them."

"Can it be so hard to understand me?" Anna Akimovna asked with amazement, and her eyes were bright with tears. "Understand, I have an immense business on my hands—two thousand workmen, for whom I must answer before God. The men who work for me grow blind and deaf. I am afraid to go on like this; I am afraid! I am wretched, and you have the cruelty to talk to me of Negroes and . . . and you smile!" Anna Akimovna brought her fist down on the table. "To go on living the life I am living now, or to marry someone as idle and incompetent as myself, would be a crime. I can't go on living like this," she said hotly, "I cannot!"

"How handsome she is!" said Lysevich, fascinated by her. "My God, how handsome she is! But why are you angry, my dear? Perhaps I am wrong; but surely you don't imagine that if, for the sake of ideas for which I have the deepest respect, you renounce the joys of life and lead a dreary existence, your workmen will be any the better for it? Not a scrap! No, frivolity, frivolity!" he said decisively. "It's essential for you; it's your duty to be frivolous and depraved! Ponder that, my dear, ponder it."

Anna Akimovna was glad she had spoken out, and her spirits rose. She was pleased she had spoken so well, and that her ideas were so fine and just, and she was already convinced that if Pimenov, for instance, loved her, she would marry him with pleasure.

Mishenka began to pour out champagne.

"You make me angry, Viktor Nikolaitch," she said, clinking glasses with the lawyer. "It seems to me you give advice and know nothing of life yourself. According to you, if a man be a mechanic or a draughtsman, he is bound to be a peasant and an ignoramus! But they are the cleverest people! Extraordinary people!"

"Your uncle and father . . . I knew them and respected them . . ." Krylin said, pausing for emphasis (he had been sitting upright as a post, and had been eating steadily the whole time), "were people of considerable intelligence and . . . of lofty spiritual qualities."

"Oh, to be sure, we know all about their qualities," the lawyer muttered, and asked permission to smoke.

When dinner was over Krylin was led away for a nap. Lysevich finished his cigar, and, staggering from repletion, followed Anna Akimovna into her study. Cosy corners with photographs and fans on the walls, and the inevitable pink or paleblue lanterns in the middle of the ceiling, he did not like, as the expression of an insipid and unoriginal character; besides, the memory of certain of his love affairs of which he was now ashamed were associated with such lanterns. Anna Akimovna's study with its bare walls and tasteless furniture pleased him exceedingly. It was snug and comfortable for him to sit on a Turkish divan and look at Anna Akimovna, who usually sat on the rug before the fire, clasping her knees and looking into the fire and thinking of something; and at such moments it seemed to him that her peasant Old Believer blood was stirring within her.

Every time after dinner when coffee and liqueurs were handed, he grew livelier and began telling her various bits of literary gossip. He spoke with eloquence and inspiration and was carried away by his own stories; and she listened to him and thought every time that for such enjoyment it was worth paying not only twelve thousand, but three times that sum, and forgave him everything she disliked in him. He sometimes told her the story of some tale or novel he had been reading, and then two or three hours passed unnoticed like a minute. Now he began rather dolefully in a failing voice with his eyes shut.

"It's ages, my dear, since I have read anything," he said when she asked him to tell her something. "Though I do sometimes read Jules Verne."

"I was expecting you to tell me something new."

"Hm! . . . new," Lysevich muttered sleepily, and he settled himself further back in the corner of the sofa. "None of the new literature, my dear, is any use for you or me. Of course, it is bound to be such as it is, and to refuse to recognize it is to refuse to recognize—would mean refusing to recognize the natural order of things, and I do recognize it, but . . ." Lysevich seemed to have fallen asleep. But a minute later his voice was heard again:

"All the new literature moans and howls like the autumn wind in the chimney. 'Ah, unhappy wretch! Ah, your life may be likened to a prison; Ah, how damp and dark it is in your prison! Ah, you will certainly come to ruin, and there is no chance of escape for you.' That's very fine, but I should prefer a literature that would tell us how to escape from prison. Of all contemporary writers, however, I prefer Maupassant." Lysevich opened his eyes. "A fine writer, a perfect writer!" Lysevich shifted in his seat. "A wonderful artist! A terrible, prodigious, supernatural artist!" Lysevich got up from the sofa and raised his right arm. "Maupassant!" he said rapturously. "My dear, read Maupassant! One page of his gives you more than all the riches of the earth! Every line is a new horizon. The softest, tenderest impulses of the soul alternate with violent tempestuous sensations; your soul, as though under the weight of forty thousand atmospheres, is transformed into the most insignificant little bit of some great thing of an undefined rosy hue which I fancy, if one could put it on one's tongue, would yield a pungent, voluptuous taste. What a fury of transitions, of motives, of melodies! You rest peacefully on the lilies and the roses, and suddenly a thought—a terrible, splendid, irresistible thought— swoops down upon you like a locomotive, and bathes you in hot steam and deafens you with its whistle. Read Maupassant, dear girl; I insist on it."

Lysevich waved his arms and paced from corner to corner in violent excitement.

"Yes, it is inconceivable," he pronounced, as though in despair; "his last thing overwhelmed me, intoxicated me! But I am afraid you will not care for it. To be carried away by it you must savour it, slowly suck the juice from each line, drink it in. . . . You must drink it in! . . ."

After a long introduction, containing many words such as daemonic sensuality, a network of the most delicate nerves, simoom, crystal, and so on, he began at last telling the story of the novel. He did not tell the story so whimsically, but told it in minute detail, quoting from memory whole descriptions and conversations; the characters of the novel fascinated him, and to describe them he threw himself into attitudes, changed the expression of his face and voice like a real actor. He laughed with delight at one moment in a deep bass, and at another, on a high shrill note, clasped his hands and clutched at his head with an expression which suggested that it was just going to burst. Anna Akimovna listened enthralled, though she had already read the novel, and it seemed to her ever so much finer and more subtle in the lawyer's version than in the book itself. He drew her attention to various subtleties and emphasized the felicitous expressions and the profound thoughts, but she saw in it, only life, life, life and herself, as though she had been a character in the novel. Her spirits rose, and she, too, laughing and clasping her hands, thought that she could not go on living such a life, that there was no need to have a wretched life when one might have a splendid one. She remembered her words and thoughts at dinner and was proud of them; and when Pimenov suddenly rose up in her imagination, she felt happy and longed for him to love her.

When he had finished the story, Lysevich sat down on the sofa, exhausted.

"How splendid you are! How handsome!" he began, a little while afterwards in a faint voice as if he were ill. "I am happy near you, dear girl, but why am I forty-two instead of thirty? Your tastes and mine do not coincide: you ought to be depraved, and I have long passed that phase, and want a love as delicate and immaterial as a ray of sunshine —this is, from the point of view of a woman of your age, I am of no earthly use."

In his own words, he loved Turgenev, the singer of virginal love and purity, of youth, and of the melancholy Russian landscape; but he loved virginal love, not from knowledge but from hearsay, as something abstract, existing outside real life. Now he assured himself that he loved Anna Akimovna platonically, ideally, though he did not know what those words meant. But he felt comfortable, snug, warm. Anna Akimovna seemed to him enchanting, original, and he imagined that the pleasant sensation that was aroused in him by these surroundings was the very thing that was called platonic love.

He laid his cheek on her hand and said in the tone commonly used in coaxing little children:

"My precious, why have you punished me?"

"How? When?"

"I have had no Christmas present from you."

Anna Akimovna had never heard before of their sending a Christmas box to the lawyer, and now she was at a loss how much to give him. But she must give him something, for he was expecting it, though he looked at her with eyes full of love.

"I suppose Nazarich forgot it," she said, "but it is not too late to set it right."

She suddenly remembered the fifteen hundred she had received the day before, which was now lying in the toilet drawer in her bedroom. And when she brought that ungrateful money and gave it to the lawyer, and he put it in his coat pocket with indolent grace, the whole incident passed off charmingly and naturally. The sudden reminder of a Christmas box and this fifteen hundred was not unbecoming in Lysevich.

"*Merci*," he said, and kissed her finger.

Krylin came in with blissful, sleepy face, but without his decorations.

Lysevich and he stayed a little longer and drank a glass of tea each and began to get ready to go. Anna Akimovna was a little embarrassed. . . . She had utterly forgotten in what department Krylin served, and whether she had to give him money or not; and if she had to, whether to give it now or send it afterwards in an envelope.

"Where does he serve?" she whispered to Lysevich.

"Goodness knows," muttered Lysevich, yawning.

She reflected that if Krylin used to visit her father and her uncle and respected them, it was probably not for nothing: apparently he had been charitable at their expense, serving in some charitable institution. As she said good-bye she slipped three hundred roubles into his hand; he seemed taken aback and looked at her for a minute in silence with his pewtery eyes, but then seemed to understand and said:

"The receipt, honoured Anna Akimovna, you can only receive on the New Year."

Lysevich had become utterly limp and heavy, and he staggered when Mishenka put on his overcoat.

As he went downstairs he looked like a man in the last stage of exhaustion, and it was evident that he would drop asleep as soon as he got into his sledge.

"Your Excellency," he said languidly to Krylin, stopping in the middle of the staircase, "has it ever happened to you to experience a feeling as though some unseen force were drawing you out longer and longer? You are drawn out and turn into the finest wire. Subjectively this finds expression in a curious voluptuous feeling which is impossible to compare with anything."

Anna Akimovna, standing at the top of the stairs, saw each of them give Mishenka a note.

"Good-bye! Come again!" she called to them, and ran into her bedroom.

She quickly threw off her dress, which she was weary of already, put on a dressing gown, and ran downstairs; and as she ran downstairs she laughed and thumped with her feet like a schoolboy; she had a great desire for mischief.

MENU:

Cabbage soup

Suckling pig

(with Kasha stuffing)

Matelote of turbots

Mushrooms in cream

Sauce Provencale made of fried oysters and crayfish,

flavored with bitter pickles

The recipes for Anna Akimovna's Franco-Russian Christmas dinner were drawn from a variety of Franco-Russian sources. The chef with the most impressive qualifications is François Tanty, from whom the cabbage soup and the mushrooms come. Trained for his profession under Carême, the 19th century's most noted French cook, Tanty became Chef de Cuisine to Emperor Napoleon III. But he was determined to see more of the world than just his native France and left that post for the even mightier one of chef to Russia's Imperial Family.

Although his cookbook, La Cuisine Française, *was published in Chicago, the rail heart of America, Tanty was not one to overlook the flaws of his audience: "I cannot protest enough," he wrote back in 1894, "against the custom so general in the United States to give to the table only the necessary time and eat like a locomotive taking water. . . ."*

CABBAGE SOUP

FROM *La Cuisine Française*, 1894, François Tanty

Tchy à la Russe

6 pounds beef breast	2-3 quarts water
½ cabbage (shredded)	(salt and pepper to taste)
2 carrots (sliced)	2 tablespoons flour
2 onions (sliced)	1 glass (1 cup) sour cream

Take 6 pounds of beef breast, cut it into pieces about 1 inch long, place it in a kettle with 2 to 3 quarts *cold* water, let boil while skimming. When the bouillon begins to be clear, add ½ cabbage, 2 carrots, 2 onions sliced quite fine (and salt and pepper), and let cook for about 3 hours. When quite ready to serve, mix in a bowl 2 tablespoonsful of flour with about 1 glass bouillon [not too warm], pour in the kettle while stirring, add 1 glass sour cream and serve hot, the soup and meat being served together in the tureen.

(Serves 10)

SUCKLING PIG

with Kasha stuffing

FROM *The Epicure in Imperial Russia,* 1941, Marie Alexandre Markevitch

a small suckling pig	kasha (buckwheat groats)
olive oil	1 tablespoon sour cream

Singe and dress a small suckling pig. Smear it with olive oil so that the skin, which is the most delicate part, will be both crisp and tender. Make a slit of moderate length in the stomach and stuff the pig with (raw, previously soaked) kasha. Sew together the slit and place in a quick oven. As soon as the little suckling pig is well-browned on all sides, lower the fire and baste with the cooking juice very frequently. Allow the same cooking time per pound as for a turkey.

The little suckling pig is cut first of all in two: from the head to the feet, the head being left whole, on the spinal column, then at right angles to the spinal column, so as to form, in addition to the feet, three equal pieces from side to side. Arrange the animal on a large plate, taking care to place the pieces next to one another, as if the little pig were whole. Serve the juice in a saucer, with a spoonful of cream. Suckling pig may be eaten hot or cold, and is accompanied by a horseradish sauce.

MATELOTE OF TURBOTS

FROM *What To Eat and How To Cook It,* 1862, Pierre Blot

The combination of turbots in matelote comes highly recommended. Martial, the Roman epigram-maker, wrote, "However great the dish that holds the turbot, the turbot is still greater than the dish," and Brillat-Savarin said, "Fish, in the hands of a skillful cook, can become an inexhaustible source of gustatory delight . . . but it is never more welcome than when it appears in the guise of a matelote."

2 or 3 pounds of filleted turbot (or substitute halibut or flounder)	1¼ cups butter
	12 small noions, lightly sautéed
	6 or 8 large mushrooms
6 sprigs of fresh parsley	pinch of allspice
½ teaspoon thyme	salt and pepper
2 bay leaves	claret wine to cover
4 cloves	1 cup French brandy
2 cloves of garlic, chopped	2 tablespoons flour

Cut the fish in pieces about 2 inches square. Put in a fish kettle large enough to hold the fish easily the parsley, thyme, bay leaves, cloves, garlic cloves, ½ cup of butter, the sautéed onions, mushrooms, allspice, salt, pepper and the fish. (Heat till butter melts.) Cover with claret wine and set it on a very brisk fire; at the first boiling throw in the brandy, light a small piece of wood and set the brandy and wine on fire; do not take the kettle from the fire for that; it will burn for a while; then put again in the kettle the rest of the butter kneaded with 2 tablespoons flour; move the kettle now and then so as to prevent the pieces of fish from sticking to the pan; when done, which will be in about half an hour (or 10-15 minutes, depending on thickness of fillets), take the fish from the kettle by the means of a dipper or skimmer, and be careful not to break the pieces; lay it gently on a dish; remove the mushrooms and strain the sauce (through a fine strainer) onto fish. Spread the mushrooms tastefully over sauce, surround the dish with croutons and serve.

(Serves 6-8)

MUSHROOMS IN CREAM

FROM *La Cuisine Française*, 1894, François Tanty

a 2-pound can of mushrooms   1 glass (1½ cups) cream
(salt and pepper)   ¼ handful parsley (¼ cup,
2 egg yolks   chopped)
1 tablespoonful cornstarch

Pour a 2-pound can of mushrooms in a saucepan with their juice and boil a while. (Add salt and pepper to taste.) Place the saucepan on a corner of the range and add 2 yolks mixed in a bowl with 1 tablespoonful cornstarch, 1 glassful cream and some chopped parsley (to mushrooms in saucepan). Heat. Serve as a garnish for fine dinners.

(Serves 5)

SAUCE PROVENÇALE MADE OF FRIED OYSTERS AND CRAYFISH, FLAVORED WITH BITTER PICKLES

Chekhov must have invented this combination, but here's a way to make it:

¼ cup olive oil
3½ cups canned tomatoes,
   strained and squashed
salt and pepper
2 cloves garlic, crushed
pinch of sugar

1 tablespoon chopped parsley
3 tablespoons butter
1 cup of crayfish or shrimp,
   cleaned
¾ cup drained oysters
minced dill pickles

Heat the olive oil, brown the garlic, then add tomatoes, a healthy pinch of salt and pepper to taste, sugar and parsley. Reduce the flame and simmer sauce for 30 minutes. Shortly before this time is up, melt butter in a separate saucepan and sauté the shrimp for 10 minutes. Three minutes before the shrimp are finished, add the oysters. Remove both from their saucepan, combine them with the tomato sauce, sprinkle the whole with minced dill pickles, and serve.

(Pour over other broiled fish or on rice as a sauce, or
eat as is—it will serve 3)

OSCAR WILDE

THE IMPORTANCE OF BEING EARNEST
1895

Jack Worthing manages to get away to town whenever he feels like escaping the responsibilities of life in the country by pretending to have a younger brother, Ernest, who lives in town, gets into scrapes, and is far too disreputable to bring home. Once in town Jack pretends to be Ernest Worthing and there he courts and proposes to Gwendolen Fairfax, a girl who swears she can only love a man named Ernest.

Back home in the country Jack's ward, little Cecily Cardew, has also fallen in love with the nonexistent city slicker Ernest. She composes letters to herself, signed "Ernest." She dreams of saving him from his sinful ways (and of learning a bit about sin herself along the way), and she even imagines he has proposed marriage to her. Thus, when Jack's city friend Algernon, aware that the lovely Cecily is enamored of Ernest, goes off to the country in Jack's absence and pretends to be the young brother Ernest, the already willing Cecily really falls in love.

In this scene Gwendolen, about to marry Jack-Ernest, has arrived at the Worthing house unexpectedly. She meets Cecily, of whose existence she was unaware, and learns that Cecily, too, is engaged to Ernest. A violent competition over "Ernest" ensues. "Do you mind if I look at you?" asks Gwendolen. "Oh, not at all," says Cecily, "I am very fond of being looked at." Each girl is out to undercut and insult the other. Trying to make the country more exciting than the city, Cecily tells Gwendolen that from the top of a certain hill one can actually have a view of five counties. "Five counties!" says Gwendolen. "I don't think I should like that. I hate crowds."

What results is the funniest tea party ever written down. Ladies in Wildean England could fight vicious duels, even though pistols were denied them, with tea cakes and bread and butter.

ENTER Gwendolen

CECILY (advancing to meet her). Pray let me introduce myself to you. My name is Cecily Cardew.

GWENDOLEN. *Cecily Cardew?* (Moving to her and shaking hands.) What a very sweet name! Something tells me that we are going to be great friends. I like you already more than I can say. My first impressions of people are never wrong.

CECILY. How nice of you to like me so much after we have known each other such a comparatively short time. Pray sit down.

GWENDOLEN (still standing up). I may call you Cecily, may I not?

CECILY. With pleasure!

GWENDOLEN. And you will always call me Gwendolen, won't you?

CECILY. If you wish.

GWENDOLEN. Then that is all quite settled, is it not?

CECILY. I hope so (A pause. They both sit down together.)

GWENDOLEN. Perhaps this might be a favorable opportunity for my mentioning who I am. My father is Lord Bracknell. You have never heard of papa, I suppose?

CECILY. I don't think so.

GWENDOLEN. Outside the family circle, papa, I am glad to say, is entirely unknown. I think that is quite as it should be. The home seems to me to be the proper sphere for the man. And certainly once a man begins to neglect his domestic duties he becomes painfully effeminate, does he not? And I don't like that. It makes men so very attractive. Cecily, mamma, whose views on education are remarkably strict, has brought me up to be extremely shortsighted; it is part of her system; so do you mind my looking at you through my glasses?

CECILY. Oh, not at all, Gwendolen. I am very fond of being looked at.

GWENDOLEN (after examining Cecily carefully through a lorgnette). You are here on a short visit, I suppose.

CECILY. Oh, no, I live here.

GWENDOLEN (severely). Really? Your mother, no doubt, or some female relative of advanced years, resides here also?

CECILY. Oh, no. I have no mother, nor, in fact, any relations.

GWENDOLEN. Indeed?

CECILY. My dear guardian, with the assistance of Miss Prism, has the arduous task of looking after me.

GWENDOLEN. Your guardian?

CECILY. Yes, I am Mr. Worthing's ward.

GWENDOLEN. Oh! It is strange he never mentioned to me that he had a ward. How secretive of him! He grows more interesting hourly. I am not sure, however, that the news inspires me with feelings of unmixed delight. (Rising and going to her.) I am very fond of you, Cecily; I have liked you ever since I met you. But I am bound to state that now that I know that you are Mr. Worthing's ward, I cannot help expressing a wish you were—well, just a little older than you seem to be—and not quite so very alluring in appearance. In fact, if I may speak candidly—

CECILY. Pray do! I think that whenever one has anything unpleasant to say, one should always be quite candid.

GWENDOLEN. Well, to speak with perfect candour, Cecily, I wish that you were fully forty-two, and more than usually plain for your age. Ernest has a strong upright nature. He is the very soul of truth and honour. Disloyalty would be as impossible to him as deception. But even men of the noblest possible moral character are extremely susceptible to the influence of the physical charms of others. Modern, no less than Ancient History supplies us with many most painful examples of what I refer to. If it were not so, indeed, History would be quite unreadable.

CECILY. I beg your pardon, Gwendolen, did you say Ernest?

GWENDOLEN. Yes.

CECILY. Oh, but it is not Mr. Ernest Worthing who is my guardian. It is his brother—his elder brother.

GWENDOLEN (sitting down again). Ernest never mentioned to me that he had a brother.

CECILY. I am sorry to say they have not been on good terms for a long time.

GWENDOLEN. Ah! that accounts for it. And now that I think of it I have never heard any man mention his brother. The subject seems distasteful to most men. Cecily, you have lifted a load from my mind. I was growing almost anxious. It would have been terrible if any cloud had come across a friendship like ours, would it not? Of course you are quite, quite sure that it is not Mr. Ernest Worthing who is your guardian?

CECILY. Quite sure. (A pause.) In fact, I am going to be his.

GWENDOLEN (enquiringly). I beg your pardon?

CECILY (rather shy and confidingly). Dearest Gwendolen, there is no reason why I should make a secret of it to you. Our little county newspaper is sure to chronicle the fact next week. Mr. Ernest Worthing and I are engaged to be married.

GWENDOLEN (quite politely, rising). My darling Cecily, I think there must be some slight error. Mr. Ernest Worthing is engaged to me. The announcement will appear in the *Morning Post* on Saturday at the latest.

CECILY (very politely, rising). I am afraid you must be under some misconception. Ernest proposed to me exactly ten minutes ago. (Shows diary.)

GWENDOLEN (examines diary through her lorgnette carefully). It is certainly very curious, for he asked me to be his wife yesterday afternoon at 5:30. If you would care to verify the incident, pray do so. (Produces diary of her own.) I never travel without my diary. One should always have something sensational to read in the train. I am so sorry, Cecily, if it is any disappointment to you, but I am afraid I have the prior claim.

CECILY. It would distress me more than I can tell you, dear Gwendolen, if it caused you any mental or physical anguish, but I feel bound to point out that since Ernest proposed to you he clearly has changed his mind.

GWENDOLEN (meditatively). If the poor fellow has been entrapped into any foolish promise I shall consider it my duty to rescue him at once, and with a firm hand.

CECILY (thoughtfully and sadly). Whatever unfortunate entanglement my dear boy may have got into, I will never reproach him with it after we are married.

GWENDOLEN. Do you allude to me, Miss Cardew, as an entanglement? You are presumptuous. On an occasion of this kind it becomes more than a moral duty to speak one's mind. It becomes a pleasure.

CECILY. Do you suggest, Miss Fairfax, that I entrapped Ernest into an engagement? How dare you? This is no time for wearing the shallow mask of manners. When I see a spade I call it a spade.

GWENDOLEN (satirically). I am glad to say that I have never seen a spade. It is obvious that our social spheres have been widely different.

ENTER Merriman, followed by the footman. He carries a salver, table-cloth, and plate-stand. Cecily is about to retort. The presence of the servants exercises a restraining influence, under which both girls chafe.

MERRIMAN. Shall I lay tea here as usual, miss?

CECILY (sternly, in a calm voice). Yes, as usual. (Merriman begins to clear and lay cloth. A long pause. Cecily and Gwendolen glare at each other.)

GWENDOLEN. Are there many interesting walks in the vicinity, Miss Cardew?

CECILY. Oh, yes, a great many. From the top of one of the hills quite close one can see five counties.

GWENDOLEN. Five counties! I don't think I should like that. I hate crowds.

CECILY (sweetly). I suppose that is why you live in town? (Gwendolen bites her lip, and beats her foot nervously with her parasol.)

GWENDOLEN (looking around). Quite a well-kept garden this is, Miss Cardew.

CECILY. So glad you like it, Miss Fairfax.

GWENDOLEN. I had no idea there were any flowers in the country.

CECILY. Oh, flowers are as common here, Miss Fairfax, as people are in London.

GWENDOLEN. Personally I cannot understand how anybody manages to exist in the country, if anybody who is anybody does. The country always bores me to death.

CECILY. Ah! This is what the newspapers call agricultural depression, is it not? I believe the aristocracy are suffering very much from it just at present. It is almost an epidemic amongst them, I have been told. May I offer you some tea, Miss Fairfax?

GWENDOLEN (with elaborate politeness). Thank you. (Aside.) Detestable girl! But I require tea!

CECILY (sweetly). Sugar?

GWENDOLEN (superciliously). No, thank you. Sugar is not fashionable any more. (Cecily looks angrily at her, takes up the tongs and puts four lumps of sugar into the cup.)

CECILY (severely). Cake or bread and butter?

GWENDOLEN (in a bored manner). Bread and butter, please. Cake is rarely seen at the best houses nowadays.

CECILY (cuts a very large slice of cake, and puts it on the tray). Hand that to Miss Fairfax. (Merriman does so, and goes out with footman. Gwendolen drinks the tea and makes a grimace. Puts down cup at once, reaches out her hand to the bread and butter, looks at it, and finds it is cake. Rises in indignation.)

GWENDOLEN. You have filled my tea with lumps of sugar, and though I asked most distinctly for bread and butter, you have given me cake. I am known for the gentleness of my disposition, and the extraordinary sweetness of my nature, but I warn you, Miss Cardew, you may go too far.

CECILY (rising). To save my poor, innocent, trusting boy from the machinations of any other girl there are no lengths to which I would not go.

GWENDOLEN. From the moment I saw you I distrusted you. I felt that you were false and deceitful. I am never deceived in such matters. My first impressions of people are invariably right.

CECILY. It seems to me, Miss Fairfax, that I am trespassing on your valuable time. No doubt you have many other calls of a similar character to make in the neighbourhood.

MENU:

Muffins and Tea Cakes

Velvet cakes
English muffins
Cocoanut biscuits
Rock cakes

Two of the recipes for the Wildean tea party were provided by Mrs. Seely, proud author of Mrs. Seely's Cook Book, a woman who deserves to be remembered not only for her cooking skills, but for her fantastic ability to command. She wrote cookbooks as if she were ordering a forced march: chambermaids should commence sweeping halls promptly at six-thirty, she intones; all beds must be changed on Saturdays; cooks must prepare all game such as canvasback and redhead duck. Damn the poor chambermaid who oversleeps, the lie-abed child who dreams late on Saturday mornings, the husband who likes his canvasback the way he himself prepares it. Mrs. Seeley seemed to picture all housewives as her lieutenants, backed up by a vast army of recruits. To make the kitchens of the world function with precision, she took care to list each and every duty of all the regular household servants from the "Lady's Maid" to the "Second Man When Three Men Are Kept" to the "Fourth or Useful Man."

The remaining recipes come from a far gentler book, My Favorite Recipes for Dainty Dishes, Cakes and Confections, *which was put together by a number of eminent but embarrassed nineteenth-century Britishers who had decided to write a cookbook in order to benefact their favorite charity. But the ladies and gentlemen discovered that their main interest in eating was sweets, hardly a dignified gastronomical pursuit. They were distressed by this discovery until at last they recalled that Descartes was once taken to task for his fondness for sweets. "What!" said an incredulous marquis to the philosopher, 'And do you philosophers eat dainties, then?" 'Do you think,' answered Descartes, 'that God made good things only for fools?' " Vindicated, the authors of the book reprinted the anecdote;* My Favorite Recipes *was published and the Cripples' Home at Gosforth was duly benefacted.*

VELVET CAKES

FROM *Mrs. Seely's Cook Book*, 1902

2 teaspoons cream of tartar   1 teaspoon baking soda
1 quart flour   1 pint milk

1 cup sugar   1/3 cup butter

Mix thoroughly and bake in greased hot earthen cups (or muffin tins) for half an hour (in a 350° oven).

(Makes 2 dozen muffins)

ENGLISH MUFFINS

FROM *Mrs. Seely's Cook Book,* 1902

1 pint flour   1 teaspoon baking powder
½ teaspoon sugar   ½ pint milk
½ teaspoon salt   2 eggs, separated

Sift flour, sugar, salt and baking powder together. Mix the yolks of the eggs with the milk and gradually stir into the flour. Last of all, add the whites, beaten stiff. Bake in greased muffin rings (in a 350° oven for 35 minutes).

(Makes 1 dozen biscuits)

COCOANUT BISCUITS

FROM *My Favorite Recipes for Dainty Dishes, Cakes and Confections,* 1896

½ cup cocoanut (flaked)   whites of 2 eggs
½ cup powdered sugar (sifted)

Mix the cocoanut and sugar with the egg whites, beating with a wooden spoon till it forms softish but thick paste. Lay the mixture out on wafer paper (brown paper) in small drops; bake in a slow oven till they are a very light brown. (A 350° oven for 20-25 minutes will do it.)

(Makes 8-10)

ROCK CAKES

FROM *My Favorite Recipes for Dainty Dishes, Cakes and Confections,* 1896

2 cups (sifted) flour   1 teaspoon baking powder
¼ cup (or more) raisins   1 teaspoon ground ginger
¼ cup (to ½ cup) brown sugar   1 egg
grated rind of 1 lemon   milk (4 tablespoons)

Mix flour and baking powder together, rub in the butter, add all the dry ingredients. Beat up the egg, add the milk, and then mix with the flour, etc. in the basin. Divide into 12 rough shapes, and bake in greased tins in a quick oven. (Bake in 375° oven for 25-30 minutes.)

(Makes 12)

MARCEL PROUST
SWANN'S WAY
1913

The intricate weblike world of Proust's Remembrance of Things Past *springs into being from a taste of tea and cake. It is a vain labor, Proust tells us, to attempt to recall the past through an effort of the intellect. The door to the past lies through some material object, some sensation. And "when from a long-distant past nothing subsists, after the people are dead, after the things are broken and scattered, still, alone, more fragile, but with more vitality, more unsubstantial, more persistent, more faithful, the smell and taste of things remain poised a long time, like souls, ready to remind us, waiting and hoping for their moment, amid the ruins of all the rest; and bear, unfalteringly, in the tiny and almost impalpable drop of their essence, the vast structure of recollection."*

Proust wrote magnificently about food, about elaborate dinners and cool picnics and the ardent cook Françoise, a "Michelangelo of the kitchen," who would exhaust herself at procuring the family's provisions just as the sculptor exhausted himself choosing the most perfect blocks of marble in the mountains of Carrara.

But all these many scenes and, humbly, the theory of this anthology itself evolve from this section embodying Proust's theory about material objects, about the smells and tastes which carry unfalteringly the structure of remembrance and of storymaking.

I feel that there is much to be said for the Celtic belief that the souls of those whom we have lost are held captive in some inferior being, in an animal, in a plant, in some inanimate object, and so effectively lost to us until the day (which to many never comes) when we happen to pass by the tree or to obtain possession of the object which forms their prison. Then they start and tremble, they call us by our name, and as soon as we have recognised their voice the spell is broken. We have delivered them: they have overcome death and return to share our life.

And so it is with our own past. It is a labour in vain to attempt to recapture it: all the efforts of our intellect must prove futile. The past is hidden somewhere outside the realm, beyond the reach of intellect, in some material object (in the sensation which that material object will give us) which we do not suspect. And as for that object, it depends on chance whether we come upon it or not before we ourselves must die.

Many years had elapsed during which nothing of Combray, save what was comprised in the theatre and the drama of my going to bed there, had any existence for me, when one day in winter, as I came home, my mother, seeing that I was cold, offered me some tea, a thing I did not ordinarily take. I declined at first, and then, for no particular reason, changed my mind. She sent out for one of those short, plump little cakes called 'petites madeleines,' which look as though they had been moulded in the fluted scallop of a pilgrim's shell. And soon, mechanically, weary after a dull day with the prospect of a depressing morrow, I raised to my lips a spoonful of the tea in which I had soaked a morsel of the cake. No sooner had the warm liquid, and the crumbs with it, touched my palate than a shudder ran through my whole body, and I stopped, intent upon the extraordinary changes that were taking place. An exquisite pleasure had invaded my senses, but individual, detached, with no suggestion of its origin. And at once the vicissitudes of life had become indifferent to me, its disasters innocuous, its brevity illusory—this new sensation having had on me the effect which love has of filling me with a precious essence; or rather this essence was not in me, it was myself. I had ceased now to feel mediocre, accidental, mortal. Whence could it have come to me, this all-powerful joy? I was conscious that it was connected with the taste of tea and cake, but that it infinitely transcended those savours, could not, indeed, be of the same nature as theirs. Whence did it come? What did it signify? How could I seize upon and define it?

I drink a second mouthful, in which I find nothing more than in the first, a third, which gives me rather less than the second. It is time to stop; the potion is losing its magic. It is plain that the object of my quest, the truth, lies not in the cup but in myself. The tea has called up in me, but does not itself understand, and can only repeat indefinitely with a gradual loss of strength, the same testimony; which I, too, cannot interpret, though I hope at least to be able to call upon the tea for it again and to find it there presently, intact and at my disposal, for my final enlightenment. I put down my cup and examine my own mind. It is for it to discover the truth. But how? What an abyss of uncertainty whenever the mind feels that some part of it has strayed beyond its own borders; when it, the seeker, is at once the dark region through which it must go seeking, where all its equipment will avail it nothing. Seek? More than that: create. It is face to face with something which does not so far exist, to which it alone can give reality and substance, which it alone can bring into the light of day.

And I begin again to ask myself what it could have been, this unremembered state which brought with it no logical proof of its existence, but only the sense that it was a happy, that it was a real state in whose presence other states of consciousness melted and vanished. I decide to attempt to make it reappear. I retrace my thoughts to the moment at which I drank the first spoonful of tea. I find again the same state, illumined by no fresh light. I compel my mind to make one further effort, to follow and recapture once again the fleeting sensation. And that nothing may interrupt it in its course I shut out every obstacle, every extraneous idea, I stop my ears and inhibit all attention to the sounds which come from the next room. And then, feeling that my mind is growing fatigued without having any success to report, I compel it for a change to enjoy that distraction which I have just denied it, to think of other things, to rest and refresh itself before the supreme attempt. And then for the second time I clear an empty space in front of it. I place in position before my mind's eye the still recent taste of that first mouthful, and I feel something start within me, something that leaves its resting-place and attempts to rise, something that has been embedded like an anchor at a great depth; I do not know yet what it is, but I can feel it mounting slowly; I can measure the resistance, I can hear the echo of great spaces traversed.

Undoubtedly what is thus palpitating in the depths of my being must be the image, the visual memory which, being linked to that taste, has tried to follow it into my conscious mind. But its struggles are too far off, too much confused; scarcely can I perceive the colourless reflection in which are blended the uncapturable whirling medley of radiant hues, and I cannot distinguish its form, cannot invite it, as the one possible interpreter, to translate to me the evidence of its contemporary, its inseparable paramour, the taste of cake soaked in tea; cannot ask it to inform me what special circumstance is in question, of what period in my past life.

Will it ultimately reach the clear surface of my consciousness, this memory, this old, dead moment which the magnetism of an identical moment has travelled so far to importune, to disturb, to raise up out of the very depths of my being? I cannot tell. Now that I feel nothing, it has stopped, has perhaps gone down again into its darkness, from which who can say whether it will ever rise? Ten times over I must essay the task, must lean down over the abyss. And each time the natural laziness which deters us from every difficult enterprise, every work of importance, has urged me to leave the thing alone, to drink my tea and to think merely of the worries of today and of my hopes for tomorrow, which let themselves be pondered over without effort or distress of mind.

And suddenly the memory returns. The taste was that of the little crumb of madeleine which on Sunday mornings at Combray (because on those mornings I did not go out before church-time), when I went to say good day to her in her bedroom, my aunt Leonie used to give me, dipping it first in her own cup of real or of lime-flower tea. The sight of the little madeline had recalled nothing to my mind before I tasted it; perhaps because I had so often seen such things in the interval, without tasting them, on the trays in pastry-cooks' windows, that their image had dissociated itself from those Combray days to take its place among others more recent; perhaps because of those memories, so long abandoned and put out of mind, nothing now survived, everything was scattered; the forms of things, including that of the little scallop-shell of pastry, so richly sensual under its severe, religious folds, were either obliterated or had been so long dormant as to have lost the power of expansion which would have allowed them to resume their place in my consciousness. But when from a long-distant past nothing subsists, after the people are dead, after the things are broken and scattered, still, alone, more fragile, but with more vitality, more unsubstantial, more persistent, more faithful, the smell and taste of things remain poised a long time, like souls, ready to remind us, waiting and hoping for their moment, amid the ruins of all the rest; and bear unfaltering, in the tiny and almost impalpable drop of their essence, the vast structure of recollection.

And once I had recognized the taste of the crumb of madeleine soaked in her decoction of lime-flowers which my aunt used to give me (although I did not yet know and must long postpone the discovery of why this memory made me so happy) immediately the old grey house upon the street, where her room was, rose up like the scenery of a theatre to attach itself to the little pavilion, opening on to the garden, which had been built out behind it for my parents (the isolated panel which until that moment had been all that I could see); and with the house the town, from morning to night and in all weathers, the Square where I was sent before luncheon, the streets along which I used to run errands, the country roads we took when it was fine. And just as the Japanese amuse themselves by filling a porcelain bowl with water and steeping in it little crumbs of paper which until then are without character or form, but, the moment they become wet, stretch themselves and bend, take on colour and distinctive shape, become flowers or houses or people, permanent and recognisable, so in that moment all the flowers in our garden and in M. Swann's park, and the water-lilies on the Vivonne and the good folk of the village and their little dwellings and the parish church and the whole of Combray and of its surroundings, taking their proper shapes and growing solid, sprang into being, town and gardens alike, from my cup of tea.

MENU:

Petites Madeleines

The recipe is based on that of the distinguished Charles Ranhofer who presided over Delmonico's receptions for the elite of the late nineteenth century, men like President Ulysses S. Grant, the Grand Duke of Russia and Charles Dickens. His elaborate cookbook, The Epicurean, *is one of the most inclusive treatises on classic French cuisine ever composed.*

PETITES MADELEINES

ADAPTED FROM *The Epicurean*, 1894, Charles Ranhofer

1⅛ cups melted butter
2 cups sugar
4½ cups sifted cake flour
5 whole eggs
4 egg yolks

2 tablespoons brandy
2 pinches of salt
grated lemon peel or ¼
   teaspoon lemon extract
1 teaspoon baking soda

Melt the butter in a saucepan. Beat well together the remaining ingredients, then add the melted butter. Mix, and fill buttered madeleine molds two-thirds full. Bake in a 350° oven for 20 minutes, until light brown.

(Makes 5 dozen petites madeleines)

SHOLOM ALEICHEM

TIT FOR TAT

c. 1915

"In Kasrielevky," says a character in one of Sholom Aleichem's stories, "there are experienced authorities on the subject of hunger, one might say specialists. On the darkest night, simply by hearing your voice, they can tell if you are hungry and would like a bite to eat, or if you are really starving." Poverty and hunger, so much a part of the life of the poor East European Jew, form the warp of Sholom Aleichem's tales. Across it, as the woof, lie his warmth, his irony and his wit. Poverty is a precondition, but how do the people live with and on top of it?

They survive with their humor. Humor is their defense, their means of making a miserable life endurable. No one is above the sharp barbs of humor. Not even God himself. "How cleverly the Eternal One has created this little world of His," says another Aleichem character, "so that every living thing, from man to a simple cow, must earn its food. Nothing is free." It is the humor of the famous Jewish concentration camp joke, "We know we are God's chosen people. But why doesn't He choose someone else for a while?" Thus, in "Tit for Tat," the petitioners can make fun of their rabbi, the rabbi make fun of his petitioners.

The food in the story is so complete that it might form the menu of a Jewish restaurant—or, rather, two Jewish restaurants, one serving meat dishes and the other dairy dishes. Aleichem seems to delight in the exact, precise detail, detail which enables him to be not just a story-teller but the full chronicler of a culture.

Once I was a rabbiner. A rabbiner, not a rabbi. That is, I was called rabbi—but a rabbi of the crown.

To old-country Jews I don't have to explain what a rabbi of the crown is. They know the breed. What are his great responsibilities? He fills out birth certificates, officiates at circumcisions, performs marriages, grants divorces. He gets his share from the living and the dead. In the synagogue he has a place of honor, and when the congregation rises, he is the first to stand. On legal holidays he appears in a stove-pipe hat and holds forth in his best Russian: *"Gospoda Prihozhane!"* To take it for granted that among our people a rabbiner is well loved— let's not say any more. Say rather that we put up with him, as we do a government inspector or a deputy sheriff. And yet he is chosen from among the people, that is, every three years a proclamation is sent us: *"Na Osnavania Predpisania. . . ."* Or, as we would say: "Your Lord, the Governor, orders you to come together in the synagogue, poor little Jews, and pick out a rabbiner for yourselves. . . ."

Then the campaign begins. Candidates, hot discussions, brandy, and maybe even a bribe or two. After which come charges and counter-charges, the elections are annulled, and we are ordered to hold new elections. Again the proclamations: *"Na Osnavania Predpisania. . . ."* Again candidates, discussions, party organizations, brandy, a bribe or two. . . . That was the life!

Well, there I was—a rabbiner in a small town in the province of Poltava. But I was anxious to be a modern one. I wanted to serve the public. So I dropped the formalities of my position and began to mingle with the people—as we say: to stick my head into the community pot. I got busy with the *Talmud Torah,* the charity fund, interpreted a law, settled disputes or just gave plain advice.

The love of settling disputes, helping people out, or advising them, I inherited from my father and my uncles. They—may they rest in peace—also enjoyed being bothered all the time with other people's business. There are two kinds of people in the world: those that you can't bother at all, and others whom you can bother all the time. You can climb right on their heads—naturally not in one jump, but gradually. First you climb into their laps, then onto their shoulders, then their heads—and after that you can jump up and down on their heads and stamp on their hearts with your heavy boots—as long as you want to.

I was that kind, and without boasting I can tell you that I had plenty of ardent followers and plain hangers-on who weren't ashamed to come every day and fill my head with their clamoring and sit around till late at night. They never refused a glass of tea, or cigarettes. Newspapers and books they took without asking. In short, I was a regular fellow.

Well, there came a day. . . . The door opened, and in walked the very foremost men of the town, the sparkling best, the very cream of the city. Four householders—men of affairs—you could almost say: real men of substance. And who were these men? Three of them were the *Troika*—that was what we called them in our town because they were together all the time—partners in whatever business any one of them was in. They always fought, they were always suspicious of each other, and watched everything the others did, and still they never separated—working always on this principle: if the business is a good one and there is profit to be made, why shouldn't I have a lick at the bone too? And on the other hand, if it should end in disaster—you'll be buried along with me, and lie with me deep in the earth. And what does God do? He brings together the three partners with a fourth one. They operate together a little less than a year and end up in a brawl. That is why they're here.

What had happened? "Since God created thieves, swindlers and crooks, you never saw a thief, swindler or crook like this one." That is the way the three old partners described the fourth one to me. And he, the fourth, said the same about them. Exactly the same, word for word. And who was this fourth one? He was a quiet little man, a little innocent-looking fellow, with thick, dark eyebrows under which a pair of shrewd, ironic, little eyes watched everything you did. Everyone called him Nachman Lekach.

His real name was Nachman Noss'n, but everybody called him Nachman Lekach, because as you know, *Noss'n* is the Hebrew for "he gave," and *Lekach* means "he took," and in all the time we knew him, no one had ever seen him give anything to anyone—while at taking no one was better.

Where were we? Oh, yes. . . . So they came to the rabbiner with the complaints, to see if he could find a way of straightening out their tangled accounts. "Whatever you decide, Rabbi, and whatever you decree, and whatever you say, will be final."

That is how the three old partners said it, and the fourth, Reb Nachman, nodded with that innocent look on his face to indicate that he too left it all up to me: "For the reason," his eyes said, "that I know that I have done no wrong." And he sat down in a corner, folded his arms across his chest like an old woman, fixed his shrewd, ironic, little eyes on me, and waited to see what his partners would have to say. And when they had all laid out their complaints and charges, presented all their evidence, said all they had to say, he got up, patted down his thick eyebrows, and not looking at the others at all, only at me, with those deep, deep, shrewd little eyes of his, he proceeded to demolish their claims and charges—so completely, that it looked as if they were the thieves, swindlers and crooks—the three partners of his—and he, Nachman Lekach, was a man of virtue and piety, the little chicken that is slaughtered before Yom Kippur to atone for our sins—a sacrificial lamb. "And every word that you heard them say is a complete lie, it never was and never could be. It's simply out of the question." And he proved with evidence, arguments and supporting data that everything he said was true and holy, as if Moses himself had said it.

All the time he was talking, the others, the *Troika*, could hardly sit in their chairs. Every moment one or another of them jumped up, clutched his head—or his heart: "Of all things! How can a man talk like that! Such lies and falsehoods!" It was almost impossible to calm them down, to keep them from tearing at the fourth one's beard. As for me—the rabbiner—it was hard, very hard to crawl out from this horrible tangle, because by now it was clear that I had a fine band to deal with, all four of them swindlers, thieves and crooks, and informers to boot, and all four of them deserving a severe punishment. But what? At last this idea occurred to me, and I said to them:

"Are you ready, my friends? I am prepared to hand down my decision. My mind is made up. But I won't disclose what I have to say until each of you has deposited twenty-five rubles—to prove that you will act upon the decision I am about to hand down."

"With the greatest of pleasure," the three spoke out at once, and Nachman Lekach nodded his head, and all four reached into their pockets, and each one counted out his twenty-five on the table. I gathered up the money, locked it up in a drawer, and then I gave them my decision in these words:

"Having heard the complaints and the arguments of both parties, and having examined your accounts and studied your evidence, I find according to my understanding and deep conviction, that all four of you are in the wrong, and not only in the wrong, but that it is a shame and a scandal for Jewish people to conduct themselves in such a manner—to falsify accounts, perjure yourselves and even act as informers. Therefore I have decided that since we have a *Talmud Torah* in our town with many children who have neither clothes nor shoes, and whose parents have nothing with which to pay their tuition, and since there has been no help at all from you gentlemen (to get a few pennies from you one has to reach down into your very gizzards) therefore it is my decision that this hundred rubles of yours shall go to the *Talmud Torah,* and as for you, gentlemen, you can go home, in good health, and thanks for your contribution. The poor children will now have some shoes and socks and shirts and pants, and I'm sure they'll pray to God for you and your children. Amen."

Having heard the sentence, the three old partners—the *Troika*— looked from one to the other—flushed, unable to speak. A decision like this they had not anticipated. The only one who could say a word was Reb Nachman Lekach. He got up, patted down his thick eyebrows, held out a hand, and looking at me with his ironic little eyes, said this:

"I thank you, Rabbi Rabbiner, in behalf of all four of us, for the wise decision which you have just made known. Such a judgment could have been made by no one since King Solomon himself. There is only one thing that you forgot to say, Rabbi Rabbiner, and that is: what is your fee for this wise and just decision?"

"I beg your pardon," I tell him. "You've come to the wrong address. I am not one of those rabbiners who tax the living and the dead." That is the way I answered him, like a real gentleman. And this was his reply:

"If that's the case, then you are not only a sage and a rabbi among men, you're an honest man besides. So, if you would care to listen, I'd like to tell you a story. Say that we will pay you for your pains at least with a story."

"Good enough. Even with two stories."

"In that case, sit down, Rabbi Rabbiner, and let us have your cigarette case. I'll tell you an interesting story, a true one, too, something that happened to me. What happened to others I don't like to talk about."

And we lit our cigarettes, sat down around the table, and Reb Nachman spread out his thick eyebrows, and looking at me with his shrewd, smiling, little eyes, he slowly began to tell his true story of what had happened to him himself.

All this happened to me a long time ago. I was still a young man and I was living not far from here, in a village near the railroad. I traded in this and that, I had a small tavern, made a living. A Rothschild I didn't become, but bread we had, and in time there were about ten Jewish families living close by—because, as you know, if one of us makes a living, others come around. They think you're shoveling up gold . . . But that isn't the point. What I was getting at was that right in the midst of the busy season one year, when things were moving and traffic was heavy, my wife had to go and have a baby—our boy —our first son. What do you say to that? "Congratulations! Congratulations everybody!" But that isn't all. You have to have a *bris,* the circumcision. I dropped everything, went into town, bought all the good things I could find, and came back with the *Mohel* with all his instruments, and for good measure I also brought the *shammes* of the synagogue. I thought that with these two holy men and myself and the neighbors we'd have the ten men that we needed, with one to spare. But what does God do? He has one of my neighbors get sick— he is sick in bed and can't come to the *bris,* you can't carry him. And another has to pack up and go off to the city. He can't wait another day! And here I am without the ten men. Go do something. Here it is— Friday! Of all days, my wife has to pick Friday to have the *bris*—the day before the Sabbath. The *Mohel* is frantic—he has to go back right away. The *shammes* is actually in tears. "What did you ever drag us off here for?" they both want to know. And what can I do?

All I can think of is to run off to the railroad station. Who knows— so many people come through every day—maybe God will send some one. And that's just what happened. I come running up to the station —the agent has just called out that a train is about to leave. I look around—a little roly-poly man carrying a huge traveling bag comes flying by, all sweating and out of breath, straight toward the lunch counter. He looks over the dishes—what is there a good Jew can take in a country railroad station? A piece of herring—an egg. Poor fellow —you could see his mouth was watering. I grab him by the sleeve. "Uncle, are you looking for something to eat?" I ask him, and the look he gives me says: "How did you know that?" I keep on talking: "May you live to be a hundred—God himself must have sent you." He still doesn't understand, so I proceed: "Do you want to earn the blessings of eternity—and at the same time eat a beef roast that will melt in your mouth, with a fresh, white loaf right out of the oven?" He still looks at me as if I'm crazy. "Who are you? What do you want?"

So I tell him the whole story—what a misfortune had overtaken us: here we are, all ready for the *bris,* the *Mohel* is waiting, the food is ready—and such food!—and we need a tenth man! "What's that got to do with me?" he asks, and I tell him: "What's that got to do with you? Why—everything depends on you—you're the tenth man! I beg you—come with me. You will earn all the rewards of heaven—and have a delicious dinner in the bargain!" "Are you crazy," he asks me, "or are you just out of your head? My train is leaving in a few minutes, and it's Friday afternoon—almost sundown. Do you know what that means? In a few more hours the Sabbath will catch up with me, and I'll be stranded." "So what!" I tell him. "So you'll take the next train. And in the meantime you'll earn eternal life—and taste a soup, with fresh dumplings, that only my wife can make . . ."

Well, why make the story long? I had my way. The roast and the hot soup with fresh dumplings did their work. You could see my customer licking his lips. So I grab the traveling bag and I lead him home, and we go through with the *bris.* It was a real pleasure! You could smell the roast all over the house, it had so much garlic in it. A roast like that, with fresh warm twist, is a delicacy from heaven. And when you consider that we had some fresh dill pickles; and a bottle of beer, and some cognac before the meal and cherry cider after the meal—you can imagine the state our guest was in! His cheeks shone and his forehead glistened. But what then? Before we knew it the afternoon was gone. My guest jumps up, he looks around, sees what time it is, and almost has a stroke! He reaches for his traveling bag: "Where is it?" I say to him, "What's your hurry? In the first place, do you think we'll let you run off like that—before the Sabbath? And in the second place—who are you to leave on a journey an hour or two before the Sabbath? And if you're going to get caught out in the country somewhere, you might just as well stay here with us."

He groans and he sighs. How could I do a thing like that to him—keep him so late? What did I have against him? Why hadn't I reminded him earlier? He doesn't stop bothering me. So I say to him: "In the first place, did I have to tell you that it was Friday afternoon? Didn't you know it yourself? And in the second place, how do you know—maybe it's the way God wanted it? Maybe He wanted you to stay here for the Sabbath so you could taste some of my wife's fish? I can guarantee you, that as long as you've eaten fish, you haven't eaten fish like my wife's fish—not even in a dream!" Well, that ended the argument. We said our evening prayers, had a glass of wine, and my wife brings the fish to the table. My guest's nostrils swell out, a new light shines in his eyes and he goes after that fish as if he hadn't eaten a thing all day. He can't get over it. He praises it to the skies. He fills a glass with brandy and drinks a toast to the fish. And then comes the soup, a specially rich Sabbath soup with noodles. And he likes that, too, and the *tzimmes* also, and the meat that goes with the *tzimmes*, a nice, fat piece of brisket. I'm telling you, he just sat there licking his fingers! When we're finishing the last course he turns to me: "Do you know what I'll tell you? Now that it's all over, I'm really glad that I stayed over for *Shabbes*. It's been a long time since I've enjoyed a Sabbath as I've enjoyed this one." "If that's how you feel, I'm happy," I tell him. "But wait. This is only a sample. Wait till tomorrow. Then you'll see what my wife can do."

And so it was. The next day, after services, we sit down at the table. Well, you should have seen the spread. First the appetizers: crisp wafers and chopped herring, and onions and chicken fat, with radishes and chopped liver and eggs and *gribbenes*. And after that the cold fish and the meat from yesterday's *tzimmes*, and then the jellied neat's foot, or *fisnoga* as you call it, with thin slices of garlic, and after that the potato *cholent* with the *kugel* that had been in the oven all night—and you know what that smells like when you take it out of the oven and take the cover off the pot. And what it tastes like. Our visitor could not find words to praise it. So I tell him: "This is still nothing. Wait until you have tasted our borsht tonight, then you'll know what good food is." At that he laughs out loud—a friendly laugh, it is true—and says to me: "Yes, but how far do you think I'll be from here by the time your borsht is ready?" So I laugh even louder than he does, and say: "You can forget that right now! Do you think you'll be going off tonight?"

And so it was. As soon as the lights were lit and we had a glass of wine to start off the new week, my friend begins to pack his things again. So I call out to him: "Are you crazy? Do you think we'll let you go off, the Lord knows where, at night? And besides, where's your train?" "What?" he yells at me. "No train? Why, you're murdering me! You know I have to leave!" But I say, "May this be the greatest misfortune in your life. Your train will come, if all is well, around dawn tomorrow. In the meantime I hope your appetite and digestion are good, because I can smell the borsht already! All I ask," I say, "is just tell me the truth. Tell me if you've ever touched a borsht like this before. But I want the absolute truth!" What's the use of talking—he had to admit it: never before in all his life had he tasted a borsht like this. Never. He even started to ask how you made the borsht, what you put into it, and how long you cooked it. Everything. And I say: "Don't worry about that! Here, taste this wine and tell me what you think of *it*. After all, you're an expert. But the truth! Remember— nothing but the truth! Because if there is anything I hate, it's flattery . . ."

So we took a glass, and then another glass, and we went to bed. And what do you think happened? My traveler overslept, and missed the early morning train. When he wakes up he boils over! He jumps on me like a murderer. Wasn't it up to me, out of fairness and decency, to wake him up in time? Because of me he's going to have to take a loss, a heavy loss—he doesn't even know himself how heavy. It was all my fault. I ruined him. I! . . . So I let him talk. I listen, quietly, and when he's all through, I say: "Tell me yourself, aren't you a queer sort of person? In the first place, what's your hurry? What are you rushing for? How long is a person's life altogether? Does he have to spoil that little with rushing and hurrying? And in the second place, you have forgotten that today is the third day since the *bris*? Doesn't that mean a thing to you? Where we come from, on the third day we're in the habit of putting on a feast better than the one at the *bris* itself. The third day—it's something to celebrate! You're not going to spoil the celebration, are you?"

What can he do? He can't control himself any more, and he starts laughing—a hysterical laugh. "What good does it do to talk?" he says. "You're a real leech!" "Just as you say," I tell him, "but after all, you're a visitor, aren't you?"

At the dinner table, after we've had a drink or two, I call out to him: "Look," I say, "it may not be proper—after all, we're Jews—to talk about milk and such things while we're eating meat, but I'd like to know your honest opinion: what do you think of *kreplach* with cheese?" He looks at me with distrust. "How did we get around to that?" he asks. "Just like this," I explain to him. "I'd like to have you try the cheese *kreplach* that my wife makes—because tonight, you see, we're going to have a dairy supper. . . ." This is too much for him, and he comes right back at me with, "Not this time! You're trying to keep me here another day, I can see that. But you can't do it. It isn't right! It isn't right!" And from the way he fusses and fumes it's easy to see that I won't have to coax him too long, or fight with him either, because what is he but a man with an appetite, who has only one philosophy, which he practices at the table? So I say this to him: "I give you my word of honor, and if that isn't enough, I'll give you my hand as well—here, shake—that tomorrow I'll wake you up in time for the earliest train. I promise it, even if the world turns upside down. If I don't, may I—you know what!' At this he softens and says to me: "Remember, we're shaking hands on that!" And I: "A promise is a promise." And my wife makes a dairy supper—how can I describe it to you? With such *kreplach* that my traveler has to admit that it was all true: he has a wife too, and she makes *kreplach* too, but how can you compare hers with these? It's like night to day!

And I kept my word, because a promise is a promise. I woke him when it was still dark, and started the samovar. He finished packing and began to say goodbye to me and the rest of the household in a very handsome, friendly style. You could see he was a gentleman. But I interrupt him: "We'll say goodbye a little later, first, we have to settle up." "What do you mean—settle up?" "Settle up," I say, "means to add up the figures. That's what I'm going to do now. I'll add them up, let you know what it comes to, and you will be so kind as to pay me."

His face flames red. "Pay you?" he shouts. "Pay you for what?" "For what?" I repeat. "You want to know for what? For everything. The food, the drink, the lodging." This time he becomes white—not red—and he says to me: "I don't understand you at all. You came and invited me to the *bris*. You stopped me at the train. You took my bag away from me. You promised me eternal life." "That's right," I interrupt him. "That's right. But what's one thing got to do with the other?

When you came to the *bris* you earned your reward in heaven. But food and drink and lodging—do I have to give you these things for nothing? After all, you're a businessman, aren't you? You should understand that fish costs money, and that the wine you drank was the very best, and the beer, too, and the cherry cider. And you remember how you praised the *tzimmes* and the puddings and the borsht. You remember how you licked your fingers. And the cheese *kreplach* smelled pretty good to you, too, Now, I'm glad you enjoyed these things; I don't begrudge you that in the least. But certainly you wouldn't expect that just because you earned a reward in heaven, and enjoyed yourself in the bargain, that I should pay for it?" My traveling friend was really sweating; he looked as if he'd have a stroke. He began to throw himself around, yell, scream, call for help. "This is Sodom!" he cried. "Worse than Sodom! It's the worst outrage the world has ever heard of! How much do you want?" Calmly I took a piece of paper and a pencil and began to add it up. I itemized everything, I gave him an inventory of everything he ate, of every hour he spent in my place. All in all it added up to something like thirty-odd rubles and some kopeks—I don't remember it exactly.

When he saw the total, my good man went green and yellow, his hands shook, and his eyes almost popped out, and again he let out a yell, louder than before. "What did I fall into—a nest of thieves? Isn't there a single human being here? Is there a God anywhere? So I say to him, "Look, sir, do you know what? Do you know what you're yelling about? Do you have to eat your heart out? Here is my suggestion: let's ride into town together—it's not far from here—and we'll find some people—there's a rabbiner there—let's ask the rabbi. And we'll abide by what he says." When he heard me talk like that, he quieted down a little. And—don't worry—we hired a horse and wagon, climbed in, and rode off to town, the two of us, and went straight to the rabbi.

When we got to the rabbi's house, we found him just finishing his morning prayers. He folded up his prayer shawl and put his philacteries away. "Good morning," we said to him, and he: "What's the news today?" The news? My friend tears loose and lets him have the whole story—everything from A to Z. He doesn't leave a word out. He tells how he stopped at the station, and so on and so on, and when he's through he whips out the bill I had given him and hands it to the rabbi. And when the rabbi had heard everything, he says: "Having heard one side I should now like to hear the other." And turning to me, he asks, "What do you have to say to all that?" I answer: "Everything he says is true. There's not a word I can add. Only one thing I'd like to have him tell you—on his word of honor: did he eat the fish, and did he drink the beer and cognac and the cider, and did he smack his lips over the borsht that my wife made?" At this the man becomes almost frantic, he jumps and he thrashes about like an apoplectic. The rabbi begs him not to boil like that, not to be so angry, because anger is a grave sin. And he asks him again about the fish and the borsht and the *kreplach,* and if it was true that he had drunk not only the wine, but beer and cognac and cider as well. Then the rabbi puts on his spectacles, looks the bill over from top to bottom, checks every line, and finds it correct! Thirty-odd rubles and some kopeks, and he makes his judgment brief: he tells the man to pay the whole thing, and for the wagon back and forth, and a judgment fee for the rabbi himself. . . .

The man stumbles out of the rabbi's house looking as if he'd been in a steam bath too long, takes out his purse, pulls out two, twenty-fives and snaps at me: "Give me the change." "What change?" I ask, and he says: "For the thirty you charged me—for that bill you gave me." "Bill? What bill? What thirty are you talking about? What do you think I am, a highwayman? Do you expect me to take money from you? I see a man at the railroad station, a total stranger; I take his bag away from him, and drag him off almost by force to our own *bris,* and spend a wonderful *Shabbes* with him. So am I going to charge him for the favor he did me, and for the pleasure I had?" Now he looks at me as if I really am crazy, and says: "Then why did you carry on like this? Why did you drag me to the rabbi?" "Why this? Why that?" I say to him. "You're a queer sort of person, you are! I wanted to show you what kind of man our rabbi was, that's all. . . ."

When he finished the story, my litigant, Reb Nachman Lekach, got up with a flourish, and the other three partners followed him. They buttoned their coats and prepared to leave. But I held them off. I passed the cigarettes around again, and said to the storyteller:

"So you told me a story about a rabbi. Now maybe you'll be so kind as to let me tell you a story—also about a rabbi, but a much shorter story than the one you told."

And without waiting for a yes or no, I started right in, and made it brief:

This happened, I began, not so long ago, and in a large city, on Yom Kippur eve. A stranger falls into the town—a businessman, a traveler, who goes here and there, everywhere, sells merchandise, collects money. . . . On this day he comes into the city, walks up and down in front of the synagogue, holding his sides with hands, asks everybody he sees where he can find the rabbi. "What do you want the rabbi for?" people ask. "What business is that of yours?" he wants to know. So they don't tell him. And he asks one man, he asks another: "Can you tell where the rabbi lives?" "What do you want the rabbi for?" "What do you care?" This one and that one, till finally he gets the answer, finds the rabbi's house, goes in, still holding his sides with both hands. He calls the rabbi aside, shuts the door, and says, "Rabbi, this is my story. I am a traveling man, and I have money with me, quite a pile. It's not my money. It belongs to my clients—first to God and then to my clients. It's Yom Kippur eve. I can't carry money with me on Yom Kippur, and I'm afraid to leave it at my lodgings. A sum like that! So do me a favor—take it, put it away in your strong box till tomorrow night, after Yom Kippur."

And without waiting, the man unbuttons his vest and draws out one pack after another, crisp and clean, the real red, crackling, hundred ruble notes!

Seeing how much there was, the rabbi said to him: "I beg your pardon. You don't know me, you don't know who I am." "What do you mean, I don't know who you are? You're a rabbi, aren't you?" "Yes, I'm a rabbi. But I don't know *you*—who you are or what you are." They bargain back and forth. The traveler: "You're a rabbi." The rabbi: "I don't know who you are." And time does not stand still. It's almost Yom Kippur! Finally the rabbi agrees to take the money. The only thing is, who should be the witnesses? You can't trust just anyone in a matter like that.

So the rabbi sends for the leading townspeople, the very cream, rich and respectable citizens, and says to them: "This is what I called you for. This man has money with him, a tidy sum, not his own, but first God's and then his clients'. He wants me to keep it for him till after Yom Kippur. Therefore I want you to be witnesses, to see how much he leaves with me, so that later—you understand?" And the rabbi took the trouble to count it all over three times before the eyes of the townspeople, wrappd the notes in a kerchief, sealed the kerchief with wax, and stamped his initials on the seal. He passed this from one man to the other, saying, "Now look. Here is my signature, and remember, you're the witnesses." The kerchief with the money in it he handed over to his wife, had her lock it in a chest, and hide the keys where no one could find them. And he himself, the rabbi, went to *shul,* and prayed and fasted as it was ordained, lived through Yom Kippur, came home, had a bite to eat, looked up, and there was the traveler. "Good evening, Rabbi." "Good evening. Sit down. What can I do for you?" "Nothing. I came for my package." "What package?" "The money." "What money?" "The money I left with you to keep for me." "You gave *me* money to keep for you? When was that?"

The traveler laughs out loud. He thinks the rabbi is joking with him. The rabbi asks: "What are you laughing at?" And the man says: "It's the first time I met a rabbi who likes to play tricks." At this the rabbi is insulted. No one, he pointed out, had ever called him a trickster before. "Tell me, my good man, what do you want here?"

When he heard these words, the stranger felt his heart stop. "Why, Rabbi, in the name of all that's holy, do you want to kill me? Didn't I give you all my money? That is, not mine, but first God's and then my clients'? I'll remind you, you wrapped it in a kerchief, sealed it with wax, locked it in your wife's chest, hid the key where no one could find it. And here is better proof: there were witnesses, the leading citizens of the city!" And he goes ahead and calls them all off by name. In the midst of it a cold sweat breaks out on his forehead, he feels faint, and asks for a glass of water.

The rabbi sends the *shammes* off to the men the traveler had named—the leading citizens, the flower of the community. They come running from all directions. "What's the matter? What's happened?" "A misfortune. A plot! A millstone around our necks! He insists that he brought a pile of money to me yesterday, to keep over Yom Kippur, and that you were witnesses to the act."

The householders look at each other, as if to say: "Here is where we get a nice bone to lick!" And they fall on the traveler: how could he do a thing like that? He ought to be ashamed of himself! Thinking up an ugly plot like that against their rabbi!

When he saw what was happening, his arms and legs went limp, he just about fainted. But the rabbi got up, went to the chest, took out the kerchief and handed it to him.

"What's the matter with you! Here! Here is your money! Take it and count it, see if it's right, here in front of your witnesses. The seal, as you see, is untouched. The wax is whole, just as it ought to be."

The traveler felt as if a new soul had been installed in his body. His hands trembled and tears stood in his eyes.

"Why did you have to do it, Rabbi? Why did you have to play this trick on me? A trick like this."

"I just wanted to show you—the kind—of—leading citizens—we have in our town."

MENU:
Chicken soup with dumplings
Beef pot roast with garlic
Fresh warm twist
(Challah)
Gefülte fish
Tzimmes, with a piece of brisket of beef
Chopped herring
Potato cholent
Kugel
Borscht
Cold beet borscht
Hot cabbage borscht
Cheese kreplach

The recipes come from The Art of Jewish Cooking *by Jennie Grossinger, one of the founders of that palace of good food and bustling rest, Grossinger's Hotel, and from Emma and Mina Kaufman, two unsung but worthy cooks who learned their recipes by word of mouth and watch of eye from their mother Elka. Their mother, they relate, who had herself learned them the same way from her mother, had some singular habits. When she baked bread and arrived at the point at which the cookbooks always say, "Cover with a towel, set in a warm place and let rise," Elka would put the challah dough gently into bed, surround it cozily with pillows and top it warmly with the thick down quilt. With such love, it would rise to great heights.*

CHICKEN SOUP WITH DUMPLINGS

Emma and Mina Kaufman

For the soup:
1 fat pullet (3-4 pounds)
3½ quarts water
1 tablespoon salt
2-3 carrots, cut up

2 sprigs of parsley (1 teaspoon
    dried parsley)
2 sprigs of dill (¼-½ teaspoon
    dried-dill)
2 onions, cut up

For the dumplings:
a pot of boiling salted water
3 eggs, separated

1 teaspoon salt
matzoth meal (about a cup)

The soup: Put a fat pullet into a saucepan with the water and salt. Bring to a boil. Simmer, skim, and add carrots, parsley, dill and onions. The dill is most important; it gives a marvelous flavor to the soup. Simmer slowly, covered, for 2½ to 3 hours. Remove the chicken and serve the soup. The chicken may be eaten separately.

The dumplings: While the soup is cooking set a pot of salted water to boil. Beat the whites of 3 eggs until frothy with a teaspoon of salt. Then add the yolks of the eggs and beat some more. Add just enough matzoth meal to make it possible to form small balls. Wet hands with cold water before making the balls so the matzoth meal doesn't stick to your hands. You must work fast now as matzoth meal will harden if allowed to stand and the dumplings will be as heavy as baseballs.

When the balls are shaped, drop them into the boiling water, cover, and cook on a medium flame for about ½ hour. The balls will expand, becoming two or three times larger in size, and will be very light and fluffy. When they are done, drop them into the chicken soup and serve together.

Contrary to what most cooks advise, do not use fat of any kind in dumplings. If no fat is used the balls will be as light as spongecake.

(Serves 6-8)

BEEF POT ROAST WITH GARLIC

Emma and Mina Kaufman

2 pounds brisket or chuck
1 large onion, sliced
salt and pepper
a little water (1 cup)

1-2 cloves garlic, halved
1-2 bay leaves
optional: a small piece of honey
cake or several ginger snaps

Sear the meat over a high flame in a heavy pot. Lower the flame, add a large sliced onion, and let the onion brown slightly in the meat's fat. Add salt and pepper to taste, a little water, and a halved clove or two of garlic. Cover tightly and cook slowly for about 2 hours. Turn the meat frequently and baste with the liquid in the pot. Add more water if necessary. One hour before it's done add a bay leaf or two. You may also add at this time some ginger snaps or a bit of honey cake, to give flavor and color to the gravy.

(Serves 4)

FRESH WARM TWIST

(Challah)

FROM *The Art of Jewish Cooking*, 1958, Jennie Grossinger

1 cake or package of yeast	2 eggs
2 teaspoons sugar	2 tablespoons salad oil
1¼ cups lukewarm water	1 egg yolk
4½ cups sifted flour	4 tablespoons poppy seeds
2 teaspoons salt	optional: ⅛ teaspoon saffron

Combine the yeast, sugar, and ¼ cup lukewarm water. Let stand 5 minutes.

Sift the flour and salt into a bowl. Make a well in the center and drop the eggs, oil, remaining water and the yeast mixture into it. Work into the flour. Knead on a floured surface until smooth and elastic. Place in a bowl and brush the top with a little oil. Cover with a towel, set in a warm place and let rise one hour. Punch down, cover again and let rise until double in bulk. Divide the dough into 3 equal parts. Between lightly floured hands roll the dough into 3 strips of even length. Braid them together and place in a baking pan. Cover with a towel and let rise until double in bulk. Brush with the egg yolk and sprinkle with the poppy seeds.

Bake in a 375° oven 50 minutes or until browned.

Makes 1 very large challah. If you wish, divide the dough in 6 parts and make 2 large loaves, or make 1 loaf and many small rolls. You may also bake the bread in a loaf pan; ⅛ teaspoon saffron can be dissolved in the water if you like additional flavor and color.

GEFÜLTE FISH

Emma and Mina Kaufman

1 pound whitefish	a carrot, cut up
1 pound yellow pike	2 teaspoons salt
1 pound winter carp	¾ teaspoon pepper
fish bones and skin	½ teaspoon sugar
a quart of boiling water	1½ tablespoons matzoth meal
2 sliced onions and their skin	2 eggs
a piece of a fresh beet	ice water

Have fish filleted and save the skin and bones. Put skin and bones into 1 quart of boiling water and add a sliced onion, a piece of a fresh beet, the carrot, a teaspoon of salt and ¼ teaspoon pepper, and let this cook. Meanwhile put the fish itself into a wooden chopping bowl, with the other onion, the rest of the salt and pepper, the sugar and matzoth meal. Start chopping the fish, turning it over and over to blend (or grind it with fine blade of grinder). Beat up an egg and add. Continue chopping. Beat up the other egg and add. Continue chopping. Now add some ice water to the mixture slowly until the fish becomes almost pasty (about ½ cup of water). When fish is thoroughly and very finely chopped, shape into balls and drop into the pot of boiling stock. After all the fish is in the pot, throw in the onion skins on top. They give the gravy an excellent flavor and make the fish turn a golden color. Simmer the whole on a small flame for about an hour and a half, making certain that the cover to the pot is slightly ajar so that steam can escape. Thorough chopping and slow cooking will make the fish fine and fluffy. Serve hot or cold, with horseradish.

(Serves 6)

TZIMMES WITH A PIECE OF BRISKET OF BEEF

FROM *The Art of Jewish Cooking,* 1958, Jennie Grossinger

"The word tzimmes," *says Mrs. Grossinger, "means a fuss or excitement. But making a tzimmes does not mean a great deal of work; most tzimmes dishes are easily prepared. Actually, it's almost any combination of meat or vegetables or fruits, limited only by the imagination of the cook."*

Sweet Potato and Prune Tzimmes

1½ pounds prunes	¼ teaspoon pepper
3 cups boiling water	3 sweet potatoes, peeled and
2 tablespoons fat	quartered
3 pounds brisket of beef	½ cup honey
2 onions, diced	2 cloves
1½ teaspoons salt	½ teaspoon cinnamon

Wash prunes and let soak in the boiling water ½ hour.

Melt the fat in a Dutch oven. Cut the beef in 6 or 8 pieces and brown with the onions. Sprinkle with the salt and pepper. Cover and cook over low heat 1 hour. Add the undrained prunes, sweet potatoes, honey, cloves and cinnamon. Replace cover loosely and cook over low heat 2 hours.

(Serves 6-8)

CHOPPED HERRING

FROM *The Art of Jewish Cooking*, 1958, Jennie Grossinger

6 fillets of salt herring
3 tablespoons chopped onion
½ cup chopped apple
2 hard-cooked eggs

3 tablespoons cider vinegar
2 slices white bread, trimmed
1 teaspoon sugar
2 tablespoons salad oil

Soak the herring in water to cover overnight. Change the water twice. Drain. Chop the onion, apple, eggs and herring together. Pour the vinegar over the bread and add to the herring with the sugar and oil. Chop until very smooth. Taste for seasoning, adding more vinegar if needed. Chill.

(Serves 8 as an appetizer or as many as 24 as a spread)

POTATO CHOLENT

FROM *The Art of Jewish Cooking*, 1958, Jennie Grossinger

6 eggs
1 cup melted fat
2 cups sifted flour
3 teaspoons salt
3 pounds flanken (or brisket of beef)

6 potatoes, peeled and cut in half
½ teaspoon pepper
2 teaspoons paprika
½ teaspoon garlic powder

Beat the eggs, fat, flour and 1 teaspoon salt together. Form into a flat mound and place in the center of a Dutch oven or baking dish. Place the meat on one side of the dough and arrange the potatoes around it. Sprinkle with the pepper, paprika, garlic powder and remaining salt. Add enough boiling water to cover all the ingredients. Cover tightly and bake in a 250° oven for 24 hours or more or in a 350° oven 4-5 hours.

Slice the meat, cut the crust and serve with the potatoes.

(Serves 6-8)

KUGEL

Emma and Mina Kaufman

Noodle Kugel

4 cups parboiled noodles
3 eggs
4 tablespoons sugar

½ cup raisins (previously soaked in hot water and drained)
½ teaspoon salt

⅛ teaspoon cinnamon
a peeled, grated apple

⅛ pound butter
¼-½ cup milk

Parboil noodles in salted water and drain them. Place in a greased casserole. Beat the eggs and the sugar together, add them with the raisins, a little salt, cinnamon, a grated, peeled apple, the butter and milk to the noodles; stir, and bake uncovered in a 350° oven for 1 hour or until browned.

(Serves 6-8)

BORSCHT

Emma and Mina Kaufman

Cold Beet Borscht

8-10 beets
2½ quarts salted water
1 lemon
2 teaspoons salt
sugar to taste (about 1½-2 tablespoons)

1-2 eggs
sour cream
garnish: chopped hard-cooked
   eggs, cucumbers, scallions or
   onions, minced

Wash the beets, remove the stems and leaves, and cook in salted water till soft. Then remove from pot, reserving the liquid. Peel beets and grate on coarse side of grater. Return them to the liquid in the pot and add the juice of a lemon, salt, and sugar to taste—the soup should taste both sweet and sour. Cook for 15 minutes on low heat, remove from fire, then beat up an egg or two, dilute with a little beet liquor, and pour into the rest of the borscht. Chill, and serve 2 tablespoons of sour cream on top of each bowl of soup. Also, add chopped hard-cooked eggs for decoration, and cut up cucumbers, scallions or onions.

(Serves 8)

Hot Cabbage Borscht

1½ pounds cabbage
1 onion, cut up
2 carrots, cut up
1½ cups canned tomatoes
1 quart water
1 teaspoon salt

pepper
sugar to taste (about 1 tablespoon)
1 pound brisket or chuck
2 tablespoons lemon juice
garlic clove, halved

Grate the cabbage on coarse side of grater or cut into slivers with knife. Put all the ingredients into a deep pot and cook slowly for 2-2½ hours. Serve with pumpernickel which has had its crust well rubbed with garlic.

(Serves 3-4)

CHEESE KREPLACH

FROM *The Art of Jewish Cooking*, 1958, Jennie Grossinger

The dough:

2 cups flour	1 tablespoon water
2 eggs	½ teaspoon salt

Place unsifted flour on a board and make a well in the center. Drop the eggs, water and salt into it. Work into the flour with one hand and knead until smooth and elastic. Roll and stretch the dough as thin as possible. The thinner it is, the better the noodles. Let the rolled dough stand until it feels dry to the touch but don't let it get too dry.

Cut into 3-inch squares and place a tablespoon of the following on each:

The filling:

½ cup minced onions	1 teaspoon salt
3 tablespoons butter	⅛ teaspoon pepper
1½ cups mashed potatoes	1 egg
½ cup pot cheese	sour cream

(Lightly brown the onions in the butter. Add the potatoes, cheese, salt, pepper and egg, beating until smooth.)

(Now) fold over the dough into a triangle. Press edges together with a little water. Cook in boiling salted water or soup 20 minutes, or until they rise to the top. Drain, if cooked in water. They can be fried or served immediately in the soup. Makes 24 or more, according to how thin you roll the dough.

VIRGINIA WOOLF

TO THE LIGHTHOUSE
1927

Mrs. Ramsay is like a legendary earth goddess. She is the mother of eight children, the mistress of her household, the arbiter and arranger of the loves and comforts of all around her. Her ability to give of herself never runs dry; she absorbs even hate unflinchingly.

At this dinner she is involved in all things: the guests, with their needs and grievances, the colors on her table, the shape of a pear, the light of a candle, the love of her husband. She is weary at first from the vast female effort of creating, "the whole of the effort of merging and flowing and creating rested on her." But her party is a triumph, just as is the main course, the Boeuf en Daube. Magically, like a goddess, she has made things so beautiful and ordered within her dining room that for one brief moment she has shut the night outside of the lives of those she watches over.

Now all the candles were lit up, and the faces on both sides of the table were brought nearer by the candle light, and composed, as they had not been in the twilight, into a party round table, for the night was now shut off by panes of glass, which, far from giving any accurate view of the outside world, rippled it so strangely that here, inside the room, seemed to be order and dry land; there, outside, a reflection in which things wavered and vanished, waterily.

Some change at once went through them all, as if this had really happened, and they were all conscious of making a party together in a hollow, on an island; had their common cause against that fluidity out there. Mrs. Ramsay, who had been uneasy, waiting for Paul and Minta to come in, and unable, she felt, to settle to things, now felt her uneasiness changed to expectation. For now they must come, and Lily Briscoe, trying to analyse the cause of the sudden exhilaration, compared it with that moment on the tennis lawn, when solidity suddenly vanished, and such vast spaces lay between them; and now the same effect was got by the many candles in the sparely furnished room, and the uncurtained windows, and the bright mask-like look of faces seen by candlelight. Some weight was taken off them; anything might happen, she felt. They must come now, Mrs. Ramsay thought, looking at the door, and at that instant, Minta Doyle, Paul Rayley, and a maid carrying a great dish in her hands came in together. They were awfully late; they were horribly late, Minta said, as they found their way to different ends of the table.

"I lost my brooch—my grandmother's brooch," said Minta with a sound of lamentation in her voice, and a suffusion in her large brown eyes, looking down, looking up, as she sat by Mr. Ramsay, which roused his chivalry so that he bantered her.

How could she be such a goose, he asked, as to scramble about the rocks in jewels?

She was by way of being terrified of him—he was so fearfully clever, and the first night when she had sat by him, and he talked about George Eliot, she had been really frightened, for she had left the third volume of *Middlemarch* in the train and she never knew what happened in the end; but afterwards she got on perfectly, and made herself out even more ignorant than she was, because he liked telling her she was a fool. And so tonight, directly he laughed at her, she was not frightened. Besides, she knew, directly she came into the room that the miracle had happened; she wore her golden haze. Sometimes she had it; sometimes not. She never knew why it came or why it went, or if she had it until she came into the room and then she knew instantly by the way some man looked at her. Yes, tonight she had it, tremendously; she knew that by the way Mr. Ramsay told her not to be a fool. She sat beside him, smiling.

It must have happened then, thought Mrs. Ramsay; they are engaged. And for a moment she felt what she had never expected to feel again—jealousy. For he, her husband, felt it too—Minta's glow; he liked these girls, these golden-reddish girls, with something flying, something a little wild and harum-scarum about them, who didn't "scrape their hair off," weren't, as he said about poor Lily Briscoe, ". . . skimpy." There was some quality which she herself had not, some lustre, some richness, which attracted him, amused him, led him to make favourites of girls like Minta. They might cut his hair from him, plait him watch-chains, or interrupt him at his work, hailing him (she heard them), "Come along, Mr. Ramsay; it's our turn to beat them now," and out he came to play tennis.

But indeed she was not jealous, only, now and then, when she made herself look in her glass a little resentful that she had grown old, perhaps, by her own fault. (The bill for the greenhouse and all the rest of it.) She was grateful to them for laughing at him. ("How many pipes have you smoked today, Mr. Ramsay?" and so on), till he seemed a young man; a man very attractive to women, not burdened, not weighted down with the greatness of his labours and the sorrows of the world and his fame or his failure, but again as she had first known him, gaunt but gallant; helping her out of a boat, she remembered; with delightful ways, like that (she looked at him, and he looked astonishingly young, teasing Minta). For herself—"Put it down there," she said, helping the Swiss girl to place gently before her the huge brown pot in which was the Boeuf en Daube—for her own part she liked her boobies. Paul must sit by her. She had kept a place for him. Really, she sometimes thought she liked the boobies best. They did not bother one with their dissertations. How much they missed, after all, these very clever men! How dried up they did become, to be sure. There was something, she thought as he sat down, very charming about Paul. His manners were delightful to her, and his sharp-cut nose and his bright blue eyes. He was so considerate. Would he tell her—now that they were all talking again—what had happened?

"We went back to look for Minta's brooch," he said, sitting down by her. "We"—that was enough. She knew from the effort, the rise in his voice to surmount a difficult word that it was the first time he had said "we." "We did this, we did that." They'll say that all their lives, she thought, and an exquisite scent of olives and oil and juice rose from the great brown dish as Marthe, with a little flourish, took the cover off. The cook had spent three days over that dish. And she must take great care, Mrs. Ramsay thought, diving into the soft mass, to choose a specially tender piece for William Bankes. And she peered into the dish, with its shiny walls and its confusion of savoury brown and yellow meats and its bay leaves and its wine, and thought. This will celebrate the occasion—a curious sense rising in her, at once freakish and tender, of celebrating a festival, as if two emotions were called up in her, one profound—for what could be more serious than the love of man for woman, what more commanding, more impressive, bearing in its bosom the seeds of death; at the same time these lovers, these people entering into illusion glittering eyed, must be danced round with mockery, decorated with garlands.

"It is a triumph," said Mr. Bankes, laying his knife down for a moment. He had eaten attentively. It was rich; it was tender. It was perfectly cooked. How did she manage these things in the depths of the country? he asked her. She was a wonderful woman. All his love, all his reverence, had returned; and she knew it.

"It is a French recipe of my grandmother's," said Mrs. Ramsay, speaking with a ring of great pleasure in her voice. Of course it was French. What passes for cookery in England is an abomination (they agreed). It is putting cabbages in water. It is roasting meat till it is like leather. It is cutting off the delicious skins of vegetables. "In which," said Mr. Bankes, "all the virtue of the vegetable is contained." And the waste, said Mrs. Ramsay. A whole French family could live on what an English cook throws away. Spurred on by her sense that William's affection had come back to her, and that everything was all right again, and that her suspense was over, and that now she was free both to triumph and to mock, she laughed, she gesticulated, till Lily thought, How childlike, how absurd she was, sitting up there with all her beauty opened again in her, talking about the skins of vegetables. There was something frightening about her. She was irresistible. Always she got her own way in the end, Lily thought. Now she had brought this off—Paul and Minta, one might suppose, were engaged. Mr. Bankes was dining here. She put a spell on them all, by wishing, so simply, so directly, and Lily contrasted that abundance with her own poverty of spirit, and supposed that it was partly that belief (for her face was all lit up—without looking young, she looked radiant) in this strange, this terrifying thing, which made Paul Rayley, sitting at her side, all of a tremor, yet abstract, absorbed, silent. Mrs. Ramsay, Lily felt, as she talked about the skins of vegetables, exalted that, worshipped that; held her hands over it to warm them, to protect it, and yet, having brought it all about, somehow laughed, led her victims, Lily felt, to the altar. It came over her too now—the emotion, the vibration, of love. How inconspicuous she felt herself by Paul's side! He, glowing, burning; she, aloof, satirical; he, bound for adventure; she, moored to the shore; he, launched, incautious; she, solitary, left-out—and, ready to implore a share, if it were disaster, in his disaster, she said shyly:

"When did Minta lose her brooch?"

He smiled the most exquisite smile, veiled by memory, tinged by dreams. He shook his head. "On the beach," he said.

"I'm going to find it," he said, "I'm getting up early." This being kept secret from Minta, he lowered his voice, and turned his eyes to where she sat, laughing, beside Mr. Ramsay.

Lily wanted to protest violently and outrageously her desire to help him, envisaging how in the dawn on the beach she would be the one to pounce on the brooch half-hidden by some stone, and thus herself be included among the sailors and adventurers. But what did he reply to her offer? She actually said with an emotion that she seldom let appear, "Let me come with you," and he laughed. He meant yes or no—either perhaps. But it was not his meaning—it was the odd chuckle he gave, as if he had said, Throw yourself over the cliff if you like, I don't care. He turned on her cheek the heat of love, its horror, its cruelty, its unscrupulosity. It scorched her, and Lily, looking at Minta, being charming to Mr. Ramsay at the other end of the table, flinched for her exposed to these fangs, and was thankful. For at any rate, she said to herself, catching sight of the salt cellar on the pattern, she need not marry, thank Heaven: she need not undergo that degradation. She was saved from that dilution. She would move the tree rather more to the middle.

Such was the complexity of things. For what happened to her, especially staying with the Ramsays, was to be made to feel violently two opposite things at the same time; that's what you feel, was one; that's what I feel, was the other, and then they fought together in her mind, as now. It is so beautiful, so exciting, this love, that I tremble on the verge of it, and offer, quite out of my own habit, to look for a brooch on a beach; also it is the stupidest, the most barbaric of human passions, and turns a nice young man with a profile like a gem's (Paul's was exquisite) into a bully with a crowbar (he was swaggering, he was insolent) in the Mile End Road. Yet, she said to herself, from the dawn of time odes have been sung to love; wreaths heaped and roses; and if you asked nine people out of ten they would say they wanted nothing but this—love; while the women, judging from her own experience, would all the time be feeling, This is not what we want; there is nothing more tedious, puerile, and inhumane than this; yet it is also beautiful and necessary. Well then, well then? she asked, somehow expecting the others to go on with the argument, as if in an argument like this one threw one's own little bolt which fell short obviously and left the others to carry it on. So she listened again to what they were saying in case they should throw any light upon the question of love.

"Then," said Mr. Bankes, "there is that liquid the English call coffee."

"Oh, coffee!" said Mrs. Ramsay. But it was much rather a question (she was thoroughly roused, Lily could see, and talked very emphatically) of real butter and clean milk. Speaking with warmth and eloquence, she described the iniquity of the English dairy system, and in what state milk was delivered at the door, and was about to prove her charges, for she had gone into the matter, when all round the table, beginning with Andrew in the middle, like a fire leaping from tuft to tuft of furze, her children laughed; her husband laughed; she was laughed at, fire-encircled, and forced to veil her crest, dismount her batteries, and only retaliate by displaying the raillery and ridicule of the table to Mr. Bankes as an example of what one suffered if one attacked the prejudices of the British Public.

Purposely, however, for she had it on her mind that Lily, who had helped her with Mr. Tansley, was out of things, she exempted her from the rest; said "Lily anyhow agrees with me," and so drew her in, a little fluttered, a little startled. (For she was thinking about love.) They were both out of things, Mrs. Ramsey had been thinking, both Lily and Charles Tansley. Both suffered from the glow of the other two. He, it was clear, felt himself utterly in the cold; no woman would look at him with Paul Rayley in the room. Poor fellow! Still, he had his dissertation, the influence of somebody upon something: he could take care of himself. With Lily it was different. She faded, under Minta's glow; became more inconspicuous than ever, in her little grey dress with her little puckered face and her little Chinese eyes. Everything about her was so small. Yet, thought Mrs. Ramsay, comparing

her with Minta, as she claimed her help (for Lily should bear her out
she talked no more about her dairies than her husband did about his
boots—he would talk by the hour about his boots) of the two, Lily at
forty will be the better. There was in Lily a thread of something; a
flare of something; something of her own which Mrs. Ramsay liked
very much indeed, but no man would, she feared. Obviously, not,
unless it were a much older man, like William Bankes. But then he
cared, well, Mrs. Ramsay sometimes thought that he cared, since his
wife's death, perhaps for her. He was not "in love" of course; it was
one of those unclassified affections of which there are so many. Oh,
but nonsense, she thought; William must marry Lily. They have so
many things in common. Lily is so fond of flowers. They are both cold
and aloof and rather self-sufficing. She must arrange for them to take
a long walk together.

Foolishly, she had set them opposite each other. That could be
remedied tomorrow. If it were fine, they should go for a picnic. Everything seemed possible. Everything seemed right. Just now (but this
cannot last, she thought, dissociating herself from the moment while
they were all talking about boots) just now she had reached security;
she hovered like a hawk suspended; like a flag floated in an element
of joy which filled every nerve of her body fully and sweetly, not
noisily, solemnly rather, for it arose, she thought, looking at them all
eating there, from husband and children and friends; all of which
rising in this profound stillness (she was helping William Bankes to
one very small piece more, and peered into the depths of the earthenware pot) seemed now for no special reason to stay there like a smoke,
like a fume rising upwards, holding them safe together. Nothing need
be said; nothing could be said. There it was, all round them. It partook, she felt, carefully helping Mr. Bankes to a specially tender piece,
of eternity; as she had already felt about something different once
before that afternoon; there is a coherence in things, a stability; something, she meant, is immune from change, and shines out (she glanced
at the window with its ripple of reflected lights) in the face of the
flowing, the fleeting, the spectral, like a ruby; so that again tonight
she had the feeling she had had once today, already, of peace, of rest.
Of such moments, she thought, the thing is made that endures.

"Yes," she assured William Bankes, "there is plenty for everybody."

"Andrew," she said, "hold your plate lower, or I shall spill it."
(The Boeuf en Daube was a perfect triumph.)

MENU:

Boeuf en daube

New York's Chateaubriand Restaurant provided the recipe for Mrs. Ramsay's triumphant Boeuf en Daube, with its "exquisite scent of olives and oil and juice . . . its confusion of savory brown and yellow meats and its bay leaves and its wine." The Chateaubriand appropriately bears on its menu the classic words of the gastronomer Brillat-Savarin: "The joys of the table belong equally to all ages, conditions, countries and times; they mix with all other pleasures and remain the last to console us for the others' loss."

BOEUF EN DAUBE

à la Provençale

The Chateaubriand Restaurant, New York City

4 pounds rump of beef
larding (strips of bacon, pork
   or ham fat; see page 298)
salt and pepper
fines herbes (finely chopped
   chervil, parsley, chives and
   tarragon)
a carrot, sliced
2 onions, halved
thyme (1 sprig or a dash of dried
   thyme)
bay leaves (3)

parsley sprigs (3)
2 cloves of garlic, crushed
10 ounces dry white wine
4 ounces cognac
3 parboiled calves' feet
2 tablespoons flour
fresh tomatoes (1-2 large ones)
stock broth, if necessary
cooked small new carrots (6-8)
cooked small white onions (6)
1 dozen black olives, blanched
   and stoned

Take 4 pounds of rump of beef and cut in four. Lard the meat with strips of larding, salt it, and roll in *fines herbes* and a little cognac (about an ounce). Then marinate it for 6 hours or more with salt and pepper, 1 sliced carrot, 2 halved onions, thyme, bay leaves, parsley sprigs, 2 cloves of crushed garlic, the wine and 3 ounces of cognac. Meanwhile, parboil 3 calves' feet for ½ hour and hold in reserve.

Drain the beef from the marinade and brown in a frying pan until well browned on both sides. Add 2 tablespoons of flour and make golden brown. Then add the marinade with the calves' feet, herbs and vegetables, and some fresh tomatoes. If the meat is not covered with liquid, add some stock broth.

Transfer to an earthenware casserole* and cook slowly for 4 hours or more in a 325–350° oven. Remove the meat into a serving dish with the calves' feet cut in small dice. Then strain the sauce, add the calves' feet to it with small new carrots, small white onions, blanched olives and *fines herbes*, and pour everything on top of the meat. This may be served hot or cold.

(Serves 6-8)

* To make this dish truly *en daube*, when you place your casserole in the oven you should seal the rim, no matter how close-fitting it is, with a paste of flour and water so that not a breath of juice may escape the pot. The technique is as old as the fourteenth century, and there is an early example of a dish cooked *en daube* in the Boccaccio section.

PART IV

•

MELTING POTS AND PEPPER POTS

•

THE NEW WORLD, 1700 TO TODAY

America's first cookbook was written by an orphan. History rarely produces a more perfect symbol. The literal-minded Amelia Simmons, so proud of her parentless state that she added to her name the phrase "an American orphan," wrote *American Cookery* in 1796 for those women who in actual fact had neither mother nor sister nor kindly aunt to teach them to boil an egg or make a hoecake.

But the whole country, culinarily speaking, was an enormous wailing orphanage. Every woman who ever came to America's shores felt herself rootless, disconnected from her heritage. However well she had mastered the secrets of cooking at her mother's knee, in the new country she had to begin the process all over again. The old familiar stand-bys were lacking; strange plants and peculiar animals proliferated. There were no parents; there was the self and the pot alone. It continued for centuries.

The first colonists asked constant advice of the Indians. What is that scrawny yellow plant you cherish? You scrape it and mash it and boil it with bear's meat? Bear's meat indeed! Fat and grease you mean. What is that dark black stuff you carry, all wrapped up in bark? You pound it between two stones and boil it into soup? Is it really dried meat? Will it really keep? Even when my husband goes West? What is that mysterious swamp grain you shake down into your canoes? It looks familiar, a wild "rice" perhaps.

Exploring and experimenting, they overcame their initial fears. They tasted buzzard and grew sick. But they munched on wild turkey and gave thanks.

Sometimes, like the abandoned orphans they were, they starved to death. Hunger plagued all the first colonists. In Jamestown, roots and herbs alone were boiled into soups. One poor Indian assisted the settlers' appetites with more than information. He was murdered and eaten by the "poor sort." Another man claimed that it was hunger alone which motivated him to kill and eat his wife, at least according to Captain John Smith, who ghoulishly adds that he doesn't know whether the wife was roasted or boiled.

The experience of the Pilgrims was even worse. They had thought they were going south to Virginia, where by the time of their sailing conditions had improved. But instead they landed in the dead of winter on the rocky shores of Massachusetts, inhospitable in any season. By the end of their first year hunger had reduced them to nearly half their original number. Even fewer might have survived had not some Indians recently abandoned the area, carelessly leaving behind them pots and bowls of the new plant, corn.

By the late 1600's in both North and South many more settlers had arrived, farming was under way, towns were being built. In warm Virginia the colonists carved out huge plantations with kitchen premises composed of many different outbuildings. One Virginia planter wrote home to his relatives in England in 1686 and made them green with envy by describing his thousand-acre farm equipped with "all things necessary & convenient, & all houses for use furnished with brick chimneys, four good Cellars, a Dairy, Dovecot, Stable, Barn, Henhouse, Kitchen & all other conveniencys & all in a manner new, . . . [and] about a mile and a half distance a good water Grist miln, whose tole I find sufficient to find my own family with wheat & Indian corn for our necessitys. . . ."

The possession of slaves made possible the reputation for hospitality Virginia early received. At parties a supper might consist of almost a hundred different dishes. "Strangers are fought over with greediness," wrote one traveler, "every comer is welcome." Pigs freely roamed the pleasant countryside, growing fat and complacent. They were smoked and eaten avidly, one rich family consuming twenty-seven thousand pounds of pork in a year. Exotic crops like rice and oranges were planted and grew copiously. Martha Washington had a cake recipe calling for forty eggs. Cookies were baked over the open fire in little cookie irons, one at a time, and sometimes it would take a young slave boy the entire day just to bake the plantation's cookies.

In New England it was different. Next to the Southern fireplace the usual chair was the shoo-fly chair, designed for the warm weather kitchen. In it, a cook might sit and peel potatoes with both hands yet keep the flies and bugs away by pushing a treadle with her feet. But the chair beside the fire in wintry New England was likely to be the settle, its front turned full toward the fire, tall enough to keep cold drafts away, wide enough to fit several members of the family. Because of the weather, kitchens were smaller affairs where much of the work was confined to single quarters. The housewife herself did most of her own cooking. Therefore she developed many boiled dishes, preferring this method which freed her from constant supervision of the pot. Her family ate venison and game birds, fish and shellfish, and great nourishing and warming soups. Maple trees provided sugar; apple trees provided tasty fruit that helped the housewife over her aversion to fruit which back home in England had most often been rotten or dry.

This was the start of regional variety in American cooking, and, as other areas got settled, other regional styles appeared. But wherever the new Americans were, one thing remained constant in their diet: Indian or corn meal. It could be made into breads, used for stuffing birds, combined with beans to make succotash. With its amazing ability to cohere it was especially useful in a land of open fires. Placed on a hoe and held over the flames it baked into a lovely hoecake. Pasted against a board tilted alongside the hearth it baked into an excellent johnnycake.

Naturally, many settlers grew tired of it. Kathleen Ann Smallzreid in *The Everlasting Pleasure* tells the story of the French "casket girls" who rebelled against corn fare. The girls had been sent early in the eighteenth century from Quebec, already a civilized city, to New Orleans, an uncivilized one, at the request of the male population who wanted women and wives. The girls came, each fitted out by the government with a casket containing the necessities she would need for life in the new place: chemises, lingerie and caps. They didn't complain about the muddy New Orleans streets or the rough-hewn homes the men carried them off to, but they hated the corn meal. Ultimately, after corn meal for breakfast and corn meal for lunch and corn meal for dinner, they revolted. They marched en masse to the governor's home declaring that they would not cook a single further dinner unless the colony imported some fine expensive French wheat flour. The governor, faced by this crowd of irate females, decided that only another woman could deal with them. He turned them over to his cook, Madame Langlois, also a Canadian but for a long time a resident of New Orleans. Madame Langlois deserves to be mentioned along with Hannah Glasse and Eliza Raffald and François Tanty, and all the other great teaching cooks of history, for, though she wrote no books, she too was a superior instructor. She took the young women and showed them that corn meal was repellent because they really didn't know how to prepare it. She taught them secrets she herself had gathered in the days of her own homesickness for wheat flour, secrets learned from Choctaw Indian squaws. She taught them how to grind the meal smoothly between two stones, how to add honey to it to make it taste good, and how to use sassafras and other local herbs. The casket girls were convinced to go home to their hungry men and try again. This they did, ultimately accepting New Orleans and starting the initial culinary skills of that French city. Later, treated to Spanish and West Indian developments too, it became the finest seat of cooking in America.

Other settlers were proud of corn meal, for it was the most truly American thing in the country. However much the English might insist that England and America could not be separated because they were culturally the same, there was always the corn meal to point to and say, "We are different; we are new." Thus in 1796 Joel Barlow wrote his poem "Hasty Pudding" in praise of Indian meal and told the world that, while Americans might live simply, they lived originally. And the proud patriot John Adams often startled the diplomatic world by serving dinners which began with a dish of Indian mush.

Later, American cooking developed an even more stratified regionalism. It was determined not by place and climate alone but by the areas in which immigrants from various foreign lands settled. Traditionally a melting pot, America was nowhere more of one than in her kitchen, where wave after wave of immigrants arrived, each new group bringing its own national imagination and delicacies.

The Dutch, who had been living in New York State, cooked much as they had back in Holland. They were exceptional farmers and exceptional cooks and they knew it. Two Dutch settlers on a trip in 1680 to that stronghold of English life, Boston, searched up and down for a countryman with whom they might spend the night—not, as one might imagine, because they wanted to talk their own language but because they wanted to be well fed. They finally did find a countryman: "We were better off at his house, for although his wife was an English-woman, she was quite a good housekeeper." Still proud, the Dutch held on to their own national style of cooking throughout the nine-teenth century. The other groups that came are legion: the Italians, bringing with them the pasta they themselves had inherited after Marco Polo's trip to China in the thirteenth century; the Irish, bring-ing stews; the Germans, bringing marvelous sausage-making tech-niques; the Chinese, the Mexicans, the Jews.

For many of these peoples the initial experience remained hunger. They had turned to the United States as a result of famine and pov-erty in Europe. It was reflected in the songs the immigrants brought with them: the Irish singing of how back home they had lived on potatoes, "skin and all," and the Jews singing of a potato diet on Mon-days, Tuesdays, Wednesdays, Thursdays, Fridays, Saturdays and even Sundays. In America too, the immigrants made songs of starvation, only here they starved on corn, not potatoes. The Homestead Act, passed in 1862, granted the right to 160 acres for a price of only $18 to any settler who would develop his land, build a house with at least one window and one door and live in it for at least five years. Many men took up land in the Great Plains, one day to be America's "bread bas-ket." But in dry weather their newly built sod houses leaked sand and in wet weather they leaked mud; there were blizzards so terrible that it was said men froze to death simply trying to get to their barn to feed their livestock. There were droughts, like the great one in 1859-60 in which no rain fell in Nebraska for over sixteen months and prairie fires burned the landscape black. There were grasshopper plagues and windstorms. Above all, there was little and bad food. One farmer sang sarcastically of life on his government claim:

> My clothes are all ragged, my language is rough,
> My bread is corn dodgers, both solid and tough;
> But yet I am happy and live at my ease
> On sorghum molasses and bacon and cheese.
>
> Hurrah for Greer County! The land of the free,
> The home of the bedbug, grasshopper and flea;
> I'll sing of its praises, I'll tell of its fame,
> While starving to death on my government claim.

Arkansas, always the butt of settlers' jokes, was given a miserable report:

> I followed my conductor into his dwelling place,
> There poverty and starvation were writ on every face,
> Their bread it was corn dodger, their meat I couldn't chaw,
> But they charged me a half a dollar, in the state of Arkansas.
>
> They fed me on corn dodgers, as hard as any rock,
> Till my teeth began to loosen, and my knees began to knock,
> I got so thin on sassafras tea, I could hide behind a straw,
> And indeed I was a different man, when I left old Arkansas.

In the South too they were bemoaning corn cuisine:

> They fed me on corn bread and beans,
> They fed me on corn bread and beans,
> They fed me on corn bread and beans, Oh Lord,
> But I ain't gonna be treated thisaway.

But despite it all there came the attempt at survival, the continuing belief that America really was a land of plenty, if one only knew how to work at it:

> When I first came to this land,
> I was not a wealthy man,
> But the land was sweet and good,
> I did what I could.

The singer of this song reports failure after failure, how his cow would give no milk, how his goose would lay no eggs: "But the land was sweet and good. I did what I could."

The wives of such pioneers were forced to develop clever skills to make the food, what little of it they had, palatable. Consequently another tradition arose in American cuisine. When there wasn't enough of any one ingredient to go around, many different and unrelated ingredients were cast into the pot. The aim was a harmonious whole, and, while occasionally the results were disastrous, more often the method produced mighty successes. American peasant cooking became known for its pepper pots and hodge pots and jambalaya and all the many soups and stews in which not one but all the gifts of the land were gathered up, tried together, weighed and found good.

By the 1850's the country's cookbooks reflected that Americans were fed with many unique dishes, unknown in Europe. A favorite author was Miss Leslie, who did a great deal to unite and define the nation. Her 1852 *New Receipts for Cooking* included such obviously "American" dishes as Carolina Grits and Hominy, Backwoods Pot Pie, Kentucky Sweet Cake, a Sea-Coast Pie, Missouri Cake, Roasted Canvas-Back Ducks, Chicken Gumbo, Venison and Chestnut Pudding and Indian Dumplings. Her awareness of American cuisine extended to a dish called Eggs Columbus in honor of the man who, in search of spices, accidentally discovered the New World. Spices are included in the recipe; they are mixed with chopped meat and stuffed into hard-cooked eggs. But these eggs had a very special culinary fillip. According to legend, when the explorer was told by a cynic that anyone could have discovered America, he answered with a parable. Placing a hard-cooked egg on the table, he asked a room full of noblemen if any of them could make an egg stand on end. When all had failed, Columbus cut off the egg's tip, giving it a flat surface to stand upon. "That is how it was with discovering the New World," Columbus reputedly declared. "Once accomplished, it seems so easy!" To commemorate this famous "egg debate," Miss Leslie's Eggs Columbus sported flattened tips.

Cookbooks like Miss Leslie's, and in fact nearly all the cookbooks of the first half of the nineteenth century, were as interested in telling women how to live as how to cook. Fulfilling a need later to be handed over to the ladies' magazines, they were the housewife's confidante, her adviser on all sorts of personal matters. Should a woman drink? Catharine Beecher in her 1846 *Domestic Receipt-Book* deliberated and announced that, while it was really improper to drink, it was even more improper to be discourteous. If a guest asked the lady of the house to join him in a glass of wine, "she is expected to have a little poured into her glass, and raise it to her lips, looking at and slightly bowing to the guest who makes the request." She also advised that, unless a husband provided his wife with an experienced cook and a well-trained waiter, it was "absolute *cruelty*" to require her to give a fancy dinner party.

Should a mother prompt her daughter to marry? Lydia Maria Child's *American Frugal Housewife* published here in 1836 vigorously said no. "It promotes envy and rivalship; it leads our young girls to spend their time between the public streets, the ball room and the toilet; and, worst of all, it leads them to contract engagements, without any knowledge of their own hearts, merely for the sake of being married as soon as their companions." She was definitely against that kind of education for girls which turned their whole beings into "man-traps."

How should a woman travel when crossing the Atlantic? Miss Leslie in *New Receipts,* told wives not to give a hoot for their skinflint husbands but always to engage a stateroom exclusively to themselves, no matter what the expense. "No one who has not been at sea can imagine the perpetual and mutual annoyance of being confined to the small limits of a state-room with a stranger; each incommoding the other all the time, and each feeling herself under the continual *surveillance* of her companion. . . ."

Then the frontier closed. Industry expanded and cookbooks turned their attention from polishing women's manners and mores to easing their work. America had begun to develop a well-to-do middle class with money to spend but with fewer servants than had families of comparable income in Europe. Women complained about how burdensome their household chores were, how much time and energy they consumed. Businessmen helped them out by creating new stoves and refrigeration devices; scholars studied means of making prompt use of leftovers; scientists explained the secrets of health and nutrition. Cooking schools mushroomed across the country in the late years of the century, proposing to educate America's women in the ways that "scientific knowledge can enable the housekeeper to maintain the health and generally promote the physical well-being of those committed to her charge. . . ." Once again cookbooks became serious, involved primarily with cooking. They offered marketing information, charts of meat cuts, discussions of the healthfulness of vegetables.

And always, now that the country had reached its furthest limits and a breathing space had occurred in which to assess how really immense America was, there came an attempt to grasp the whole of the diverse land, to push its too-gawky frame onto a Procrustean bed and shrink it, make it more comprehensible. "In Philadelphia," wrote Miss Parloa in her 1884 scientifically oriented cookbook, "they cut meat more as is done in Boston, than they do in New York. The following diagram shows a hind-quarter as it appears in Boston. The dotted lines show wherein the New York cutting differs from the Boston." By the time Miss Parloa wrote it had become virtually impossible for a cookbook to reflect and appeal to the entire nation and between her lines one can almost read her scholar's impatience with a country so huge and so various that its cuisine actually defied any orderly representation.

America's fiction writers reacted in the opposite fashion. To them, the immense variety of local custom was a boon. There is hardly a single nineteenth-century American writer who does not at some point use the naming of food as a stylistic device to differentiate his heroes from the overwhelming American whole. Of the writers included in this section, nearly every one describes foods which are clearly regional specialties. Washington Irving tells of the abundant baked goods of the Hudson Valley Dutch; Lafcadio Hearn describes Creole delicacies; Melville writes of New England fishy fare, and Dreiser of the sirloin found in that butchershop to the world, Chicago.

Peculiarly, each and every one of these foods may be called American and each and every one may be called not-American. That is what is today so confusing about American cuisine. What is it? Does it exist at all? Actually no one yet knows. Those who point to our regional varieties overlook the fact that our public fare is monotonous. Those who point to our public fare overlook the regional varieties. Foreign critics have taken American cooking to task, insisting that if America can be honored with possessing a national cuisine at all, its components are: for wine, a Coke; for dessert, a blueberry glue-pie more glue than berries; for the *pièce de résistance*, a charcoal-broiled hamburger. Native authors like Henry Miller have deplored our omnipresent catchup and mustard, our failure in particular to produce a decent bread (our bread, "the staff of our unsavory and monotonous life," writes Miller, is so unpalatable that under no circumstances should it be fed to birds. "The birds of North America are already on the decline," and this would do them in). We have, it is true, excellent steak, excellent fruits and vegetables. But it is also true that we have poor bread, and true that our public fare is singularly bad with few worthwhile restaurants outside the big cities. (With few restaurants at all in fact. The Chinese restaurant is the one happy exception, ubiquitous, ever providing its welcoming dishes in the most obscure corners of the country, ever charging modest prices for wholesome multicourse and unique meals.)

No one has ever quite figured out what went wrong with America's cuisine. Some say the fault lay within the method itself, that there were too many national strands and too much territory to be covered, that whenever something good was eaten in America, delicious Jewish rye bread, or spicy shrimp Creole, or crisp cheesy Italian pizza, someone could always say, "Yes, but that's not American; it came here from somewhere else." Some say the fault lay in our lack of an aristocratic tradition, in our having no taste-makers to emulate. Some say that our quick wealth, the ease with which provisions and canned goods became available, discouraged the need for imagination. Others say just the opposite, that the initial poverty hindered us by making men and women satisfied with any meal, any flavor, so long as it filled the belly.

Fortunately, fixing the blame can be held in abeyance because changes are still on the way. In recent years there has been a surge of interest in cooking, in particular, in regional cooking. Housewives, aware that at one time America's cuisine was widely acclaimed, are turning to the excellent recipes of the past to see what went wrong and when. Our melting-pot hodge-pot culture, which once predicted that America would produce a cuisine greater than any the world had ever known, has perhaps not yet cooked long enough on the kind of slow gentle heat a well-combined dish requires. It is still seething. We can dip into it and have a taste, and another taste, but the final results won't be known until a lot of steam has escaped and a lot of time gone by.

JOEL BARLOW
HASTY PUDDING
1796

Corn, unknown in Europe, was the gift of the New World. It was not at first so lucrative as the spices the discoverers of America had hoped to find, but it proved just as valuable. The Pilgrims were saved from starvation in their first dreary winter by discovering hidden caches of it in abandoned Indian clay pots and woven baskets. In Jamestown, too, famine-ridden settlers traded corn from the Indians and were nourished.

Because it was so central a part of the colonists' diet and because it was something unique to America it became a symbol of the new country, as much as any flag or anthem. John Adams served chaste puddings made of corn at diplomatic dinners; Joel Barlow wrote his "Hasty Pudding" to commemorate it. The full poem, which praises America's simplicity of manners, describes the growing of the corn, the husking ceremony, the mixing of the meal and the many delicious dishes to be prepared from it, particularly the queen of them all, a corn meal hasty pudding.

The first First Lady, like ours today, had a dual role: she was a patron of the arts and culture and a molder of the rough country's tastes and manners. Barlow dedicated his poem to Martha Washington in honor of her task. Her husband too has an indelible connection to this symbol of America: in the famous revolutionary song "Yankee Doodle" the singer relates how he has seen the men and boys of Washington's army lined up "as thick as hasty pudding."

Thee the soft nations round the warm Levant
Polanta call; the French of course, *Polante.*
E'en in thy native regions, how I blush
To hear the Pennsylvanians call thee *Mush!*
On Hudson's banks, while men of Belgic spawn
Insult and eat thee by the name *Suppawn.*
All spurious appelations, void of truth;
I've better known thee from my earliest youth:
Thy name is *Hasty Pudding!* thus my sire
Was wont to greet thee fuming from his fire;
And while he argued in thy just defense
With logic clear he thus explained the sense:
"In haste the boiling caldron, o'er the blaze,
Receives and cooks the ready powdered maize;
In haste 'tis served, and then in equal haste,
With cooling milk, we make the sweet repast.
No carving to be done, no knife to grate
The tender ear and wound the stony plate;
But the smooth spoon, just fitted to the lip,
And taught with art the yielding mass to dip,
By frequent journeys to the bowl well stored,
Performs the hasty honors of the board."

Such is thy name, significant and clear,
A name, a sound to every Yankee dear,
But most to me, whose heart and palate chaste
Preserve my pure, hereditary taste.

There are who strive to stamp with disrepute
The luscious food, because it feeds the brute;
In tropes of high-strained wit, while gaudy prigs
Compare thy nursling, man, to pampered pigs;
With sovereign scorn I treat the vulgar jest,
Nor fear to share thy bounties with the beast.
What though the generous cow gives me to quaff
The milk nutritious: am I then a calf?
Or can the genius of the noisy swine,
Though nursed on pudding, claim a kin to mine?
Sure the sweet song I fashion to thy praise,
Runs more melodious than the notes they raise.

My song, resounding in its grateful glee,
No merit claims: I praise myself in thee.
My father loved thee through his length of days!
For thee his fields were shaded o'er with maize;
From thee what health, what vigor he possessed,
Ten sturdy freemen from his loins attest;
Thy constellation ruled my natal morn,
And all my bones were made of Indian corn.
Delicious grain, whatever form it take,
To roast or boil, to smother or to bake,
In every dish 'tis welcome still to me
But most, my Hasty Pudding, most in thee.

Let the green succotash with thee contend;
Let beans and corn their sweetest juices blend;
Let butter drench them in its yellow tide,
And a long slice of bacon grace their side;
Not all the plate, how famed soe'er it be,
Can please my palate like a bowl of thee.
Some talk of hoecake, fair Virginia's pride!
Rich johnny cake this mouth has often tried;
Both please me well, their virtues much the same,

Alike their fabric, as allied their fame,
Except in dear New England, where the last
Receives a dash of pumpkin in the paste,
To give it sweetness and improve the taste.
But place them all before me, smoking hot,
The big, round dumpling, rolling from the pot;
The pudding of the bag, whose quivering breast,
With suet lined, leads on the Yankee feast;
The charlotte brown, within whose crusty sides
A belly soft the pulpy apple hides;
The yellow bread whose face like amber glows,
And all of Indian that the bakepan knows—
You tempt me not; my favorite greets my eyes,
To that loved bowl my spoon by instinct flies.

MENU:

Hasty pudding

Succotash

Hoecake

Dumpling from the pot

Apple charlotte

Yellow bread

The recipes for the corn meal dishes in Barlow's poem come from a variety of early American cookbooks. Amelia Simmons' 1796 American Cookery, *written the same year as "Hasty Pudding," has the distinction of being the oldest; Miss Leslie's* New Receipts for Cooking *is the most complete. But Mary Randolph's* Virginia Housewife *is the most delightful. The men of the Randolph family of Virginia were all engrossed in early American politics, and some of their interests seem to have rubbed off on Mary. "The government of a family bears a Lilliputian resemblance to the government of a nation," she wrote in 1824. "The contents of the Treasury must be known, and great care taken to keep the expenditures from being equal to the receipts. A regular system must be introduced into each department, which may be modified until matured, and then pass into inviolable law."*

HASTY PUDDING

FROM *The Virginia Housewife*, 1824, Mary Randolph

1 quart of corn meal
3 quarts of milk*
3 eggs

a gill (½ cup) of molasses
(4 teaspoons salt)

Mix 1 quart of corn meal with 3 quarts of milk (and add salt), take care it be not lumpy; add 3 eggs and 1 gill of molasses; it must be put on at sunrise, to eat at three o'clock; the great art in this pudding is tying the bag properly, at the meal swells very much. (It may be boiled in a lightly greased and tightly covered can or pudding mold as well.)

(*Serves about 16*)

* You may want to add more milk. Today's corn meal puddings are made with 4-6 quarts of liquid to every quart of meal.

SUCCOTASH

FROM *New Receipts for Cooking*, 1852, Miss Leslie

Although corn dishes had been cooked constantly on every American hearth long before Joel Barlow wrote "Hasty Pudding," the early cookbooks paid them only scant attention, giving but few corn and corn meal recipes. By the time Miss Leslie wrote, however, corn meal could no longer be ignored. Wisely, she included an entire lengthy section in New Receipts *called "The Indian Meal Book."*

1 cup young beans, broken into
    pieces, or 1 cup fresh lima
    beans
boiling (salted) water

6-9 ears of young Indian corn
1 teaspoon salt
butter, at least the size of an egg
pepper

String ¼ peck of young beans, and cut each bean into three pieces and do not split them. Have by you a pan of cold water, and throw the beans into it as you cut them. Have ready over the fire a pot or saucepan of boiling (salted) water (just to cover), and put in the beans, and boil them hard near 20 minutes. Afterwards take them up, and drain them well through a cullender. (Save about a cup of the liquid.) Take ½ dozen ears of young but full-grown Indian corn and cut the grains down from the cob. Mix together the corn and the beans, adding 1 very small teaspoonful of salt, and boil them (in reserved bean water) about 20 minutes.* Then take up the saccatash, drain it well through a sieve, put it into a deep dish, and while hot, mix in a large

* Today we would find these vegetables overcooked. When the corn and beans are mixed together, boil them only 4-5 minutes or until the liquid has evaporated.

piece of butter at least the size of an egg, add some pepper, and send it to table. It is generally eaten with salted or smoked meat.

(Serves 4-6)

Fresh lima beans are excellent cooked in this manner, with green corn. They must be boiled for ½ hour or more before they are cooked with the corn. Dried beans and dried corn will do very well for saccatash, but they must be soaked all night before boiling. The water poured on them for soaking should be hot.

HOECAKE

FROM *American Cookery,* 1796, Amelia Simmons

Hoecake got its name because corn meal cakes used to be baked right in an open fire on the flat of a hoe. Today, bake the cake in a hot oven for some 30-35 minutes on a well-greased skillet or in a baking pan.

1 pint of milk, scalded	salt
3 pints Indian corn meal	molasses (about ¼ cup)
½ pint flour	shortening (about 3 tablespoons)
cold water (about 3 pints)	

Scald 1 pint of milk and put to 3 pints of Indian meal, and ½ pint of flour (and the cold water)—bake before the fire. Or scald with milk ⅔ of the Indian meal, or wet ⅔ with boiling water; add salt, molasses and shortening, work up with cold water pretty stiff, and bake as above.

(Serves about 20)

DUMPLING FROM THE POT

FROM *New Receipts for Cooking,* 1852, Miss Leslie

Indian corn meal (about 1 cup)	flour (¼ cup to each cup of corn
1 saltspoon of salt to each quart	meal)
of meal (use ½ teaspoon to each	(2 eggs)
cup of meal)	(1 tablespoon melted butter)
boiling water sufficient to make	
a thick dough (about ½ cup)	

Sift some Indian meal into a pan; add about 1 salt-spoon of salt to each quart of meal; and scald it with sufficient boiling water to make a stiff dough. Pour in the water gradually, stirring as you pour. (Add eggs and butter for a richer dumpling.) When the dough becomes a stiff lump, divide it into equal portions; flour your hands, and make it into thick, flat dumplings about as large around as the top of a glass tumbler, or a breakfast cup. Dredge the dumplings on all sides with flour, put them into a pot of boiling water (if made sufficiently stiff they need not be tied in cloths) and keep them boiling hard till thoroughly done. Try them with a fork, which must come out quite clean, and with no clamminess sticking to it. They are an excellent appendage to salt pork or bacon, serving them up with meat; or they can be eaten afterwards with butter and molasses, or with milk, sweetened well with brown sugar, and flavoured with a little ground spice.

(Serves about 5)

APPLE CHARLOTTE

FROM *American Domestic Cookery*, 1823, Maria Eliza Rundell

thin slices of trimmed white
   bread (or cornbread) to cover
   and line a baking dish
butter (½ pound to a middling-
   sized dish)

apples, pared, cored and cut in
   thin slices
sugar
warm milk

Cut as many thin slices of white bread (or cornbread) as will cover the bottom and line the sides of a baking dish: but first rub it thick with butter (or pour in melted butter). Put apples in thin slices into the dish (on top of the bread), in layers, till full, strewing sugar between, and bits of butter.* In the meantime soak as many thin slices of bread as will cover the whole, in warm milk (lay them in the dish on top of the apples), over which lay a plate, and a weight to keep the bread close on the apples. Bake slowly 3 hours.* To a middling-sized dish use ½ pound of butter in the whole.

* If you precook the apples for about 5 minutes in just a touch of sugar and water, the baking time will be reduced to an hour or less.

YELLOW BREAD

FROM *The Virginia Housewife*, 1824, Mary Randolph

butter, the size of an egg (use
   about 2 tablespoons)
a pint of corn meal
2 eggs
some new milk (1 cup or enough
   to make a stiff dough)

1 spoonful of yeast (use 1
   package powdered, dissolved
   yeast)
(¾ teaspoon salt)
(2 tablespoons sugar)

Rub a piece of butter the size of an egg into a pint of corn meal, make a batter with 2 eggs and some new milk (and salt and sugar), add 1 spoonful of yeast, set it by the fire (or any warm place) an hour to rise, butter little pans (muffin pans), and bake it (25-30 minutes in a 425° oven).

(Makes 1 dozen muffins)

WASHINGTON IRVING

THE LEGEND OF SLEEPY HOLLOW
1820

Colonial schoolmasters worked hard at disciplining their charges, just as schoolteachers do today, but they had an added labor. They had to work equally hard at maintaining good relations with their pupils' families, for the little salaries schoolteachers were paid were hardly enough to keep a man in bread, let alone to fill his stomach, and the teachers found themselves dependent upon the community for decent

*meals. Ichabod Crane, a particularly funny hungry schoolmaster, man-
ages to make himself useful and charming among those neighbors who
keep well-stocked cupboards. He is always dreaming of food. One day
he visits Baltus Van Tassel's farm and sees its opulence. He imagines
every pig roasted and with an apple in its mouth, every pigeon tucked
into a comfortable pie, and all the ducks "pairing cozily in dishes, like
snug married couples, with a decent competency of onion sauce." From
that time forward Ichabod abandons all concerns except how to woo
and win Van Tassel's delectable daughter Katrina.*

*But Ichabod has a formidable rival in Brom Bones, a young wild
one of the community, a player of practical jokes. And pretty Katrina
leads both suitors on. In this scene she has invited them both to a
quilting party, a scene of fabulous abundance. For poor Ichabod the
charms of the buxom Dutch lasses fade before the ample charms of a
Dutch country tea table. The women are pretty but the food is more
glorious than any man could resist.*

As Ichabod jogged slowly on his way, his eye, ever open to every
symptom of culinary abundance, ranged with delight over the treasures of jolly autumn. On all sides he beheld vast stores of apples, some
hanging in oppressive opulence on the trees, some gathered into baskets
and barrels for the market, others heaped up in rich piles for the cider
press. Farther on he beheld great fields of Indian corn, with its golden
ears peeping from their leafy coverts and holding out the promise of
cakes and hasty pudding; and the yellow pumpkins lying beneath
them, turning up their fair round bellies to the sun, and giving ample
prospects of the most luxurious of pies; and anon he passed the fragrant
buckwheat fields, breathing the odor of the beehive, and as he beheld
them, soft anticipations stole over his mind of dainty slapjacks, well
buttered and garnished with honey or treacle, by the delicate little
dimpled hand of Katrina Van Tassel.

Thus feeding his mind with many sweet thoughts and "sugared
suppositions," he journeyed along the sides of a range of hills which
look out upon some of the goodliest scenes of the mighty Hudson. The
sun gradually wheeled his broad disk down into the west. The wide
bosom of the Tappan Zee lay motionless and glassy, excepting that
here and there a gentle undulation waved and prolonged the blue
shadow of the distant mountain. A few amber clouds floated in the
sky, without a breath of air to move them. The horizon was of a fine

golden tint, changing gradually into a pure apple green, and from that into the deep blue of the mid-heaven. A slanting ray lingered on the woody crests of the precipices that overhung some parts of the river, giving greater depth to the dark-gray and purple of their rocky sides. A sloop was loitering in the distance, dropping slowly down with the tide, her sail hanging uselessly against the mast; and as the reflection of the sky gleamed along the still water, it seemed as if the vessel was suspended in the air.

It was toward evening that Ichabod arrived at the castle of the Heer Van Tassel, which he found thronged with the pride and flower of the adjacent country. Old farmers, a spare leathern-faced race, in homespun coats and breeches, blue stockings, huge shoes, and magnificent pewter buckles. Their brisk withered little dames, in close-crimped caps, long-waisted short gowns, homespun petticoats, with scissors and pincushions and gay calico pockets hanging on the outside. Buxom lasses, almost as antiquated as their mothers, excepting where a straw hat, a fine ribbon, or perhaps a white frock gave symptoms of city innovation. The sons, in short square-skirted coats with rows of stupendous brass buttons, and their hair generally queued in the fashion of the times, especially if they could procure an eel skin for the purpose, it being esteemed throughout the country as a potent nourisher and strengthener of the hair.

Brom Bones, however, was the hero of the scene, having come to the gathering on his favorite steed Dare-devil, creature, like himself, full of mettle and mischief, and which no one but himself could manage. He was, in fact, noted for preferring vicious animals, given to all kinds of tricks, which kept the rider in constant risk of his neck, for he held a tractable well-broken horse as unworthy of a lad of spirit.

Fain would I pause to dwell upon the world of charms that burst upon the enraptured gaze of my hero as he entered the state parlor of Van Tassel's mansion. Not those of the bevy of buxom lasses, with their luxurious display of red and white, but the ample charms of a genuine Dutch country tea table, in the sumptuous time of autumn. Such heaped-up platters of cakes of various and almost indescribable kinds, known only to experienced Dutch housewives! There was the doughty doughnut, the tenderer oly koek, and the crisp and crumbling cruller; sweet cakes and shortcakes, ginger cakes and honey cakes, and the whole family of cakes. And then there were apple pies and peach pies and pumpkin pies; beside slices of ham and smoked beef; and moreover delectable dishes of preserved plums, and peaches, and pears, and quinces; not to mention broiled shad and roasted chickens; together with bowls of milk and cream, all mingled higgledy-piggledy, pretty much as I have enumerated them, with the motherly teapot sending up its clouds of vapor from the midst—Heaven bless the mark! I want breath and time to discuss this banquet as it deserves, and am too eager to get on with my story. Happily, Ichabod Crane was not in so great a hurry as his historian, but did ample justice to every dainty.

He was a kind and thankful creature whose heart dilated in proportion as his skin was filled with good cheer, and whose spirits rose with eating as some men's do with drink. He could not help, too, rolling his large eyes around him as he ate, and chuckling with the possibility that he might one day be lord of all this scene of almost unimaginable luxury and splendor. Then, he thought, how soon he'd turn his back upon the old schoolhouse; snap his fingers in the face of Hans Van Ripper, and every other niggardly patron, and kick any itinerant pedagogue out of doors that should dare to call him comrade!

Old Baltus Van Tassel moved about among his guests with a face dilated with content and good humor, round and jolly as the harvest moon. His hospitable attentions were brief, but expressive, being confined to a shake of the hand, a slap on the shoulder, a long laugh, and a pressing invitation to "fall to, and help themselves."

And now the sound of the music from the common room, or hall, summoned to the dance. The musician was an old grey-headed Negro, who had been the itinerant orchestra of the neighborhood for more than half a century. His instrument was as old and battered as himself. The greater part of the time he scraped on two or three strings, accompanying every movement of the bow with a motion of the head; bowing almost to the ground and stamping with his foot whenever a fresh couple were to start.

Ichabod prided himself upon his dancing as much as upon his vocal powers. Not a limb, not a fiber about him was idle; and to have seen his loosely hung frame in full motion, and clattering about the room, you would have thought Saint Vitus himself, that blessed patron of the dance, was figuring before you in person. He was the admiration of all Negroes, who, having gathered, of all ages and sizes, from the farm and the neighborhood, stood forming a pyramid of shining black faces at every door and window, gazing with delight at the scene, rolling their white eyeballs, and showing grinning rows of ivory from ear to ear. How could the flogger of urchins be otherwise than animated and joyous? The lady of his heart was his partner in the dance, and smiling graciously in reply to all his amorous oglings, while Brom Bones, sorely smitten with love and jealousy, sat brooding by himself in one corner.

MENU:

Doughnuts
(Oliebollen)

Oly koek

Crullers

Sweet cake
(Almond cake)

Ginger cake
(Ginger cookies)

Molasses cake
(Stroophoek)

Pumpkin pie

Dutch cooking has been sadly neglected. Very few collections of Dutch recipes exist, and virtually none describe the culinary successes of the early Dutch in America. Old Dutch Receipts, *from which a number of the recipes here are drawn, was such an attempt. In 1885 the Lafayette Reformed Church of Newark realized with alarm that the famous local Dutch heritage of hospitality and fine cooking was beginning to fade; the old people were dying, the young leaving the community or changing their way of life. To salvage some bit of the past before it entirely disappeared, the church put together* Old Dutch Receipts *by interviewing members of the community. But it was already a little too late. The recipes are given in kindly but grandmotherly style. Occasionally an author grows forgetful and leaves out important ingredients, or stops in the midst of the instructions to wander to another dish, or even entirely omits her instructions, believing youth uncaring and unkind.*

DOUGHNUTS

Oliebollen

FROM *Dine with the Dutch,* 1945, Mary Hartree

1 pound flour (4½ cups cake flour)
1 egg
1 ounce (dissolved) yeast
salt (¼-½ teaspoon)
(½–1 tablespoon sugar)

1 pint milk
½ pound raisins, currants and
   candied peel
sugar and ground cinnamon

(Dissolve yeast in some lukewarm milk.) Make a rather stiff batter from the flour, egg, yeast, salt (sugar) and 1 pint lukewarm milk. Add the washed dried fruits and let it rise for 1 hour. Then make the fat hot and with the help of 2 tablespoons let small balls of dough fall in the fat and fry for a few minutes till they are brown and done. Drip in rough brown paper and then roll through a mixture of sugar and ground cinnamon.

(Makes about 40)

OLY KOEK

FROM *Breakfast, Dinner and Tea,* 1859, Julia C. Andrews

1 pint raised bread dough
1 cup sugar
½ cup butter

spice to taste (cinnamon, nutmeg)
raisins
lard for frying

To 1 pint of raised bread dough, add 1 cup of sugar and ½ cup of butter, with spice to your taste. Work these last well into the dough and set it to rise. When it becomes light, and while the lard for frying them in is heating, roll out part of the dough, cut it into squares 1½ inch in size, lay 2 or 3 raisins in each and close the dough over them to prevent any opening. Before frying, try the heat of the lard first with a small bit of dough; if it rises immediately to the surface, the lard is sufficiently hot; then drop in your balls.

(Makes about 20)

CRULLERS

FROM *Old Dutch Receipts,* 1885

1 egg (preferably 4 eggs)
1½ cups sugar
butter, the size of an egg (about
   ½ cup
1 cup sweet milk
flour, enough to roll (about
   6 cups)

2 teaspoons cream of tartar
1 teaspoon soda
(shortening for frying)
(confectioner's sugar)

(Beat the eggs. Slowly add sifted sugar. Blend. Add butter and milk. Sift together flour, cream of tartar and soda. Stir into egg mixture. Chill. Roll out the dough to about ¼-inch thickness, cut it into strips and twist sets of 2 strips together into circles.) Fry in boiling lard (until brown, about 3-4 minutes. Drain and sprinkle with confectioner's sugar.)

(Makes about 40)

SWEET CAKE

Almond Cake

FROM *Old Dutch Receipts,* 1885

3 cups raisins
½ pound citron (or candied
   orange or lemon peel)
½ pound chopped almonds
1 pound butter
2 cups sugar
9 eggs

4 cups flour
1 nutmeg (about 1 tablespoon)
(1 teaspoon salt)
(1 teaspoon baking powder)
1 small wineglass brandy, curdled
   with a little cream (¼ cup
   brandy, ¼ cup cream)

(Dredge raisins, citron and nuts in a little flour. This will keep the fruits and nuts from settling to the bottom of the pan. Cream butter and sugar. Add eggs, one at a time, beating well after each addition. Sift dry ingredients. Add to creamed mixture alternating with brandy. Add a little more brandy or cream if batter seems too dry. Mix in fruits and nuts. This amount of batter makes two good-sized cakes. Pour batter into two lightly greased 1½-quart baking tins and bake at 325° for 1 hour and 20 minutes.)

GINGER CAKE

Ginger Cookies

FROM *Old Dutch Receipts, 1885*

1 cupful of sugar	1 teaspoon soda
1 cupful of butter (use ¾ cup)	1 tablespoon ginger
1 cupful of molasses	(flour, about 4 cups)
½ cupful of prepared coffee	(1 teaspoon salt)
(½-¾ cup)	(1-2 eggs)

(Cream shortening and sugar. Add eggs and molasses, beat well. Sift dry ingredients. Add to creamed mixture alternating with coffee. Drop by spoonfuls onto greased cookie sheet. Bake at 350° 15 minutes.)

(Makes 2-3 dozen cookies)

MOLASSES CAKE

Stroophoek

FROM *Old Holland Dishes, 1936, Mrs. J. B. Hornbeck*

Although Washington Irving describes honey cake on the Van Tassel's table, the Dutch cookbooks themselves speak only of molasses cakes. Stroophoek, writes Mrs. Hornbeck, is a recipe over one hundred years old. "The dough will be almost liquid but the result perfect."

2 cups boiling water	2¾ cups flour
2½ tablespoons lard	¼ teaspoon salt
1½ teaspoons soda	spices (½-1 teaspoon each of
1 cup light brown sugar	allspice, cinnamon and
½ cup molasses	powdered cloves)
	raisins (1 cup)

Pour boiling water over lard and soda. (Sift the brown sugar and add. Stir in the molasses. Sift together flour, salt and spices.) Put washed raisins in flour. (Add to molasses mixture and pour into cake pan.) When (cake) shrinks from the sides of the tin it is done. It takes about 30 to 40 minutes in a (375°) oven.

PUMPKIN PIE

FROM *Old Dutch Receipts*, 1885

medium-sized pumpkin, pared,
    cut in pieces and boiled
(5 eggs)
6 butter crackers, rolled fine
butter, the size of an egg
1 tablespoon ginger

1 tablespoon salt
1 tablespoon nutmeg
2 large cups (brown) sugar
1½ quarts milk
(piecrust)

A medium-sized pumpkin, pared, cut in small pieces and boiled. When done, take out and strain through a cullender. (Add eggs one at a time when pumpkin is cool.) Six butter crackers, rolled fine, and a piece of butter the size of an egg should be put in while the pumpkin is hot. Add ginger, salt, nutmeg, sugar and milk. (Pour mixture into a pie crust.) Bake in a moderate (425°) oven ¾ hour.

HERMAN MELVILLE

MOBY DICK

1851

Ishmael has decided to "sail about a little and see the watery part of the world." Arriving in New Bedford, he seeks a place to stay and lands at the overcrowded inn of Peter Coffin. There the only bed available is one he must share with the savage harpooner, Queequeg, who jumps under their mutual blanket with a tomahawk between his teeth. But the tomahawk turns out to be only a pipe, and Queequeg turns out to be the most noble of savages. Ishmael and Queequeg decide to cast their lots together. Ishmael clings to Queequeg and Queequeg, expressing his own version of the White Man's Burden, says, "It's a mutual joint-stock world in all meridians. We cannibals must help these Christians."

Although ultimately Ishmael will be the only survivor of Captain Ahab's terrible pursuit of the white whale, Moby Dick, in this scene he and Queequeg, still happy, enjoy an ecstatic fishy meal that captures the spirit of the robust New England of whaling days.

It was quite late in the evening when the little Moss came snugly to anchor, and Queequeg and I went ashore; so we could attend to no business that day, at least none but a supper and a bed. The landlord of the Spouter-Inn had recommended us to his cousin Hosea Hussey of the Try Pots, whom he asserted to be the proprietor of one of the best hotels in all Nantucket, and moreover he had assured us that Cousin Hosea, as he called him, was famous for his chowders. In short, he plainly hinted that we could not possibly do better than try pot-luck at the Try Pots. But the directions he had given us about keeping a yellow warehouse on our starboard hand till we opened a white church to the larboard, and then keeping that on the larboard hand till we made a corner three points to the starboard, and that done, then ask the first man we met where the place was; these crooked directions of his very much puzzled us at first, especially as, at the outset, Queequeg insisted that the yellow warehouse—our first point of departure—must be left on the larboard hand, whereas I had understood Peter Coffin to say it was on the starboard. However, by dint of beating about a little in the dark, and now and then knocking up a peaceful inhabitant to inquire the way, we at last come to something which there was no mistaking.

Two enormous wooden pots painted black, and suspended by asses ears, swung from the cross-trees of an old top-mast, planted in front of an old doorway. The horns of the cross-trees were sawed off on the other side, so that this old top-mast looked not a little like a gallows. Perhaps I was over sensitive to such impressions at the time, but I could not help staring at this gallows with a vague misgiving. A sort of crick was in my neck as I gazed up to the two remaining horns; yes, *two* of them, one for Queequeg, and one for me. It's ominous, thinks I. A Coffin my Innkeeper upon landing in my first whaling port; tombstones staring at me in the whalemen's chapel, and here a gallows! and a pair of prodigious black pots too! Are these last throwing out oblique hints touching Tophet?

I was called from these reflections by the sight of a freckled woman with yellow hair and a yellow gown, standing in the porch of the inn, under a dull red lamp swinging there, that looked much like an injured eye, and carrying on a brisk scolding with a man in a purple woollen shirt.

"Get along with ye," said she to the man, "or I'll be combing ye!"

"Come on, Queequeg," said I, "all right. There's Mrs. Hussey."

And so it turned out; Mr. Hosea Hussey being from home, but leaving Mrs. Hussey entirely competent to attend to all his affairs. Upon making known our desires for a supper and a bed, Mrs. Hussey, postponing further scolding for the present, ushered us into a little room, and seating us at a table spread with the relics of a recently concluded repast, turned round to us and said—"Clam or Cod?"

"What's that about Cods, ma'am?" said I, with politeness.

"Clam or Cod?" she repeated.

"A clam for supper? a cold clam; is *that* what you mean, Mrs. Hussey?" says I! "but that's a rather cold and clammy reception in the winter time, ain't it, Mrs. Hussey?"

But being in a great hurry to resume scolding the man in the purple shirt who was waiting for it in the entry, and seeming to hear nothing but the word "clam," Mrs. Hussey hurried towards an open door leading to the kitchen, and bawling out "clam for two," disappeared.

"Queequeg," said I, "do you think that we can make a supper for us both on one clam?"

However, a warm savory steam from the kitchen served to belie the apparently cheerless prospect before us. But when that smoking chowder came in, the mystery was delightfully explained. Oh! sweet friends, hearken to me. It was made of small juicy clams, scarcely bigger than hazel nuts, mixed with pounded ship biscuits, and salted pork cut up into little flakes! the whole enriched with butter, and plentifully seasoned with pepper and salt. Our appetites being sharpened by the frosty voyage, and in particular, Queequeg seeing his favorite fishing food before him, and the chowder being surpassingly excellent, we despatched it with great expedition: when leaning back a moment and bethinking me of Mrs. Hussey's clam and cod announcement, I thought I would try a little experiment. Stepping to the kitchen door, I uttered the word "cod" with great emphasis, and resumed my seat. In a few moments the savoury steam came forth again, but with a different flavor, and in good time a fine cod-chowder was placed before us.

We resumed business; and while plying our spoons in the bowl, thinks I to myself, I wonder now if this here has any effect on the head? What's that stultifying saying about chowder-headed people? "But look, Queequeg, ain't that a live eel in your bowl? Where's your harpoon?"

Fishiest of all fishy places was the Try Pots, which well deserved its name; for the pots there were always boiling chowders. Chowder for breakfast, and chowder for dinner, and chowder for supper, till you began to look for fish-bones coming through your clothes. The area before the house was paved with clam-shells. Mrs. Hussey wore a polished necklace of codfish vertebra; and Hosea Hussey had his account books bound in superior old shark-skin. There was a fishy flavor to the milk, too, which I could not at all account for, till one morning happening to take a stroll along the beach among some fishermen's boats, I saw Hosea's brindled cow feeding on fish remnants, and marching along the sand with each foot in a cod's decapitated head, looking very slipshod, I assure ye.

Supper concluded, we received a lamp, and directions from Mrs. Hussey concerning the nearest way to bed; but, as Queequeg was about to precede me up the stairs, the lady reached forth her arm, and demanded his harpoon; she allowed no harpoon in her chambers. "Why not?" said I; "every true whaleman sleeps with his harpoon—but why not?" "Because it's dangerous," says she. "Ever since young Stiggs coming from that unfort'nt v'y'ge of his, when he was gone four years and a half, with only three barrels of *ile*, was found dead in my first floor back, with his harpoon in his side; ever since then I allow no boarders to take sich dangerous weepons in their rooms at night. So, Mr. Queequeg" (for she had learned his name), "I will just take this here iron, and keep it for you till morning. But the chowder; clam or cod to-morrow for breakfast, men?"

"Both," says I; "and let's have a couple of smoked herring by way of variety."

MENU:

Clam chowder

à la Miss Beecher
à la Mrs. Chadwick

Cod chowder

Several New England housewives of Melville's time provided the chowder recipes. The most interesting of them is Catharine Beecher, 1846 author of Miss Beecher's Domestic Receipt-Book. *Catharine was the sister of Harriet Beecher Stowe, and like Harriet she was a crusader. A staunch believer in female equality, she devoted her life to educating and enlightening women. She was the founder of several women's schools and a radical proponent of the theory that women should be taught how to be housewives, that learning to be a housewife was as much a subject of honor as any other study.*

But Catharine had one minor flaw. She herself was a rather crude organizer, and on at least one occasion it pushed her into making a slur on humanity. In a chapter in her book headed, "Women Should Know How to Take Care of Domestic Animals," Miss Beecher covers some of the following subjects:

> *Care of a horse*
> *Care of a cow*
> *Poultry*
> *Comfort of guests*

CLAM CHOWDER

à la Miss Beecher

FROM *Miss Beecher's Domestic Receipt Book*, 1846, Catharine Beecher

Most New England cookbooks of the period did not include milk in their clam chowders. Miss Beecher's book is one of the few that did and, while this makes the recipe into what we today think of as a New England chowder, an equally good chowder, without milk, is the one that follows, by Mrs. Chadwick, who includes the salt pork and the crackers which Melville praises.

1 peck of unshucked clams (or
  1 quart shucked clams or a
  20-ounce can minced clams)
1 pint of water (or the juice of
  the canned clams and enough
  added water to equal 1 pint of
  liquid)

1 quart of milk
2½ tablespoons flour
3 tablespoons butter
pepper (cayenne)
mace
other spices to taste

Wash 1 peck of clams and boil them in 1 pint of water, till those on the top open and they come out easily. Strain the liquor (to obtain 1 pint) and add (this liquor and) 1 quart of milk (to the clams). When it boils, thicken with 2½ spoonfuls of flour, worked into 3 of butter, with pepper, mace and other spices to taste. It is better without spice.*

(Serves 6-8)

* No, it isn't. A good chowder should tingle the tongue. Use cayenne pepper and sprinkle minced chives on each bowl of soup before serving.

CLAM CHOWDER

à la Mrs. Chadwick

FROM *Home Cookery*, 1853, Mrs. J. Chadwick

1 quart shucked clams (or a
    20-ounce can minced clams)
finely diced salt pork (¼ cup)
2 onions, chopped
4-5 cups water (or the juice of
    the canned clams and enough
    water to equal 4-5 cups liquid)

flour (about 2 tablespoons)
½ teaspoon pepper
5 potatoes, sliced
hard crackers (use 5-6 pilot
    crackers)
(1 quart scalded milk)*
(2 tablespoons butter)*

After the clams are picked out, fry the pork, and cut up 2 onions (which fry in the pork fat. Drain and chop the clams, separating the hard and the soft parts, and save the water you drain off). Put in some of the clams (hard parts only), then some onions and pepper; pare and slice the potatoes, and put a layer of them and then some of the pork, and some hard crackers split, then more clams (still only hard parts), and so on, until all is in, shaking in flour each time. Then put in the water you drained the clams with, and you will have a delicious chowder (after it has cooked, covered, for 35-40 minutes on a low flame).

(Serves 6-8)

* To make this into a modern New England chowder, add 1 quart of milk and 2 table-spoons butter when the potatoes are nearly, but not quite, soft. At the same time, add the soft parts of the clams. Heat the chowder to boiling, taste and add salt and more pepper if needed, and serve.

COD CHOWDER

FROM *The Skillful Housewife's Book,* 1852, Mrs. L. Abell

¼ cup diced salt pork
1 pound codfish, sliced
crackers
1 onion, sliced
3½ cups water

2 cups potatoes, sliced
salt and pepper
flour (about 2 tablespoons)
optional: sliced lemon, clams

Lay salt pork in the bottom of the pot, let it cook slowly that it may not burn; when done brown, take it out and lay in fish cut in lengthwise slices, then a layer of crackers, sliced onions, and very thin sliced potatoes, with some of the pork that was fried, and then a layer of fish again and so on. Strew a little salt and pepper over each layer; over the whole pour flour and water well stirred up, enough to come up even with what you have in the pot.

A sliced lemon adds to the flavor. A few clams improve it. Let it be so covered that the steam cannot escape. It must not be opened until cooked, to see if it is well seasoned. (Let it cook about 20-30 minutes.)

(Makes 5 servings)

LAFCADIO HEARN

THE LAST
OF THE VOUDOOS
1885

Lafcadio Hearn was a tormented man. Abandoned by his parents when he was a boy, brought up by an aunt who forced upon him a religion he disliked, penniless throughout most of his youth, blinded through a careless and horrible childhood accident, and convinced, always, that he himself was not quite right enough, quite good enough for the rest of society, he developed a sympathy for all the wounded in life. He wrote compellingly of the lowly and the poor and especially of the Negroes of nineteenth-century New Orleans and the West Indies.

In "The Last of the Voudoos" he describes Jean Montanet, "this possible son of a Bambara prince," a legendary figure out of America's past. Montanet, despite being a slave, despite being unlettered and superstitious, yet retains his princely dignity throughout his life. And, like a prince, even when he is down and out he distributes largesse in the form of food to the less fortunate of his neighborhood.

In the death of Jean Montanet, at the age of nearly a hundred years, New Orleans lost, at the end of August, the most extraordinary African character that ever gained celebrity within her limits. Jean Montanet, or Jean La Ficelle, or Jean Latanié, or Jean Racine, or Jean Grisgris, or Jean Macaque, or Jean Bayou, or "Voudoo John," or "Bayou John," or "Doctor John" might well have been termed "The Last of the Voudoos"; not that the strange association with which he was affiliated has ceased to exist with his death, but that he was the last really important figure of a long line of wizards or witches whose African titles were recognized, and who exercised an influence over the colored population. Swarthy occultists will doubtless continue to elect their "queens" and high-priests through years to come, but the influence of the public school is gradually dissipating all faith in witchcraft, and no black hierophant now remains capable of manifesting such mystic knowledge or of inspiring such respect as Voudoo John exhibited and compelled. There will never be another "Rose," another "Marie," much less another Jean Bayou.

It may reasonably be doubted whether any Negro of African birth who lived in the South had a more extraordinary career than that of Jean Montanet. He was a native of Senegal, and claimed to have been a prince's son, in proof of which he was wont to call attention to a number of parallel scars on his cheek, extending in curves from the edge of either temple to the corner of the lips. This fact seems to me partly confirmatory of his statement, as Berenger-Feraud dwells at some length on the fact that the Bambaras, who are probably the finest Negro race in Senegal, all wear such disfigurations. The scars are made by gashing the cheeks during infancy, and are considered a sign of race. Three parallel scars mark the freemen of the tribe; four distinguish their captives or slaves. Now Jean's face had, I am told, three scars, which would prove him a free-born Bambara, or at least a member of some free tribe allied to the Bambaras, and living upon their territory. At all events, Jean possessed physical characteristics answering to those by which the French ethnologists in Senegal distinguish the Bambaras. He was of middle height, very strongly built, with broad shoulders, well-developed muscles, an inky black skin, retreating forehead, small bright eyes, a very flat nose, and a wooly beard, gray only during the last few years of his long life. He had a resonant voice and a very authoritative manner.

At an early age he was kidnapped by Spanish slavers, who sold him at some Spanish port, whence he was ultimately shipped to Cuba. His West Indian master taught him to be an excellent cook, ultimately became attached to him, and made him a present of his freedom. Jean soon afterward engaged on some Spanish vessel as ship's cook, and in the exercise of this calling voyaged considerably in both hemispheres. Finally tiring of the sea, he left his ship at New Orleans, and began life on shore as a cotton-roller. His physical strength gave him considerable advantage above his fellow-blacks; and his employers also discovered that he wielded some peculiar occult influence over the Negroes, which made him valuable as an overseer or gang leader. Jean, in short, possessed the mysterious obi power, the existence of which has been recognized in most slave-holding communities, and with which many a West Indian planter has been compelled by force of circumstances to effect a compromise. Accordingly Jean was permitted many liberties which other blacks, although free, would never have presumed to take. Soon it became rumored that he was a seer of no small powers, and that he could tell the future by the marks upon bales of cotton. I have never been able to learn the details of this queer method of telling fortunes; but Jean became so successful in the exercise of it that thousands of colored people flocked to him for predictions and counsel, and even white people, moved by curiosity or by doubt, paid him to prophesy for them. Finally he became wealthy enough to abandon the levee and purchase a large tract of property on the Bayou Road, where he built a house. His land extended from Prieur Street on the Bayou Road as far as Roman, covering the greater portion of an extensive square, now well built up. In those days it was a marshy green plain, with a few scattered habitations.

At his new home Jean continued the practice of fortune-telling, but combined it with the profession of Creole medicine, and of arts still more mysterious. By and by his reputation became so great that he was able to demand and obtain immense fees. People of both races and both sexes thronged to see him—many coming even from faraway Creole towns in the parishes, and well-dressed women, closely veiled, often knocked at his door. Parties paid from ten to twenty dollars for advice, for herb medicines, for recipes to make the hair grow, for cataplasms supposed to possess mysterious virtues, but really made with scraps of shoe-leather triturated into paste, for advice what ticket to buy in the Havana Lottery, for aid to recover stolen goods, for love powers, for counsel in family troubles, for charms by which to obtain revenge upon an enemy. Once Jean received a fee of fifty dollars for a potion. "It was water," he said to a Creole confidant, "with some common herbs boiled in it. I hurt nobody; but if folks want to give me fifty dollars, I take the fifty dollars every time!" His office furniture consisted of a table, a chair, a picture of the Virgin Mary, an elephant's tusk, some shells which he said were African shells and enabled him to read the future, and a pack of cards in each of which a small hole had been burned. About his person he always carried two small bones wrapped around with a black string, which bones he really appeared to revere as fetiches. Wax candles were burned during his performances; and as he bought a whole box of them every few days during "flush times," one can imagine how large the number of his clients must have been. They poured money into his hands so generously that he became worth at least $50,000!

Then, indeed, did this possible son of a Bambara prince begin to live more grandly than any black potentate of Senegal. He had his carriage and pair, worthy of a planter, and his blooded saddle-horse, which he rode well, attired in a gaudy Spanish costume, and seated upon an elaborately decorated Mexican saddle. At home, where he ate and drank only the best—scorning claret worth less than a dollar the *litre*—he continued to find his simple furniture good enough for him; but he had at least fifteen wives—a harem worthy of Boubakar-Segou. White folks might have called them by a less honorific name, but Jean declared them his legitimate spouses according to African ritual. One of the curious features in modern slavery was the ownership of blacks by freedmen of their own color, and these Negro slave-holders were usually savage and merciless masters. Jean was not; but it was by right of slave purchase that he obtained most of his wives, who bore him children in great multitude. Finally he managed to woo and win a white woman of the lowest class, who might have been, after a fashion, the Sultana-Validé of this Seraglio. On grand occasions Jean used to distribute largess among the colored population of his neighborhood in the shape of food—bowls of *gombo* or dishes of *Jimbalaya*. He did it for popularity's sake in those days, perhaps; but in after-years, during the great epidemics, he did it for charity, even when so much reduced in circumstances that he was himself obliged to cook the food to be given away.

But Jean's greatness did not fail to entail certain cares. He did not know what to do with his money. He had no faith in banks, and had seen too much of the darker side of life to have much faith in human nature. For many years he kept his money underground, burying or taking it up at night only, occasionally concealing large sums so well that he could never find them again himself; and now, after many years, people still believe there are treasures entombed somewhere in the neighborhood of Prieur Street and Bayou Road. All business negotiations of a serious character caused him much worry, and as he found many willing to take advantage of his ignorance, he probably felt small remorse for certain questionable actions of his own. He was notoriously bad pay, and part of his property was seized at last to cover a debt. Then, in an evil hour, he asked a man without scruples to teach him how to write, believing that financial misfortunes were mostly due to ignorance of the alphabet. After he had learned to write his name, he was innocent enough one day to place his signature by request at the bottom of a blank sheet of paper, and, lo! his real estate passed from his possession in some horribly mysterious way. Still he had some money left, and made heroic efforts to retrieve his fortunes. He bought other property, and he invested desperately in lottery tickets. The lottery craze finally came upon him, and had far more to do with his ultimate ruin than his losses in the grocery, the shoemaker's shop, and other establishments into which he had put several thousand dollars as the silent partner of people who cheated him. He might certainly have continued to make a good living, since people still sent for him to cure them with his herbs, or went to see him to have their fortunes told; but all his earnings were wasted in tempting fortune. After a score of seizures and a long succession of evictions, he was at last obliged to seek hospitality from some of his numerous children; and of all he had once owned nothing remained to him but his African shells, his elephant's tusk, and the sewing-machine table that had served him to tell fortunes and to burn wax candles upon. Even these, I think, were attached a day or two before his death, which occurred at the house of his daughter by the white wife, an intelligent mulatto with many children of her own.

Jean's ideas of religion were primitive in the extreme. The conversion of the chief tribes of Senegal to Islam occurred in recent years, and it is probable that at the time he was captured by slavers his people were still in a condition little above gross fetichism. If during his years of servitude in a Catholic colony he had imbibed some notions of Romish Christianity, it is certain at least that the Christian ideas were always subordinated to the African—just as the image of the Virgin Mary was used by him merely as an auxiliary fetich in his witchcraft, and was considered as possessing much less power than the "elephant's toof." He was in many respects a humbug; but he may have sincerely believed in the efficacy of certain superstitious rites of his own. He stated that he had a Master whom he was bound to obey; that he could read the will of this Master in the twinkling of the stars; and often of clear nights the neighbors used to watch him standing alone at some street corner staring at the welkin, pulling his wooly beard, and talking in an unknown language to some imaginary being. Whenever Jean indulged in this freak, people knew that he needed money badly, and would probably try to borrow a dollar or two from someone in the vicinity next day.

Testimony to his remarkable skill in the use of herbs could be gathered from nearly every one now living who became well acquainted with him. During the epidemic of 1878, which uprooted the old belief in the total immunity of Negroes and colored people from yellow fever, two of Jean's children were "taken down." "I have no money," he said, "but I can cure my children," which he proceeded to do with the aid of some weeds plucked from the edge of the Prieur Street gutters. One of the herbs, I am told, was what our Creoles call the "parasol." "The children were playing on the *banquette* next day," said my informant.

Montanet, even in the most unlucky part of his career, retained the superstitious reverence of colored people in all parts of the city. When he made his appearance even on the American side of Canal Street to doctor some sick person, there was always much subdued excitement among the colored folks, who whispered and stared a great deal, but were careful not to raise their voices when they said, "Dar's Hoodoo John!" That an unlettered African slave should have been able to achieve what Jean Bayou achieved in a civilized city, and to earn the wealth and the reputation that he enjoyed during many years of his life, might be cited as a singular evidence of modern popular credulity, but it is also proof that Jean was not an ordinary man in point of natural intelligence.

MENU:
Jimbalaya
Gombo

The recipes for the dishes mentioned in Hearn's story come from his own 1885 cookbook, La Cuisine Creole. *Throughout his life Hearn took a great interest in the conviviality of eating. He often wrote about food and for a short while even tried, unsuccessfully, to run a restaurant. Years later this old interest flowered into* La Cusine Creole, *an attempt at conveying the cosmopolitan nature of New Orleans with its unique blend of American, French, Spanish, Italian, West Indian and Mexican cooking.*

JIMBALAYA

FROM *La Cuisine Creole*, 1885, Lafcadio Hearn

a fowl	1 slice cooked, minced ham
1 cup raw rice	salt and pepper
(1 onion)	(¼ teaspon powdered sassafras or
(1-2 stalks celery)	filée powder)
(1-1½ quarts water)	

Cut up and stew a fowl (with an onion and 1-2 stalks celery in 1-1½ quarts water); when half done, add 1 cup of raw rice, 1 slice of ham minced, and pepper and salt; let all cook together (covered) until the rice swells and absorbs all the gravy of the stewed chicken, but it must not be allowed to get hard or dry. (Now add the powdered sassafras or filée powder.) Serve in a deep dish. Southern children are very fond of this; it is said to be an Indian dish, and very wholesome as well as palatable; it can be made of many things.

GOMBO

FROM *La Cuisine Creole*, 1885, Lafcadio Hearn

2 pounds cold roasted chicken,
  turkey, game or any other
  meat°
salt and pepper
1 gallon boiling water to every
  2 pounds of meat and bones°
½ pound of ham, or less of
  (Canadian) bacon

1 quart sliced okra or a coffee-
  cupful (use 1½ tablespoons)
  of gombo filée, for every
  gallon of water
optional: oysters, crabs or
  shrimp; tomatoes, green corn,
  other vegetables

This is a most excellent form of soup, and is an economical way of using up the remains of any cold roasted chicken, turkey, game or other meats.° Cut up and season the chicken, meat or other material to make the soup; fry to a light brown in a pot, and add boiling water in proportion to your meat. Two pounds of meat or chicken (bones and all), with ½ pound of ham, or less of breakfast (Canadian) bacon, will flavor a gallon of soup, which, when boiled down, will make gombo for 6 people. When the boiling water is added to the meat, let it simmer for at least 2 hours. Take the large bones from the pot, and add okra or a preparation of dried and pounded sassafras leaves, called filée. This makes the difference in gombo. For gombo for 6 people use 1 quart of sliced okra; if filée be used, put in a coffee-cupful. Either gives the smoothness so desirable in this soup. Oysters, crabs and shrimp may be added when in season, as all improve the gombo. Never strain gombo. Add green corn, tomatoes, etc., if desired. Serve gombo with plain boiled rice.

(Serves 6 or more)

° Lafcadio Hearn's gombo is a poor man's soup. While it is true, as he says, that two pounds of meat will flavor a gallon of liquid, a more nourishing soup should contain less water per pound of meat. The following hints are offered to adapt this recipe to more modern gombos: 1) use either leftovers or an uncooked chicken. 2) simmer until meat no longer adheres to bones. 3) add only 4-6 cups of water to every two pounds of meat and bones. 4) add the optional items and the okra when the meat is soft; a cup of okra will be sufficient for every quart and a half of water; if you use gombo filée, add it at the very end and do not boil. 5) cook covered until the vegetables are tender, and serve.

THEODORE DREISER

SISTER CARRIE
1900

When Sister Carrie leaves her small town life in Columbia City to come live with her sister Minnie in Chicago she is only eighteen, timid and innocent and filled with illusions. Unaware of the difficulties of advancement in a city as large and inhumane as turn-of-the-century Chicago, Carrie thinks that merely having a job in so fine a city, even a four dollars and fifty cents a week job, will open to her a world of beauty

*and opulence. But when she does find a job—as a machine operator—
it opens nothing. And when she grows sick and loses her job, and can
find no other, her nebulous longings increase.*

*Hungry and cold, Carrie one day runs into Drouet, a salesman she
met on the train coming to Chicago. Drouet buys her the meal in this
scene, and the meal starts Carrie on the path away from her timidity,
and innocence. She will live with Drouet, she will then live with
Drouet's friend Hurstwood, she will achieve success on the stage, but
her life will still feel empty to her, still be filled with nebulous longings
and unfulfilled dreams. For nothing of reality that ever touches Carrie
has for her the vibrancy of her dreams.*

*The meal itself, while it is one of the most expensive meals on the
menu, is plain, hardly the kind of glamorous meal with which a French
Sister Carrie could have been seduced. Yet it is the kind of unadorned
grass-roots fare that Americans, men and women, innocent and sophisticated alike, are all familiar with and all enjoy eating.*

There came a day when the first premonitory blast of winter swept over
the city. It scudded the fleecy clouds in the heavens, trailed long, thin
streamers of smoke from the tall stacks, and raced about the streets and
corners in sharp and sudden puffs. Carrie now felt the problem of
winter clothes. What was she to do? She had no winter jacket, no hat,
no shoes. It was difficult to speak to Minnie about this, but at last she
summoned the courage.

"I don't know what I'm going to do about clothes," she said one
evening when they were together. "I need a hat."

Minnie looked serious.

"Why don't you keep part of your money and buy yourself one?"
she suggested, worried over the situation which the withholding of
Carrie's money would create.

"I'd like to for a week or so, if you don't mind," ventured Carrie.

"Could you pay two dollars?" asked Minnie.

Carrie readily acquiesced, glad to escape the trying situation, and
liberal now that she saw a way out. She was elated and began figuring
at once. She needed a hat first of all. How Minnie explained to Hanson
she never knew. He said nothing at all, but there were thoughts in the
air which left disagreeable impressions.

The new arrangement might have worked if sickness had not inter-
vened. It blew up cold after a rain one afternoon when Carrie was still

without jacket. She came out of the warm shop at six and shivered as the wind struck her. In the morning she was sneezing, and going down town made it worse. That day her bones ached and she felt light-headed. Toward evening she felt very ill, and when she reached home was not hungry. Minnie noticed her drooping actions and asked her about herself.

"I don't know," said Carrie. "I feel real bad."

She hung about the stove, suffered a chattering chill, and went to bed sick. The next morning she was thoroughly feverish.

Minnie was truly distressed at this, but maintained a kindly demeanour. Hanson said perhaps she had better go back home for a while. When she got up after three days, it was taken for granted that her position was lost. The winter was near at hand, she had no clothes, and now she was out of work.

"I don't know," said Carrie; "I'll go down Monday and see if I can't get something."

If anything, her efforts were more poorly rewarded on this trial than the last. Her clothes were nothing suitable for fall wearing. Her last money she had spent for a hat. For three days she wandered about, utterly dispirited. The attitude of the flat was fast becoming unbearable. She hated to think of going back there each evening. Hanson was so cold. She knew it could not last much longer. Shortly she would have to give up and go home.

On the fourth day she was down town all day, having borrowed ten cents for lunch from Minnie. She had applied in the cheapest kind of places without success. She even answered for a waitress in a small restaurant where she saw a card in the window, but they wanted an experienced girl. She moved through the thick throng of strangers, utterly subdued in spirit. Suddenly a hand pulled her arm and turned her about.

"Well, well!" said a voice. In the first glance she beheld Drouet. He was not only rosy-cheeked, but radiant. He was the essence of sunshine and good-humour. "Why, how are you, Carrie?" he said. "You're a daisy. Where have you been?"

Carrie smiled under his irresistible flood of geniality.

"I've been out home," she said.

"Well," he said, "I saw you across the street there. I thought it was you. I was just coming out to your place. How are you, anyhow?"

"I'm all right," said Carrie, smiling.

Drouet looked her over and saw something different.

"Well," he said, "I want to talk to you. You're not going anywhere in particular, are you?"

"Not just now," said Carrie.

"Let's go up here and have something to eat. George! but I'm glad to see you again."

She felt so relieved in his radiant presence, so much looked after and cared for, that she assented gladly, though with the slightest air of holding back.

"Well," he said, as he took her arm and there was an exuberance of good-fellowship in the word which fairly warmed the cockles of her heart.

They went through Monroe Street to the old Windsor dining-room, which was then a large, comfortable place, with an excellent cuisine and substantial service. Drouet selected a table close by the window, where the busy rout of the street could be seen. He loved the changing panorama of the street—to see and be seen as he dined.

"Now," he said, getting Carrie and himself comfortably settled, "what will you have?"

Carrie looked over the large bill of fare which the waiter handed her without really considering it. She was very hungry, and the things she saw there awakened her desires, but the high prices held her attention. "Half broiled spring chicken—seventy-five. Sirloin steak with mushrooms—one twenty-five." She had dimly heard of these things, but it seemed strange to be called to order from the list.

"I'll fix this," exclaimed Drouet. "Sst! waiter."

That officer of the board, a full-chested, round-faced negro, approached, and inclined his ear.

"Sirloin with mushrooms," said Drouet. "Stuffed tomatoes."

"Yassah," assented the negro, nodding his head.

"Hashed brown potatoes."

"Yassah."

"Asparagus."

"And a pot of coffee."

Drouet turned to Carrie. "I haven't had a thing since breakfast. Just got in from Rock Island. I was going off to dine when I saw you."

Carrie smiled and smiled.

"What have you been doing?" he went on. "Tell me all about yourself. How is your sister?"

"She's well," returned Carrie, answering the last query.

He looked at her hard.

"Say," he said, "you haven't been sick, have you?"

Carrie nodded.

"Well, now, that's a blooming shame, isn't it? You don't look very well. I thought you looked a little pale. What have you been doing?"

"Working," said Carrie.

"You don't say so! At what?"

She told him.

"Rhodes, Morgenthau and Scott—why, I know that house. Over here on Fifth Avenue, isn't it? They're a close-fisted concern. What made you go there?"

"I couldn't get anything else," said Carrie frankly.

"Well, that's an outrage," said Drouet. "You oughtn't to be working for those people. Have the factory right back of the store, don't they?"

"Yes," said Carrie.

"That isn't a good house," said Drouet. "You don't want to work at anything like that, anyhow."

He chattered on at a great rate, asking questions, explaining things about himself, telling her what a good restaurant it was, until the waiter returned with an immense tray, bearing the hot savoury dishes which had been ordered. Drouet fairly shone in the matter of serving. He appeared to great advantage behind the white napery and silver platters of the table and displaying his arms with a knife and fork. As he cut the meat his rings almost spoke. His new suit creaked as he stretched to reach the plates, break the bread, and pour the coffee. He helped Carrie to a rousing plateful and contributed the warmth of his spirit to her body until she was a new girl. He was a splendid fellow in the true popular understanding of the term, and captivated Carrie completely.

That little soldier of fortune took her turn in an easy way. She felt a little out of place, but the great room soothed her and the view of the well-dressed throng outside seemed a splendid thing. Ah, what was it not to have money! What a thing it was to be able to come in here and dine! Drouet must be fortunate. He rode on trains, dressed in such nice clothes, was so strong, and ate in these fine places. He seemed quite a figure of a man, and she wondered at his friendship and regard for her.

"So you lost your place because you got sick, eh?" he said. "What are you going to do now?"

"Look around," she said, a thought of the need that hung outside this fine restaurant like a hungry dog at her heels passing into her eyes.

"Oh, no," said Drouet, "that won't do. How long have you been looking?"

"Four days," she answered.

"Think of that!" he said, addressing some problematical individual. "You oughtn't to be doing anything like that. These girls," and he waved an inclusion of all shop and factory girls, "don't get anything. Why, you can't live on it, can you?"

He was a brotherly sort of creature in his demeanour. When he had scouted the idea of that kind of toil, he took another tack. Carrie was really very pretty. Even then in her commonplace garb, her figure was evidently not bad, and her eyes were large and gentle. Drouet looked at her and his thoughts reached home. She felt his admiration. It was powerfully backed by his liberality and good-humour. She felt that she liked him—that she could continue to like him ever so much. There was something even richer than that, running as a hidden strain, in her mind. Every little while her eyes would meet his, and by that means the interchanging current of feeling would be fully connected.

"Why don't you stay down town and go to the theatre with me?" he said, hitching his chair closer. The table was not very wide.

"Oh, I can't," she said.

"What are you going to do to-night?"

"Nothing," she answered, a little drearily.

"You don't like out there where you are, do you?"

"Oh, I don't know."

"What are you going to do if you don't get work?"

"Go back home, I guess."

There was the least quaver in her voice as she said this. Somehow, the influence he was exerting was powerful. They came to an understanding of each other without words—he of her situation, she of the fact that he realized it.

"No," he said, "you can't make it!" genuine sympathy filling his mind for the time. "Let me help you. You take some of my money."

"Oh, no!" she said, leaning back.

"What are you going to do?" he said.

She sat meditating, merely shaking her head.

He looked at her quite tenderly for his kind. There were some loose bills in his vest pocket—greenbacks. They were soft and noiseless, and he got his fingers about them and crumpled them up in his hand.

"Come on," he said, "I'll see you through all right. Get yourself some clothes."

It was the first reference he had made to that subject, and now she realized how bad off she was. In his crude way he had struck the key-note. Her lips trembled a little.

She had her hand out on the table before her. They were quite alone in their corner, and he put his larger, warmer hand over it.

"Aw, come, Carrie," he said, "what can you do alone? Let me help you."

He pressed her hand gently and she tried to withdraw it. At this he held it fast, and she no longer protested. Then he slipped the greenbacks he had into her palm, and when she began to protest, he whispered:

"I'll loan it to you—that's all right. I'll loan it to you."

He made her take it. She felt bound to him by a strange tie of affection now. They went out, and he walked with her far out south toward Polk Street, talking.

"You don't want to live with those people?" he said in one place, abstractedly. Carrie heard it but it made only a slight impression.

"Come down and meet me to-morrow," he said, "and we'll go to the matinee. Will you?"

Carrie protested a while, but acquiesced.

"You're not doing anything. Get yourself a nice pair of shoes and a jacket."

She scarcely gave a thought to the complication which would trouble her when he was gone. In his presence, she was of his own hopeful, easy-way-out mood.

"Don't you bother about those people out there," he said at parting. "I'll help you."

Carrie left him, feeling as though a great arm had slipped out before her to draw off trouble. The money she had accepted was two soft, green, handsome, ten-dollar bills.

MENU:

Sirloin steak with mushrooms

Stuffed tomatoes

Hashed brown potatoes

Asparagus

(with Cream)

In America a new type of cookbook emerged in the late nineteenth century. No longer was its author the chef of a famous epicure or the head cook at an elegant restaurant. Most often now it was a woman, and her credentials were that she ran a cooking school or was familiar with the new "science" of domestic economy. The recipes for Sister Carrie's dinner come from the works of two such authors, Miss Parloa and Linda Hull Larned. Both were standard-bearers in the nineteenth century's crusade to free women from drudgery. Linda Hull Larned's specialty was studying the timesaving uses to which leftovers could be put and she even produced a recipe for "Second Edition Cake" which required mixing the crumbs of yesterday's cake with today's new milk, butter and eggs.

SIRLOIN STEAK WITH MUSHROOMS

FROM *The Hostess of Today*, 1899, Linda Hull Larned

sirloin steak (4 pounds)	1 pound large mushrooms
3 tablespoons butter	1-2 tablespoons cream
salt and pepper	dash of nutmeg

Put steak on greased broiler close to hot coals, sear over quickly on both sides, broil 10 minutes, turning constantly. Place on warm dish, spread with 1 tablespoon butter, salt and pepper on both sides, cover with broiled mushrooms (see below) and serve at once.

To make the mushroom accompaniment, peel the mushrooms. Select 6 (caps) of the largest and cover them with one tablespoon (melted) butter. Let them stand while you chop the remainder, with their stems, and sauté in the rest of the butter, cream, dash of salt, pepper and nutmeg. Now broil the large mushrooms, place them on the steak and place the rest beside the steak to serve.

(Serves 5-6)

STUFFED TOMATOES

FROM *Miss Parloa's New Cook Book*, 1884

12 large, smooth tomatoes	1 cup bread crumbs
1 teaspoon salt	1 teaspoon onion juice (or a
pepper to taste	small chopped onion)
1 tablespoon butter	(capers)
1 tablespoon sugar (or less, to	(chopped salty olives)
taste)	parsley

Arrange the tomatoes in a baking pan. Cut a thin slice from the smooth end of each. With a small spoon, scoop out as much of the pulp and juice as possible without injuring the shape. When all have been treated in this way, mix the pulp and juice with the other ingredients, and fill the tomatoes with this mixture. Put on the tops, and bake slowly ¾ hour (20-30 minutes should be sufficient; bake at 325°). Slide the cake turner under the tomatoes and lift gently onto a flat dish. Garnish with parsley and serve.

(Serves 6-12)

HASHED BROWN POTATOES

ADAPTED FROM *Miss Parloa's New Cook Book*, 1884

4 cups parboiled potatoes, peeled and finely diced	1 tablespoon chopped onion
	¼ cup butter
salt and pepper	1 tablespoon chopped parsley

Season the potatoes with the salt and pepper. Sauté the onion in the butter and when it turns yellow, add the potatoes. Stir with a fork, and pat them down into a flat cake. Cover the pan and cook the potatoes until the bottom is brown. Flip them over and brown on the other side. Add parsley. Serve immediately on a hot dish.

(Serves 4)

ASPARAGUS

with Cream

FROM *Miss Parloa's New Cook Book*, 1884

asparagus, in bundles	1 tablespoon butter
boiling water (to cover)	1 generous teaspoon flour
1 teaspoon salt to a quart of water	salt and pepper
1 cup cream or milk to every quart asparagus	

Have the asparagus tied in bundles. Wash, and plunge into boiling water in which there is 1 teaspoonful of salt for every quart of water. Boil rapidly for (10 to) 15 minutes. Take up, and cut off the tender heads. Put the heads in a clean saucepan with 1 generous cupful of cream or milk to every quart of asparagus. Simmer 10 minutes more.* Mix 1 tablespoonful of butter and 1 generous teaspoonful of flour together for every cup of cream. When creamy, stir in with the asparagus. Add salt and pepper to taste, and simmer 5 minutes longer.*

---

* If you do this, your vegetables, in typical nineteenth-century fashion, will be over-cooked. Try letting the milk or cream just come to a simmer, add the butter and flour, make sure everything is hot, simmer a moment or two and serve.

HENRY JAMES

THE AMBASSADORS
1903

Lambert Strether has come to Europe on an errand of morality; his employer and potential spouse, the wealthy Mrs. Newsome, wants him to convince her son Chad to return to America and the family business. But Strether himself, the messenger, succumbs to the self-same sense of interior gain that the young man found in Europe, and even to the self-same woman, Madame de Vionnet, who has wooed young Chad away from his responsibilities. Before he came to Europe Strether was always in terror, the terror of "always considering something else; something else, I mean, than the thing of the moment." He was unable to fully experience life, unable to enjoy. But ultimately he comes to declare: "Live all you can, it's a mistake not to. It doesn't so much matter what you do in particular, so long as you have had your life. If you haven't had that, what have you had?"

The change in Strether is marked, among other ways, by the dinners he has or has not shared with the various women of his life. Early in the trip he dines with Maria Gostrey, his introduction to Europe, a woman more subtly civilized than any he has known, and he compares her to Mrs. Newsome: "He had been to the theatre, even to the opera, in Boston, with Mrs. Newsome, and been more than once her only escort; but there had been no little confronted dinner, no pink lights, no whiff of vague sweetness, as a preliminary." Later in the trip, when he has met the beautiful Madame de Vionnet who represents Europe to him, who doesn't go about sifting and selecting what is best in European culture but who simply transmits it, he has another revelatory dinner. He and Madame de Vionnet go to a place where the knowing make pilgrimages. They have a perfect meal, just an omelette and a bottle of Chablis, but Strether knows at that moment that not only has he dived deep into experience but that he has actually, for that once, "touched bottom." Tastes and perceptions become important; for once he sees "reasons enough" for living simply in the meal he has eaten, the woman who sits opposite him, the way life comes through to them from the open window.

The end of it was that, half an hour later, they were seated together, for an early luncheon, at a wonderful, a delightful house of entertainment on the left bank—a place of pilgrimage for the knowing, they were both aware, the knowing who came, for its great renown, the homage of restless days, from the other end of the town. Strether had already been there three times—first with Miss Gostrey, then with Chad, then with Chad again and with Waymarsh and little Bilham, all of whom he had himself sagaciously entertained; and his pleasure was deep now on learning that Mme. de Vionnet had not yet been initiated. When he had said, as they strolled round the church, by the river, acting at last on what, within, he had made up his mind to, "Will you, if you have time, come to *déjeuner* with me somewhere? For instance, if you know it, over there on the other side, which is so easy a walk—" and then had named the place; when he had done this she stopped short, as for quick intensity, and yet deep difficulty, or response. She took in the proposal as if it were almost too charming to be true; and there had perhaps never yet been for her companion so unexpected a moment of pride—so fine, so odd a case, at any rate, as his finding himself thus able to offer to a person in such universal possession a new, a rare amusement. She had heard of the happy spot, but she asked him in reply to a further question how in the world he could suppose her to have been there. He supposed himself to have supposed that Chad might have taken her, and she guessed this the next moment, to his no small discomfort.

"Ah, let me explain," she smiled, "that I don't go about with him in public; I never have such chances—not having them otherwise—and it's just the sort of thing that, as a quiet creature living in my hole, I adore." It was more than kind of him to have though of it—though, frankly, if he asked whether she had time, she hadn't a single minute. That, however, made no difference—she would throw everything over. Every duty, at home, domestic, maternal, social, awaited her; but it was a case for a high line. Her affairs would go to smash; but hadn't one a right to one's snatch of scandal when one was prepared to pay? It was on this pleasant basis of costly disorder, consequently, that they eventually seated themselves, on either side of a small table, at a window adjusted to the busy quay and the shining, barge-burdened Seine; where, for an hour, in the matter of letting himself go, of diving deep, Strether was to feel that he had touched bottom. He was to feel many things on this occasion, and one of the first of them was that he had travelled far since that evening, in London, before the theatre, when his dinner with Maria Gostrey, between the pink-shaded candles, had struck him as requiring so many explanations. He had at that time gathered them in, the explanations—he had stored them up; but it was at present as if he had either soared above or sunk below them—he couldn't tell which; he could somehow think of none that didn't seem to leave the appearance of collapse and cynicism easier for him than lucidity. How could he wish it to be lucid for others, for any one, that he, for the hour, saw reasons enough in the mere way the bright, clean, ordered water-side life came in at the open window?—the mere way Mme. de Vionnet, opposite him over their intensely white table-linen, their *omelette aux tomates*, their bottle of straw-colored Chablis, thanked him for everything almost with the smile of a child, while her gray eyes moved in and out of their talk, back to the quarter of the warm spring air, in which early summer had already begun to throb, and then back again to his face and their human questions.

MENU:

Omelette aux tomates

This gentle omelette comes from the 1901 French Cookery for American Homes, *a reserved little book but one which contains a number of far-out recipes, including "Cooking Last Year's Bird," indexed, remarkably, under the letter L.*

OMELETTE AUX TOMATES

FROM *French Cookery for American Homes,* 1901

4 ripe tomatoes
2 tablespoons butter
pinch of salt and pepper
chopped chives

8 eggs
salt and pepper
1 tablespoon melted butter
¼ pound butter

Peel very ripe tomatoes (plunge them into boiling water for an instant; the peel will come off easily); cut them in halves; take out the pips; slice them. Put 2 tablespoons of butter in a stewpan; place in the tomatoes with a pinch of salt and pepper, let them cook gently until all moisture has disappeared; add a little chopped chives.

Now break the eggs; season with salt, pepper, and 1 tablespoon of melted butter; beat up for an instant. Dissolve in (a 12-inch) omelet pan ¼ pound of butter; pour the eggs into this pan; tilt the pan toward yourself, keeping the omelet spread over only half of it, and taking an oval form (as edges set, pull them toward center of omelet and let raw egg run under); when it has taken color and substance the one side, tilt the pan in the opposite direction; turn the omelet over with a palette knife (spatula); give it a nice color on the other side; turn into a hot dish,; make an incision lengthwise in the omelet; pour into this opening the tomato mixture.

(Serves 5)

THOMAS WOLFE

*OF TIME
AND THE RIVER*

1935

*The language used here by Thomas Wolfe to describe Eugene Gant
raiding a refrigerator is almost the language of cannibalism. Ravenous,
Eugene longs to devour the "red ripe heart" of the melon; the chicken
seems to beg "for the sweet and savage pillage of the tooth." His is a
savage hunger, intent on plunder and possession. Like primitive men
who thought they became invested with the power of the lion when*

they ate its liver, it is not nourishment that he seeks but some mystical incorporation of the very attributes of the food.

At the time this scene occurs Eugene has just left his turbulent life in New York City to spend a few peaceful days on an estate up the Hudson. His friend Joel and Joel's sister provide the food and love he craves.

When they got into the kitchen they found Rosalind there: she was standing by the long white table drinking a glass of milk. Joel, in the swift and correct manner with which he gave instructions, at once eager, gentle and decisive, began to show his guest around.

"And look," he whispered with his soft, and yet incisive slowness, as he opened the heavy shining doors of the great refrigerator—"here's the icebox: if you find anything there you like, just help yourself—"

Food! Food, indeed! The great icebox was crowded with such an assortment of delicious foods as he had not seen in many years: just to look at it made the mouth begin to water, and aroused the pangs of a hunger so ravenous and insatiate that it was almost more painful than the pangs of bitter want. One was so torn with desire and greedy gluttony as he looked at the maddening plenty of that feast that his will was rendered impotent. Even as the eye glistened and the mouth began to water at the sight of a noble roast of beef, all crisp and crackly in its cold brown succulence, the attention was diverted to a plump broiled chicken, whose brown and crackly tenderness fairly seemed to beg for the sweet and savage pillage of the tooth. But now a pungent and exciting fragrance would assail the nostrils: it was the smoked pink slices of an Austrian ham—should it be brawny bully beef, now, or the juicy breast of a white tender pullet, or should it be the smoky pungency, the half-nostalgic savor of the Austrian ham? Or that noble dish of green lima beans, now already beautifully congealed in their pervading film of melted butter; or that dish of tender stewed young cucumbers; or those tomato slices, red and thick and ripe, and heavy as a chop; or that dish of cold asparagus, say; or that dish of corn; or, say, one of those musty fragrant, deep-ribbed cantaloupes, chilled to the heart, now, in all their pink-fleshed taste and ripeness; or a round thick slab cut from the red ripe heart of that great watermelon; or a bowl of those red raspberries, most luscious and most rich with sugar, and a bottle of that thick rich cream which filled one whole compartment of that treasure chest of gluttony, or —

What shall it be now? What shall it be? A snack! A snack!—Before we prowl the meadows of the moon to-night, and soak our hearts in the moonlight's magic and the visions of our youth—what it shall be before we prowl the meadows of the moon? Oh, it shall be a snack, a snack—hah! hah!—it shall be nothing but a snack because—hah! hah! —you understand, we are not hungry and it is not well to eat too much before retiring—so we'll just investigate the icebox as we have done so oft at midnight in America—and we are the moon's man, boys—and all that it will be, I do assure you, will be something swift and quick and ready, something instant and felicitous, and quite delicate and dainty—just a snack!

I think—now let me see—h'm, now!—well, perhaps I'll have a slice or two of that pink Austrian ham that smells so sweet and pungent and looks so pretty and so delicate there in the crisp garlands of the parsley leaf!—and yes, perhaps, I'll have a slice of this roast beef, as well—h'm now!—yes, I think that's what I'm going to do—say a slice of red rare meat there at the centre—ah-h! there you are! yes, that's the stuff, that does quite nicely, thank you—with just a trifle of that crisp brown crackling there to oil the lips and make its passage easy, and a little of that cold but brown and oh—most—brawny gravy—and, yes, sir! I think I *will*, now that it occurs to me, a slice of that plump chicken—some white meat, thank you, at the breast—ah, there it is!— how sweetly doth the noble fowl submit to the swift and keen persuasion of the knife—and, now, perhaps, just for our diet's healthy balance, a spoonful or two of those lima beans, as gay as April and as sweet as butter, a tomato slice or two, a speared forkful of those thin-sliced cucumbers—ah! what a delicate and toothsome pickle they do make— what sorcerer invented them, a little corn perhaps, a bottle of this milk, a pound of butter and that crusty loaf of bread—and even this moon-haunted wilderness were paradise enow—with just a snack—a snack— a snack—

He was aroused from this voluptuous and hypnotic revery by the sound of Rosalind's warm sweet laugh, her tender and caressing touch upon his arm, and Joel's soundless and astonished mouth, the eager incandescence of his gleeful smile, his whole face uplifted in its fine and gentle smile, his voice cast in its frequent tone of whispering astonishment:—

"*Simply* incredible!" he was whispering to his sister. "I've never seen such an expression on *any* one's face in all my life! It's simply diabolical! When he sees food, he looks as if he's just getting ready to rape a woman!"

MENU:
A snack, containing
Baked ham
Roast beef
Gravy
Roast chicken
Lima beans
Cucumbers
Corn

A SNACK

BAKED HAM

Mrs. John William Harless, Garrison, N. Y.

a precooked ham	1 teaspoon prepared mustard
½ cup brown sugar	canned pineapple rings
4 tablespoons of the juice of	cloves
canned pineapple rings	¼ cup Cointreau

Spread over a precooked ham a mixture of ½ cup brown sugar, 4 tablespoons of the juice of canned pineapples, and 1 teaspoon prepared mustard. Stud the ham with canned pineapple rings and cloves. Bake in a 300° oven for 15 minutes per pound. Five minutes before serving, pour Cointreau over the ham.

ROAST BEEF

Mrs. John William Harless, Garrison, N. Y.

3-6-pound roast	salt to taste
garlic clove, sliced	

Slice 1 clove of garlic and insert pieces of garlic into slits in the roast. Roast the meat at 300° for 25 to 30 minutes per pound. Slice, remove the garlic, and add salt. Serve *au jus* or with gravy.

GRAVY

Mrs. John William Harless, Garrison, N. Y.

roast beef pan juice
water
beef bouillon cubes

flour and butter (1-2 teaspoons
kneaded together till smooth)
salt and pepper

Skim off all but 3 to 4 tablespoons of fat from the beef residue in your roasting pan. Add enough water to the remainder to make the desired amount of gravy (use 1 cup of water to the juice of a 3-4 pound roast) and 1 beef bouillon cube for each ½ cup of water used. Thicken the gravy with a mixture of flour and butter. Heat this till the gravy thickens, then simmer it for 5 minutes. Add salt and pepper to taste.

ROAST CHICKEN

Mrs. John William Harless, Garrison, N. Y.

3-6-pound chicken
garlic cloves
poultry seasoning
salt and pepper

4 tablespoons melted butter
a few drops Worcestershire
sauce

Season the chicken by rubbing with garlic cloves and sprinkling with poultry seasoning and salt and pepper, both inside and out. Place the chicken on a rack in roasting pan and cover with a clean cloth which has been soaked in a mixture of 4 tablespoons of melted butter and a few drops of Worcestershire sauce. If the cloth is kept thoroughly soaked, frequent basting will not be necessary.

Roast the chicken 35-40 minutes per pound at 325°. Remove the cloth about 45 minutes before the chicken is done. Skin will be brown and crisp.

LIMA BEANS

Mrs. John William Harless, Garrison, N. Y.

1½ cups dried lima beans
3 cups water
a ham bone

1½ teaspoons salt
pepper
a pinch of baking soda

Dried lima beans need not be soaked before cooking. Cover them with water and add a ham bone, salt and pepper and a pinch of baking soda. Cook them over a low flame until they are soft (about 40-50 minutes).

(Serves 4)

CUCUMBERS

Mrs. John William Harless, Garrison, N. Y.

cucumbers	¼ tablespoon pepper
ice water	2 tablespoons sugar
2 tablespoons salt	½ cup wine vinegar

Do not peel, but score cucumbers lengthwise with a fork. Slice and soak in ice water in the refrigerator for an hour, then drain them and sprinkle salt, pepper and sugar on them. Mix ½ cup of ice water and ½ cup of vinegar, pour this over them and let them stay in refrigerator another hour at least before eating.

CORN

Mrs. John William Harless, Garrison, N. Y.

"Corn," says Mrs. Harless, "must be grown in one's own garden if it is to be really good. It should be picked while the kernels are small and tender."

corn	salted water

Begin boiling lightly salted water in a large pot. *Then* pick and husk the corn. Drop the ears into boiling water and cook 5-7 minutes, no longer. Serve with lots of butter and salt.

A pleasant courtesy to family or guests is to relieve them of the struggle of buttering their own corn. Try putting several lumps of butter in the bottom of a platter just before you take out the corn. Then place the hot corn in the buttered platter and roll till corn is well coated.

JOHN STEINBECK

BREAKFAST

1938

*This story was one of the many working items Steinbeck developed
for inclusion in* The Grapes of Wrath, *but it was not used in that novel
and it has an entity all its own. Some people say that no other story
has ever made them as hungry as this one. It isn't the food, which is
simple fare—just eggs, bacon and biscuits. But so gentle and optimistic
is this feeding of the hungrier by the hungry that the breaking of these
biscuits has a religious quality.*

This thing fills me with pleasure. I don't know why, I can see it in the smallest detail. I find myself recalling it again and again, each time bringing more detail out of a sunken memory, remembering brings the curious warm pleasure.

It was very early in the morning. The eastern mountains were black-blue, but behind them the light stood up faintly colored at the mountain rims with a washed red, growing colder, grayer and darker as it went up and overhead until, at a place near the west, it merged with pure night.

And it was cold, not painfully so, but cold enough so that I rubbed my hands and shoved them deep into my pockets, and I hunched my shoulders up and scuffled my feet on the ground. Down in the valley where I was, the earth was that lavender gray of dawn. I walked along a country road and ahead of me I saw a tent that was only a lighter gray than the ground. Beside the tent there was a flash of orange fire seeping out of the cracks of an old rusty iron stove. Gray smoke spurted up out of the stubby stovepipe, spurted up a long way before it spread out and dissipated.

I saw a young woman beside the stove, really a girl. She was dressed in a faded cotton skirt and waist. As I came close I saw that she carried a baby in a crooked arm and the baby was nursing, its head under her waist out of the cold. The mother moved about, poking the fire, shifting the rusty lids of the stove to make a greater draft, opening the oven door; and all the time the baby was nursing, but that didn't interfere with the mother's work, nor with the light quick gracefulness of her movements. There was something very precise and practiced in her movements. The orange fire flicked out of the cracks in the stove and threw dancing reflections on the tent.

I was close now and I could smell frying bacon and baking bread, the warmest, pleasantest odors I know. From the east the light grew swiftly. I came near to the stove and stretched my hands out to it and shivered all over when the warmth struck me. Then the tent flap jerked up and a young man came out and an older man followed him. They were dressed in new blue dungarees and in new dungaree coats with the brass buttons shining. They were sharp-faced men, and they looked much alike.

The younger had a dark stubble beard and the older had a gray stubble beard. Their heads and faces were wet, their hair dripped with water, and water stood out on their stiff beards and their cheeks shone with water. Together they stood looking quietly at the lightening east;

they yawned together and looked at the light on the hill rims. They turned and saw me.

"Morning," said the older man. His face was neither friendly nor unfriendly.

"Morning, sir," I said.

"Morning," said they young man.

The water was slowly drying on their faces. They came to the stove and warmed their hands at it.

The girl kept to her work, her face averted and her eyes on what she was doing. Her hair was tied back out of her eyes with a string and it hung down her back and swayed as she worked. She set tin cups on a big packing box, set the plates and knives and forks out too. Then she scooped fried bacon out of the deep grease and laid it on a big tin platter, and the bacon cricked and rustled as it grew crisp. She opened the rusty oven door and took out a square pan full of high big biscuits.

When the smell of that hot bread came out, both of the men inhaled deeply. The young man said softly, "Kee-rist!"

The elder man turned to me, "Had your breakfast?"

"No."

"Well, sit down with us, then."

That was the signal. We went to the packing case and squatted on the ground about it. The young man asked, "Picking cotton?"

"No."

"We had twelve days' work so far," the young man said.

The girl spoke from the stove. "They even got new clothes."

The two men looked down at their new dungarees and they both smiled a little.

The girl set out the platter of bacon, the brown high biscuits, a bowl of bacon gravy and a pot of coffee, and then she squatted down by the box too. The baby was still nursing, its head up under her waist out of the cold. I could hear the sucking noises it made.

We filled our plates, poured bacon gravy over our biscuits and sugared our coffee. The older man filled his mouth full and he chewed and chewed and swallowed. Then he said, "God Almighty, it's good," and he filled his mouth again.

The young man said, "We been eating good for twelve days."

We all ate quickly, frantically, and refilled our plates and ate quickly again until we were full and warm. The hot bitter coffee scalded our throats. We threw the last little bit with the grounds in it on the earth and refilled our cups.

There was color in the light now, a reddish gleam that made the air seem colder. The two men faced the east and their faces were lighted by the dawn, and I looked up for a moment and saw the image of the mountain and the light coming over it reflected in the older man's eyes.

Then the two men threw the grounds from their cups on the earth and they stood up together. "Got to get going," the older man said.

The younger turned to me. "'Fyou want to pick cotton, we could maybe get you on."

"No. I got to go along. Thanks for breakfast."

The older man waved his hand in a negative. "O.K. Glad to have you." They walked away together. The air was blazing with light at the eastern skyline. And I walked away down the country road.

That's all. I know, of course, some of the reasons why it was pleasant. But there was some element of great beauty there that makes the rush of warmth when I think of it.

MENU:
Biscuits
(Southern style)

BISCUITS

(Southern style)

Mrs. Lucius Morgan, Union Point, Georgia

2½ cups flour	1 teaspoon salt
1 teaspoon sugar	½ cup soft shortening
½ teaspoon baking soda	¾-1 cup buttermilk
1½ teaspoons baking powder	

Sift flour, sugar, baking soda and powder and salt. Blend in shortening. Add buttermilk as you knead dough to make a soft ball. Knead briefly. Roll out on floured surface to about ½-inch thickness and cut with small cutter (to make the dainty-sized biscuits Southerners prefer) or break off small pieces of dough by hand and shape into biscuits. Bake on a greased baking sheet in a preheated oven (450-500°) for 10-15 minutes until brown. The sugar is added to make the biscuits brown nicely.

(Makes 15-18 biscuits)

INDEX OF RECIPES